Subsidizing Culture

Subsidizing Culture

Taxpayer Enrichment of the Creative Class

James T. Bennett

Routledge
Taylor & Francis Group
LONDON AND NEW YORK

First published 2016 by Transaction Publishers

Published 2017 by Routledge
2 Park Square, Milton Park, Abingdon, Oxon OX14 4RN
711 Third Avenue, New York, NY 10017, USA

Routledge is an imprint of the Taylor & Francis Group, an informa business

Library of Congress Catalog Number: 2015043823

Library of Congress Cataloging-in-Publication Data

Names: Bennett, James T., author.
Title: Subsidizing culture : taxpayer enrichment of the creative class / James T. Bennett.
Description: New Brunswick : Transaction Publishers, 2016. | Includes index.
Identifiers: LCCN 2015043823 (print) | LCCN 2015044754 (ebook) | ISBN 9781412862820 (hardcover) | ISBN 9781412863353 (pbk.) | ISBN 9781412862325 ()
Subjects: LCSH: Federal aid to the arts--United States--History--20th century. | Federal aid to the arts--United States--History--21st century. | United States--Cultural policy--History--20th century. | United States--Cultural policy--History--21st century.
Classification: LCC NX730 .B46 2016 (print) | LCC NX730 (ebook) | DDC 700.79/73--dc23
LC record available at http://lccn.loc.gov/2015043823

ISBN 13: 978-1-4128-6282-0 (hbk)
ISBN 13: 978-1-4128-6335-3 (pbk)

This book is dedicated to the memory of Irving Louis Horowitz

Contents

Acknowledgments

I am grateful to many for their assistance with and support of the research and editing of this book. The research would not have been possible without the generous financial support of the Sunmark Foundation. Colin Harris provided excellent research assistance. I also owe profuse thanks to my editor, Bill Kauffman, for I am indebted to him for significant contributions to this study.

James T. Bennett
George Mason University
Fairfax, VA

Introduction

British novelist Kingsley Amis remarked, "When the State takes a really passionate interest in the work and other activities of its artists, creative and executive alike, the artists had better start running. . . . Any kind of totalitarian hates all artists, not only writers, because he can never own or direct their talent, what makes them artists."[1]

And yet today, many artists pursue state funding. They seem heedless of Amis-type warnings, or dismissive of those who caution against the entanglement of art and state. Likewise, many writers and intellectuals, who from long experience might be wary of co-optation or exploitation by the powers-that-be, discount the pitfalls inherent in government sponsorship. The state, far from being the menace of Kingsley Amis's imagination, is to them a benefactor, a partner, an agency of enlightenment. How did this shift come about in the United States? By what series of steps did the government cease to look inimical and instead assume the mask, or the mantle, of benevolence?

In *Subsidizing Culture: Taxpayer Enrichment of the Creative Class*, we will examine the development of and controversies surrounding landmark US government programs that have directly benefited writers, artists, and intellectuals.

State subsidization of the arts and artists was long associated in the American mind with monarchies and, in the twentieth century, socialist states. The support these regimes gave to intellectuals was understood to come with a cost; no one pretended that one could accept subvention from king or state and not incur an implicit, if not explicit, obligation toward king or state.

The degree of outright propaganda embedded in government cultural policy of course varied, depending on the nature of the regime. Britain's Royal Academy of Music had a different matrix than did, say, the Propaganda Ministry of Nazi Germany. Official support of artists and intellectuals derived from a complex of motives, some of which might be termed benevolent (e.g., celebrating a nation's cultural heritage, encouraging promising new artists or musicians or writers). Still, it can be sobering to realize that even the most heinous dictatorships used metrics of the sort that the most anodyne contemporary cultural organizations use. For instance, the Nazis encouraged theater as part of their cultural program; attendance at plays "tripled from 520,000 in 1932 to 1.6 million in 1936 and continued to rise until 1943."[2]

Government sponsorship of intellectuals, and particularly artists, long predates the brutal regimes of twentieth-century Germany and Russia. Supporters of this practice like to point to the magnificent treasures of the Renaissance, which often "were commissioned by princes and popes."[3] These benefactions of feudal lords and religious leaders cannot be credited to the modern nation-state, whose artistic progeny have been born or at least midwifed by such bureaucracies as the French Ministry of Cultural Affairs (created in 1959) and the British Arts Council (b. 1945).

By the late twentieth century, as editors Milton C. Cummings Jr. and Richard S. Katz note in their comparative survey, *The Patron State: Government and the Arts in Europe, North America, and Japan*, "an extensive public involvement in the arts seemed to be a permanently established government responsibility."[4] France, in particular, had developed a cultural bureaucracy of formidable size. By the late 1980s, noted Annette Zimmer and Stefan Toepler in the *Journal of Cultural Economics*, the French government's spending on culture dwarfed that of all other European nations. The corollary, however, was that "private patronage and, especially, sponsoring by the business community were actively discouraged until the 1980s," and were still scarce in the twenty-first century.[5] Where the state expands, the private sector contracts.

Despite a brief surge of dissent in the United States in the late 1980s and early 1990s, government patronage of artists and intellectuals has encountered only scattered opposition in the contemporary Western world, where "arts and culture had become a more or less accepted field of public policy."[6] Ministries of culture dispense public monies to writers, just as social-welfare departments dispense aid to dependent persons and families. The welfare state, though far more extensive and expensive, preceded the cultural welfare state by only a matter of a few years, though the latter, because it "promoted activities that were patronized and enjoyed mainly by the wealthiest and best educated.... lacked the compelling moral logic of subsidies for hospitals, colleges of engineering, or the interest on mortgages," as Daniel S. Fox, a scholar of philanthropy, has written.[7] The claim to food and shelter by those in need of such has an urgency that cantos, exegeses, and experimental novels lack.

Yet the institutionalization of government support for the arts in the late twentieth century may not have been solely due to the elevated taste and heightened sense of aesthetic responsibility of politicians. As Dutch professor of cultural studies Kees Vuyk argued in the *International Journal of Cultural Policy*, "The arts world may have thought that after World War II it was supported by governments because of its intrinsic value; in fact, even in this period, the arts were a politicians' toy."[8] If painters were not commissioned to render majestic portraits of royal personages, as in the age of monarchy, their patronage was nevertheless vouchsafed from "ideological motives," says Vuyk; specifically, its purpose was to promote the democratic West in its hot and cold wars against the communist East and the threat, however remote, of a recrudescent fascism.[9] We will take a closer look at this deployment of art as a Cold War weapon in the second section of this book.

Our focus in *Subsidizing Culture* is on the United States, which is typically held up as a relative laggard in the development of a cultural policy. The nations of Europe, Americans are told with harrumphing periodicity, are more generous in honoring writers and artists and clutch their creative class closer to the national bosom. The implication is that the United States is both less cultured and less generous.

But beginning with the New Deal's Federal Writers,' Art, Music, and Theatre Projects, which were lumped under the rubric of Federal One, a new policy argument—which would, in less than two score years, become a consensus—asserted that by offering financial support to its writers and intellectuals, the federal government was not co-opting them but rather affirming their importance to the nation. Like the nations of Europe, the United States was said to finally be paying deserved tribute to its artists.

Today the federal government subsidizes intellectuals through numerous conduits, among them the National Science Foundation, the Smithsonian Institution, the Corporation for Public Broadcasting, the Institute of Museum and Library Services, the US Information Agency, and many others, most notably federal support of higher education generally. (One could have—several have—devoted a separate book to the interplay of universities and government.)

In *Subsidizing Culture*, we investigate four case studies in US government support of intellectuals and artists: (1) The New Deal's Federal Writers,' Art, Music, and Theatre Projects, which introduced such subsidies in the guise of relief but came to be championed—and memorialized by New Deal-friendly historians—as the first great expression of Uncle Sam's appreciation of his artists and intellectuals; (2) The vigorous promotion, in the post-World War II and early Cold War eras, of Abstract Expressionism and other forms of modern art by the US State Department and the Central Intelligence Agency, which viewed such nontraditional painting as a symbol of American freedom and a useful weapon in the "cultural Cold War"; we also take stock of the headquarters from which this "cultural Cold War" was waged: the government-subsidized Congress for Cultural Freedom; (3) The National Endowment for the Arts (NEA), progeny of President Lyndon B. Johnson, which over an alternately tumultuous and placid half-century has fortified its position as the preeminent arts bureaucracy (though it has not realized the ambition of some of its conceptualizers that it might become a US Ministry of Culture); (4) The National Endowment for the Humanities (NEH), the NEA's less embattled, less glamorous twin, which funnels monies to scholars. (Both endowments have been used, by presidents of both parties, to bolster political links to influential intellectuals.)

Our focus is on the creation of and the debate over these government programs, giving special attention to the critics, who are usually given short shrift and caricatured as philistine clods. Undoubtedly some of them were—but the chorus of antisubsidy voices has included such disparate figures as writers William Faulkner, John Updike, and Edward Abbey; artists John Sloan, Wheeler Williams, and Larry Rivers; social critics Jacques Barzun, H. L. Mencken, and Christopher Lasch; and a colorful gallery of libertarian, conservative, and populist politicians. Whatever the merits of the arguments on both sides, these debates have emphatically *not* been lopsided spats between the forces of enlightenment and the ignorant and obscurantist forces of darkness. American political and intellectual life is far too complex and multifarious for such cartoonish morality plays.

Subsidizing Culture is informed by a public choice perspective in that it refuses to take the proponents of subsidizing intellectuals entirely at face value. Surely those who sought a federal role in cultivating the arts and literature of the United States were sincere in their belief that Washington's intervention would contribute to their flourishing, but it is just as certain that specific individuals as well as broad classes of people benefitted materially from this intervention. To pretend otherwise is to hold onto civics book fantasies. For whenever tax dollars are to be distributed, the mechanism for the distribution thereof will be contested over by those who desire access to those dollars.

***

The Nobel laureate economist George Stigler, in his classic essay "The Intellectual and the Marketplace" (1963), explained, "The intellectual has never felt kindly toward the marketplace: to him it has always been a place of vulgar men and base motives. Whether this intellectual be an ancient Greek philosopher, who viewed economic life as an unpleasant necessity that should never be allowed to become obtrusive or dominant, or whether this intellectual be a modern man, who focuses his scorn on gadgets and Madison Avenue, the basic similarity of view has been pronounced."[10]

Yet vulgarity, cheapness, and bad taste are not necessarily the hallmarks of American culture. Amidst the Miley Cyruses and Britney Spearses one also finds, in the half-century since Stigler wrote his essay, the *Godfather*, Barbra Streisand, Andrew Wyeth, Cormac McCarthy, Saul Bellow, indeed hundreds, even thousands, of talented American artists who have appealed to general audiences and have not needed to be kept alive by the transfusion of federal subsidies.

Subsidies can be addictive. What first seems like manna from heaven becomes one's daily bread. Its removal can be a traumatic event. To intellectuals and artists accustomed to life on the dole, the federal stipend becomes an entitlement. Joseph Wesley Zeigler, in his book *Arts in Crisis*, elucidates the mindset: By the time of the National Endowment for the Arts controversies of the 1980s and '90s, artists "had come to believe that they were entitled to federal funding. 'You, the United States, should be paying for me to create, because I'm here and I'm creating. As an artist, I'm an important member of the society—and so the society should be supporting me.'"[11]

Society, or at least many unenlightened members thereof, sometimes begs to differ. Questions of equity and justice enter the debate. Why, critics of the NEA have asked since its inception half a century ago, should a truck driver or waitress have taxes mulcted from his or her weekly paycheck and sent, via the circuitous route of federal funding, to a novelist whose audience is far more affluent than are those who live in the neighborhood of the truck driver or waitress? Why should the truck driver or waitress pay the market price for a ticket to see a country music concert while a bond-trader on Wall Street has his ticket to the Metropolitan Opera partially subsidized by the taxes paid by the truck driver and the waitress? And why should a supermarket cashier, a born-again Christian, have taxes seized from her paycheck and sent to a performance artist whose act mocks the religious faith of that cashier?

Economist William D. Grampp labeled the behavior of those artists pursuing subsidies "rent-seeking," a concept developed by Gordon Tullock and denominated by Anne O. Krueger in her pathbreaking article "The Political Economy of the Rent-Seeking Society."[12] It means, simply, "[t]he expenditure of resources in order to bring about an uncompensated transfer of goods or services from another person or persons to one's self as the result of a decision on some public policy."[13] Lobbyists engage in rent-seeking all the time. The ranks of artists and writers include enough individualistic or contrary or hermetic sorts who are resistant to political organization, but arts institutions have formed potent lobbies, though they dislike the word, suggestive as it is of backroom deals and sleazy log-rolling.

Public arts advocates like to think they are above all that. If they lobby, they are lobbying not for their own aggrandizement but for the edification of the public. And as Grampp sharply notes, those "who question their claim on other people's resources are put down as Philistines or Vandals."[14] Unlike, say, sugar beet growers, who lobby Congress sedulously for special treatment, lobbyists for subsidies to artists and writers invoke a higher cause. They are not agitating for the transfer of wealth from others to themselves; rather, they are seeking the moral, intellectual, and aesthetic elevation of the entire country. Who but a churl or a rube could object?

The public endorses artists through voluntary exchanges within the marketplace. It rewards handsomely Stephen King, Andy Warhol, Thomas Kinkaid, Bruce Springsteen, Sue Grafton, Lady Gaga, Tony Kushner, Brad Pitt, Beyoncé. . . . practitioners of various arts, at varying levels of brilliance or competence. There is no need for the aforementioned to seek government assistance (though more than one has lent his or her name to pleas for greater state subsidies to cultural organizations). But for some of those whose vocations have proved less remunerative, lobbying—rent-seeking—exerts a powerful attraction.

Joel Feinberg, in an essay in *Public Affairs Quarterly* on the philosophical challenges posed by arts subsidies, writes, "The problem raised by the indignant taxpayer is whether there is justification for using government funds derived from mandatory taxation of all citizens in order to promote the esoteric projects of a small number of people."[15]

Phrased that way, government-arts advocates are forced into an elitist corner from which they are uncomfortable making an argument. So they reject the phrasing. They deny that their projects are esoteric or that Joe and Josephine Taxpayer are shelling out for things far removed from their daily lives. And they turn the tables on the questioner, asking why he or she is unsympathetic to artists, unappreciative of the arts, and hostile to freedom of expression. As we shall see, this line of defense reached its high-water mark in the early 1990s debate over the activities, and even existence, of the National Endowment for the Arts, when indignant arts advocates asked how dare those with tin ears, those whose lips move when they read, those who wouldn't know Jackson Pollock from Norman Rockwell, stand between the artist and his or her deserved rewards?

Lest one think that the marketplace rewards a handful of artists and writers with great riches while subjecting the rest to penury, it should be noted that hundreds of thousands, if not millions, of artists, loosely defined, make liveable wages in the United States.

According to the Bureau of Labor Statistics (BLS) of the US Department of Labor, the 2014 US labor force consisted of 146,305,000 persons, of whom 2.9 million fell under the subcategory "Arts, Design, Entertainment, Sports, and Media Occupations." Excluding athletes, umpires, announcers, public relations specialists, news analysts and reporters, broadcast technicians, and sundry nonartistic occupations, artists and those who make their living with words cut this profile in the labor force:

Actors 43,000

Producers and Directors 161,000

Artists and Related Workers 203,000

Dancers and choreographers 18,000

Designers 830,000

Editors 163,000

Entertainers and performers, sports and related workers, all others 38,000

Musicians, Singers, and Related Workers 194,000

Photographers 174,000

Technical writers 61,000

Writers and authors 221,000[16]

These add up to just over two million, or about 1.4 percent of the labor force. Now, within these categories are persons who engage in activities (wedding photographer, writer of technical manuals for refrigerator owners, editor of a corporate newsletter, choir director) which are not called immediately to mind when one thinks of a working artist or intellectual. Nor are these jobs targeted for support by even the most generous advocate of bounties for intellectual or artistic work. Moreover, *employment* is defined with considerable elasticity. The BLS says that "people are considered employed if they did any work at all for pay or profit during the survey reference week."[17] One hour of paid work a week is enough to qualify one as an "artist" or "writer" in the eyes of the BLS.

But over a million people are making a living, or a piece of a living, in these jobs. Not many are getting rich: struggling novelists outpace Nicholas Sparks by a factor of thousands, and photographing a happy if obscure couple pays much less than Annie Liebovitz charges. But the median earnings of people in these fields are well above the minimum wage, and often they are securely middle class. The BLS reports that the median pay is $23.50 per hour for musicians, $14.16 for dancers, $18.33 for choreographers, $20.26 for actors, $34.31 for producers and directors (a field in which for every Steven Spielberg there are a hundred directors begging work in the film industry), $26.89 for writers and authors, $25.90 for editors, $13.70 for photographers, and $21.34 for craft and fine artists.[18]

These rates of pay are problematic for those, like actors, who work sporadically, but much less for those, such as editors, whose work is more regular.

Despite the often modest (and at times wildly variable) rates of pay, the profession of artist or writer remains desirable, not only for the psychic benefits but as a source of prestige. Since 1947, the University of Chicago's National Opinion Research Center (NORC) has conducted periodic surveys of Americans to measure the relative prestige of close to one hundred occupations. Its most recent survey, in 1989, found that physicians, who scored 86.06 out of a possible one hundred points, had the highest prestige occupation. Dishwashers (16.78) filled the lowest prestige occupation. The mean score of all occupations was 42.88, a figure easily exceeded by such artistic categories as architects (73.15), authors (63.05), actors and directors (57.62), dancers (53.49), and painters, sculptors, craft artists, and artist printmakers (52.38). Closer to the mean were designers (46.53), musicians and composers (46.56), and photographers (45.11).[19]

So Americans, who will often be disparaged in the pages ahead as materialistic money-grubbers by those seeking federal support of the culture industry, generally admire those who work in the arts.

But does society owe the artist anything beyond tolerating his or her freedom of expression? Is liberty—imperfect as it may be—enough? Or should it be accompanied by a government check?

William Faulkner didn't think so. The Nobel laureate Mississippi novelist told an interviewer, "The writer doesn't need economic freedom. All he needs is a pencil and paper. I've never known anything good in writing to come from having accepted any free gift of money. The good writer never applies to a foundation. He's too busy writing."[20] Writing, that is, for an audience. Faulkner, who had many lean years, assumed that a writer writes to be read. If he is good, he will find an audience. Perhaps not a large audience, perhaps not even an audience that will save him the necessity of taking a job at the post office or the pizza shop, but an audience.

Following the same groove, the American novelist John Updike was also sharply critical of taking government money: "I would rather have as my patron a host of anonymous citizens digging into their own pockets for the price of a book or a magazine than a small body of enlightened and responsible men administering public funds."[21]

In their disdain for small committees of enlightened men, and their preference for the ordinary book buyer, Updike and Faulkner echoed the views of a long line of American independents.

The philosopher Virginia Held, in a 1983 contribution to an American Philosophical Society symposium on "the Social Responsibility of Intellectuals," argued for a greater obligation on the part of society through the state. Held first defines her term (*intellectual*) as "a person enabled by the society to occupy a social role in which he or she either cultivates intellect for its own sake (rather than merely instrumentally) or uses intellect to evaluate society and culture."[22] Discarding "the traditional models of property and property rights," Held denies the distinction between an intellectual earning a salary *qua* intellectual (say, by writing books that the public buys) and one receiving a check from a government agency.[23] They are, in essence, she says, the same thing.

"Whether we 'earn a salary' or receive a 'welfare payment,'" Held writes, pointedly placing quotation marks around "earn a salary" and "welfare payment," as if contesting the commonly understood meaning of each phrase, "we are in either case receiving 'social support,' though at very different levels. Whether the society allows us to be employed or forces us to be unemployed, it provides the conditions within which we can live well or poorly or not at all."[24]

The idea that we are "forced" to be unemployed and "allowed" to be employed seems to discount the possibility of agency, of free choice. The market, in this view, holds a kind of dictatorial power over us, permitting some to find employment and consigning others to the scrap heap of poverty. Those who eke out a living in this market do so less because of talent or drive or ambition or work ethic than they do as a result of a cluster of circumstances—birth, geography, demographic characteristics—over which they may have no control at all.

Held's preferred policy response, with regard to intellectuals trapped in this seeming tyranny, is for "massively increased public funding for. . . . cultural production, insulated by guarantees of noninterference."[25] The state, it appears, can be trusted to dispense "massive" sums of money and to then take a hands-off approach to those it has supported. This bespeaks a faith in government that can only be called fervent. It partakes of a wishful thinking not shared by the critic Russell Lynes of *Harper's*, who in a 1962 essay in the *New York Times Magazine* vainly protesting the onrushing federal arts freight train stated as an axiom that "when the Government is involved in subsidizing the arts, it cannot and will not keep its hands off them."[26]

The antithesis of Held's case for public support of artists is the libertarian position that the state should neither promote nor discourage the production of culture and the maintenance of artists and intellectuals. We will encounter this view in the pages that follow. But there is also a tradition that sees asceticism, even poverty, as a virtue, and the "starving artist" as an ennobled figure. This was expressed in classic form by the English art critic Clive Bell in the early years of the twentieth century. Bell wrote: "Let the artist be a beggar living on public charity; let him have just enough to eat and the tools of his trade: ask nothing of him. Materially make the life of the artist sufficiently miserable to be unattractive, so that no one will take to art save those in whom the daemon is absolute. . . . Art and Religion are not professions; they are not occupations for which men can be paid. The artist and the saint do what they have to do, not to make a living, but in obedience to some mysterious necessity. They do not produce to live—they live to produce. . . . You must make pariahs of them, since they are not a part of society but the salt of the earth."[27]

This is considerably romanticized, and as Bell's father had made a fortune in coal-mining, young Clive was never in danger of missing a meal or sleeping under a bridge. But his own circumstances do not necessarily vitiate his point. For many other writers have argued that the artist, and the intellectual, needs to maintain a critical distance from the apparatus of power and influence and wealth in order to follow his or her calling in the direction of truth rather than cooptation.

Bell's argument was not solely that hunger is a motivator, or that privation winnows out the poseurs and strengthens those whose passion for art, for creation, is so all-encompassing that they simply have no other choice than to paint, to write, to create. "Planned art," he said, "is a contradiction in terms. Art is made by artists and not by soviets or government departments." The artist must maintain his or her independence from the machinery of state or else he or she becomes a mere propagandist.

"The modern state is a bad patron generally for one of three reasons," wrote Bell: "it is propagandist or it expects artists to satisfy a vulgar and stupid majority or it compromises." This first charge is a theme that winds itself around the debate over government-sponsored culture from the New Deal through the National Endowment for the Arts. Would the state—any state, outside some ideal that exists only in a philosopher's imagination—subsidize intellectuals or writers or artists out of purely altruistic or aesthetic motivations? While "generosity is a virtue which has existed under all governments," writes Bell, "genuine respect for art is unlikely to be common under any." Moreover, he concludes, "An art department means bureaucratic art, and bureaucratic art means death."[28]

Those who have championed a government role in the creation of culture would argue that government indifference means death, and that the patronage of the state, while perhaps proceeding from mixed motives, is on the whole a force for enrichment. The alternative is a dispirited and impecunious cultural community whose financially ambitious members pitch their work to wealthy patrons or the lowest common denominator.

The eminent polymath Jacques Barzun wondered if the age of subsidized art hasn't actually created a surfeit, or glut, of art. "Art is not a subject like milk, of which the need and use are self-evident," wrote Barzun in a widely discussed 1986 essay.[29] If the art being generated by government grants is bad art, then perhaps we have an oversupply of art.

Don't feed Barzun any sanctimonious lectures about our societal lack of appreciation for art being due to a crass materialism. "All known societies have been materialist," he insists; "human society exists solely for material purposes. Ours is unusual precisely in its generous expenditures on art, education, philanthropy, and other good works."

Nor does he fall for the idealized image of the artist, suffering for his vision. He traces this fantasy to the nineteenth century, with its "glorification" of the artist as "a hero, a seer, a genius; and geniuses must be allowed to do as they please while the rest of mankind gratefully brings its offerings to the altar."[30] The result of this exaltation of the artist is that more people—even those of meager talents—wanted to become artists, not bound by convention, not answerable to society's petty expectations, not punching a time clock or milking the cows at dawn or showing up for work at a regular hour.

The growth of government grants to artists has encouraged those without sufficient talent to enter the field, argues Barzun. The result is too much bad art created by too many bad artists. This echoes, as we shall see, some of the criticism of the Federal Art and Writers' Projects of the 1930s.

"We can pay farmers not to grow crops," says Barzun, "but we cannot pay artists to stop making art." We can, however, stop paying artists to make bad art. (Noted that Barzun favors state subvention of museums, operas, theaters, libraries, orchestras, and the like—just not individual artists or writers.)

Besides, says Barzun, there is nothing glamorous about the life of the painter, the poet, the playwright. "It is a test of endurance, willpower, and maniacal faith in oneself."[31] It is not suited for those who need sanction from the authorities. Those with fragile egos or breakable work ethics need not apply. As the historian of the modern culture war, Richard Jensen, puts it, "Artists will work for peanuts or for caviar, whichever is offered."[32]

The artist must often be in opposition to the powers-that-be, whether in the artistic or political world. "Official art," says Barzun, is "competent and safe"—boring and unnecessary. Or as Ernest Hemingway put it, "A writer is an outlier like a Gypsy. . . . If he is a good writer he will never like any government he lives under. His hand should be against it and its hand will always be against him."[33] That hand, therefore, should not be bearing an application for a government grant.

As the preceding examples suggest, there are several strains of thought within the antisubsidy school. There is, first and most comprehensively, the libertarian view that the involuntary transfer of resources from taxpayer to artists is, in principle, unjustified, and in the American context unconstitutional to boot. This view was most potent in the 1930s, when a significant number of writers and political figures adhered to a variation of laissez-faire or even anarchistic thought. There is the populist critique, which flared in the 1980s–'90s assault on the National Endowment for the Arts, and which protests that federal aid to artists and museums amounts to a regressive tax whereby the middle and working classes subsidize the entertainments (or, in the view of some, the perversions) of well-off artists and art patrons. The populist critique was also brought to bear against the New Deal art projects, with their heavily New York City-centric bias. Finally, there is the elitist case against art subsidies, à la Jacques Barzun. The elitist seldom objects to subvention of established institutions or classical forms; his or her gravamen is that subsidies to the arts cultivate and encourage the mediocre.

Even taken in concert, these views represent a distinct minority position in the debate—to the extent the subject is anymore debated—over subsidies to intellectuals and artists. But it was not always thus. . . .

Notes

1. Kingsley Amis, "An Arts Policy?," *Policy Review* 14 (September 1980): 84.
2. Kelly K. Ronayne, *Stages of Modernity: The Federal Theatre Project and the New American Welfare State* (Dr. Kelly K. Ronayne, D.A. diss., St. John's University, 2010), 20.
3. Milton C. Cummings Jr. and Richard S. Katz, "Government and the Arts: An Overview," in *The Patron State: Government and the Arts in Europe, North America, and Japan*, ed. Milton C. Cummings Jr. and Richard S. Katz (New York: Oxford University Press, 1987), 3.
4. Cummings and Katz, "Government and the Arts in the Modern World," 350.
5. Annette Zimmer and Stefan Toepler, "The Subsidized Muse: Government and the Arts in Western Europe and the United States," *Journal of Cultural Economics* 23, no. 1/2 (1999): 37.
6. Ibid., 33.
7. Daniel M. Fox, "Revisiting the Politics of Art Museums," *Society* 32, no. 2 (January/February 1995): 44.
8. Kees Vuyk, "The Arts as an Instrument? Notes on the Controversy Surrounding the Value of Art," *International Journal of Cultural Policy* 16, no. 2 (2010): 174.
9. Ibid., 176.
10. George J. Stigler, "The Intellectual and the Marketplace," in *The Essence of Stigler*, ed. Kurt R. Leube and Thomas Gale Moore (Stanford, CA: Hoover Institution Press, 1986), 79.
11. Quoted in Mark Bauerlein, *National Endowment for the Arts: A History 1965–2008* (Washington, DC: National Endowment for the Arts, 2008), 38.
12. David R. Henderson, "Rent Seeking," *The Concise Encyclopedia of Economics*, accessed October 9, 2015, http://www.econlib.org/library/Enc/RentSeeking.

html; Anne O. Krueger, "The Political Economy of the Rent-Seeking Society," *American Economic Review* 64, no. 3 (June 1974): 291–303.

13. "Rent-seeking Behavior," *A Glossary of Political Economy Terms*, accessed October 9, 2015, http://www.auburn.edu/~johnspm/gloss/rent-seeking_behavior.
14. William D. Grampp, "Rent-seeking in Arts Policy," *Public Choice* 60, no. 2 (1989): 114.
15. Joel Feinberg, "Not with My Tax Money: The Problem of Justifying Government Subsidies for the Arts," *Public Affairs Quarterly* 8, no. 2 (April 1994): 102.
16. "Labor Force Statistics from the Current Population Survey," U.S. Department of Labor Bureau of Labor Statistics, accessed October 9, 2015, http://www.bls.gov/cps/cpsaat11.htm.
17. "Frequently Asked Questions," accessed October 9, 2015, http://www.bls.gov/cps/faq.htm#Ques3.
18. "Occupational Outlook Handbook," U.S. Department of Labor Bureau of Labor Statistics, accessed October 9, 2015, http://www.bls.gov/ooh.
19. Harold Horowitz, "The Status of Artists in the U.S.A.," *Journal of Cultural Economics* 17, no. 1 (June 1993): 41–42.
20. Malcolm Cowley, ed., *Writers at Work* (New York: Viking, 1958), 125.
21. John Updike, *Hugging the Shore* (New York: Vintage, 1984), 868.
22. Virginia Held, "The Independence of Intellectuals," *Journal of Philosophy* 80, no. 10 (October 1983): 574.
23. Ibid., 582.
24. Ibid., 573.
25. See note 23 above.
26. Russell Lynes, "The Case against Government Aid to the Arts," *New York Times Magazine*, March 25, 1962, 86.
27. Clive Bell, "Art in the Planned State," *Forum and Century* XCVII, no. 5 (May 1937): 306.
28. Ibid., 307–9.
29. Jacques Barzun, "A Surfeit of Art," *Harper's* (July 1986): 45.
30. Ibid., 46.
31. Ibid., 47–48.
32. Richard Jensen, "The Culture Wars, 1965–1995: A Historian's Map," *Journal of Social History* 29 Supplement (1995): 18.
33. Carlos Baker, *Ernest Hemingway: A Life Story* (New York: Charles Scribner's Sons, 1986), 277.

Part One

A New Deal or a New Dole?: Artists, Writers, and Federal One

Among the functions that the authors of the Constitution never even considered vesting in the national government was the encouragement of the arts. According to James Madison's extensive notes of the Constitutional Convention of 1787, no one broached the subject.[1] Sponsorship of artistic endeavors was not among the enumerated powers in Article 1, Section 8 of the Constitution. The Congress was given the power to "promote the progress of science and the useful arts," but this was defined as "securing for limited times to authors and inventors the exclusive right to their respective writings and discoveries." That is, patents and copyrights. Not grants or outright gifts.

One of the first proposals for federal subsidy of artists came from the quill of painter John Trumbull, president of the American Academy of the Fine Arts and the creator of numerous patriotic works, most notably four large historical paintings in the Capitol Rotunda that had been commissioned by Congress in 1817: *Declaration of Independence*, *Surrender of General Burgoyne*, *Surrender of Lord Cornwallis*, and *General George Washington Resigning his Commission to Congress*. He received $8,000 per painting. It would take Trumbull seven years to complete the last of these twelve by eighteen-foot paintings. The glacial pace at which Trumbull painted was in part the result of political interference: President James Madison demanded that the persons depicted be "as large as life," which was difficult for Trumbull, who had but one functioning eye and did his best work, or so many believed, in miniatures.[2]

Trumbull was no stranger to the mix of art and politics. His father had served as governor of Connecticut, and he had been an aide to General George Washington during the Revolutionary War. Trumbull would serve as a secretary to John Jay as Jay negotiated the 1795 treaty that established the postindependence terms of the US-British relationship. Yet his enduring accomplishments were artistic: not only depictions of events during the Revolution but iconic images of George Washington, John Adams, and Alexander Hamilton, among others.

As you might guess from his background and his choice of subjects, Trumbull's political sympathies were Federalist, which is to say, in the context of his era, nationalist. He was a friend to energetic government. And he was in financial straits. That combination will almost always lead to the rattling sound of the beggar's cup. And so on Christmas Day, 1826, almost a decade after he had received his commission for the paintings in the Capitol Rotunda for which he would be remembered, Trumbull transmitted a letter to President John Quincy Adams detailing his plan "for the permanent encouragement of the Fine Arts in the United States."

Flattery first, then the ask. That has been the tactic of many a supplicant through the ages. Trumbull praised the President's efforts to afford "public protection" to other industries and he suggested a "very simple and unexpensive [*sic*] means" by which to encourage the fine arts. No tariff on foreign paintings was necessary. Rather, this suggestion involved, not surprisingly, given Trumbull's history, the commissioning of artistic renderings of historic incidents. To wit: "whenever an Event, political, naval, or military, shall occur, which shall be regarded by the Government as of sufficient importance to be recorded as matter of History, the most eminent painter of the time [say, John Trumbull . . .], be ordered to paint a picture of the same, to be placed in some of the national buildings—that an artist of secondary talent be employed to make a copy of the same, which shall be given to the Minister, Admiral, or General under whose direction or command the event shall have taken place, as a testimony of the approbation and gratitude of the nation."[3] This would, speculates Trumbull, encourage public servants to greater exertions and reward the nation's finest artists. It was, to use anachronistic parlance, a win-win proposition.

Trumbull went on to propose that "the most distinguished engraver of the day should be employed to engrave a copperplate from the painting so executed, and that one thousand impressions, first printed from this plate, be reserved by Government."[4] These would be given to ambassadors for installation in their residences and presented to appropriate foreign ministers as well. Other impressions would be printed and sold to citizens desirous of commemorating such events on the walls of their homes or businesses.

The War of 1812, asserted Trumbull, had been insufficiently memorialized by the nation's artists. What better way to make the fine arts "subservient to the highest moral purposes of human society" and redeem them from "the disgraceful and false imputation under which they have long been oppressed, of being only the base and flattering instruments of royal and aristocratic luxury and vice," than to put these artists to remunerative labor celebrating the glorious triumphs of this young, monarch-less republic?[5]

"All civilized nations have made of the arts useful auxiliaries of history," concluded Trumbull, who in a subsequent letter of December 28 estimated the cost of the paintings and engravings for each event to total $6,500—a sum equal, *mirabile dictu*, to the proceeds of the sale of 1,000 engravings to the public at $10 each, minus commissions, losses, and damage.[6]

Adams, that most nationalist of the early presidents, did not take Trumbull up on his offer. Internal improvements-wise, he had his eyes on the skies, having issued a ringing call for a national observatory—a light-house of the skies—in his annual message to Congress of December 6, 1825.[7] Patriotic paintings, however, may not have contributed sufficiently to the "improvement of the condition of men," the extra-constitutional hook on which Adams based his support for a national astronomy program.[8]

Between 1817 and 1865, wrote historian Ray Allen Billington in his survey of government and the arts, about $4,000 per year of federal funds was directed to artists and sculptors.[9] A pittance, though in that era working artists did find sustenance, usually as portraitists. And it was anything but a Dark Age of American art, for this was the age of the Hudson River School, perhaps the best-known and most loved tradition in American art.

A New Dealer, A New Deck

John Trumbull's name was invoked with regularity a century-plus later, when in Franklin D. Roosevelt's first term provision was made for federal employment of writers, artists, musicians, actors, directors, playwrights, and historians. Collectively, the five elements of this initiative—the Art, Music, Theatre, Writers', and Historical Records programs of the Works Progress Administration—were called, in bureaucratese, Federal One. The stimulus was the Great Depression; the ostensible purpose was relief. But to those charged with administering the project, the stakes were far higher than a mere paycheck.

The forerunner of Federal One was the Public Works of Art Project (PWAP), a section of the public-employment program known as the Civil Works Administration (CWA), which was born at the end of 1933 and closed up shop less than a year later. The PWAP's birth was of the bluest blood. Its genesis might be traced to FDR's old Groton and Harvard classmate George Biddle, who on May 9, 1933, wrote the President suggesting that the United States, like Mexico, hire artists "at plumber's wages" to adorn government buildings, the US Department of Justice for starters, with murals. (Biddle had studied with Diego Rivera, the dean of the Mexican mural movement.)

Biddle explained to the President: "The younger artists of America are conscious as they have never been of the social revolution that our country and civilization are going through; and they would be eager to express these ideals in a permanent art form if they were given the government's cooperation. They would be contributing to and expressing in living monuments the social ideals that you are struggling to achieve."[10]

At Roosevelt's urging, Biddle drew up "A Revival of Mural Painting," which he circulated to Eleanor Roosevelt and various members of the Roosevelt Brain Trust. Despite a series of starts and stops, Biddle's conception found life in the PWAP, a Treasury Department program under the direction of Edward Bruce, an attorney-artist who before hooking on with the New Deal had been a lobbyist for a San Francisco-based sugar concern. Bruce shrewdly invited Eleanor Roosevelt to the first organizational meeting of what would become the PWAP, and though she sat knitting throughout much of the meeting, her presence "gave the idea impetus" and the apparent imprimatur of the President. Edward Bruce later called Mrs. Roosevelt "the patron saint of the arts projects."[11]

The PWAP, which put painters and sculptors to work decorating public buildings, ran from December 1933 until June 30, 1934. Over its brief life it would employ about 3,500 artists at plumber's wages (from $38 to $46.50 a week) and generate about 400 murals, 650 sculptures, and about 6,800 paintings.[12] Its central idea, according to Bruce, was "paying salaries to artists, and allowing them to work in a medium selected by them. . . . allowing them, in fact, complete liberty to express themselves, with the single provision that their work, in the broadest sense, should be appropriate in design and quality for the adornment of public buildings."[13]

The PWAP, situated within the venerably grand Treasury Department rather than some fly-by-night ameliorative agency, was viewed by its advocates as no mere relief program for the indigent. Director

Bruce envisioned the PWAP through the eyes of an aesthetician, not an almoner. He announced at the outset, "It is going to take a fine sense of discrimination in all of us to select only those needy artists whose artistic ability is worthy of their employment. . . . We are putting artists to work and not trying to make artists out of bums."[14] If Bruce's language hinted at snobbery, so be it. As New Deal administrator Jerre Mangione recalled, "Because it employed artists on the basis of recognized competence rather than economic need, [the PWAP's] critics attacked it for paying salaries to affluent artists who were not in need of work."[15]

PWAP artists submitted their drawings anonymously; those selected to bedizen public buildings were chosen by juries. The murals typically featured Americana motifs, often with regional tie-ins; many remain among the best-loved examples of public art in America.

Its projects tended to the noncontroversial, though in San Francisco, English-born artist Clifford Wright caused a minor tempest by painting a hammer and sickle and "Workers of the World Unite" in a mural in the Coit Memorial Tower. Wright's allies protested when regional PWAP chairman Walter Heil, at the direction of Edward Bruce, insisted on the elimination of Wright's communist message. The local artists' union picketed, but Bruce was immovable. "They are welcome to all the propaganda they want," he said, "but I don't see why they should do it on our money."[16] (Almost twenty years later, controversy attended another work of public art in San Francisco: Anton Refregier's mural in the Rincon Annex Post Office. Refregier, who was awarded $26,000 for the commission, which was finished in 1949, was accused of depicting such figures as Franklin D. Roosevelt, Spanish missionaries, pioneers, and waterfront strikers unfavorably or ahistorically. Rep. Hubert Scudder, a California congressman, sought, unsuccessfully, to have Refrieger's work removed from the post office.[17] Rep. Scudder enlisted the rabid Rep. George Dondero, whom we shall meet later, in the effort, but these right-wingers were no match for the Bay Citizen's Committee to Protect the Rincon Annex Murals, the San Francisco Museum, the San Francisco Art Association, and a phalanx of "leaders in business, finance, the arts, and society." The art establishment won that tussle, as it usually does.)[18]

In general, however, the 3,479 artists who were employed at one time or another by the PWAP shied from overt politicization of their work.[19] Nor were flagrant or transgressive sexual images an issue. As Edward B. Rowan, Assistant Technical Director of the PWAP, remarked, "Any artist who paints a nude for the PWAP should have his head examined."[20]

Yet the professionalism evident in the PWAP may also have worked against the spark of artistic creativity. Art historian Francis V. O'Connor, a scholar of American mural painting, has noted that the PWAP was "an excellent example of a government patron tightly controlling all aspects of the creative process in order to acquire the 'best' art at minimum financial and political risk to itself. While it occasionally got what it wanted, it did so by stifling the very mural movement it hoped to establish and maintain."[21] In doing George Biddle's bidding, the federal government did not unleash a Diego Rivera-like national muraling of America. The regimentation inherent in government does not encourage adventurousness.

Director Bruce spoke of the psychic rewards to the artists engaged by the PWAP. "[T]he receipt of a check from the United States Government meant much more than the amount for which it was drawn," he wrote. "It brought to the artist for the first time in America the realization that he was not a solitary worker. It symbolized a people's interest in his achievement. . . . Symbolically, he had become the spokesman of his community."[22] The paycheck was secondary, said Bruce, for while "the economic relief afforded [artists] by the project was enormously appreciated and greatly needed, the spiritual stimulus to them in finding that they were recognized as useful and valuable members of the body politic and the government desired their work has been simply amazing."[23]

This craving of the government's approval was not universal among American artists, even those of the starving variety, but the feeling of validation by many of those who were chosen in juried competitions to design public artwork was no doubt real and considerable. Talented artists, whatever their politics, like to have their talents recognized.

The PWAP expired June 30, 1934. Its artists had produced over 16,000 works. But a more comprehensive federal program for artists was waiting to be born. And it would include not only painters but writers as well, for many who had made a living at the typewriter were in dire straits. "In March 1935," notes historian Monty Noam Penkower in *The Federal Writers' Project: A Study in Government Patronage of the Arts* (1977), "about 1,400 writers who had been sacked from various journalism posts were listed on the relief rolls."[24] A cynic might see this as a hungry and ready-made army of propagandists.

There had been halting and fragmentary efforts to offer vocation-specific relief to writers. Despite the popular image of President Herbert

Hoover as an inert, almost paralyzed chief executive whose response to the Great Depression was a shrug of the shoulders, in many ways the Hoover administration was a precursor of the New Deal. For instance, the Emergency Relief Administration (renamed the Federal Emergency Relief Administration, or FERA, in 1933) was a direct forerunner of FDR's Works Progress Administration. FERA was a pioneer in work relief. ("Make work," to its critics.) It made grants to the states for the purpose of hiring the unemployed to perform jobs ranging from construction to custodial to the manufacture of consumer goods. FDR placed his confidant Harry Hopkins in charge of FERA. Hopkins sought to include white-collar workers, including writers and artists, within FERA's ambit, though at the state level, where the practical decisions were made, there was precious little enthusiasm for using FERA monies to pay out-of-work novelists—unless they were willing to pick up a broom or a rake. Several states did put men of the pen to work at archival or historical projects, but these were scattered and on a very small scale.

One exception was California, where more than fifty out-of-work newspapermen and women were put to work writing "reports on subsistence homesteads, histories of the Los Angeles police department and school system, and studies of racial groups in Southern California."[25] FERA monies also went toward the production of *The Connecticut Guide: What to See and Where to Find It*, a forerunner of the American Guide series of the Federal Writers' Project (FWP). But for the most part, as FWP director Henry Alsberg fretted, "no work relief was provided" under FERA for "these highly trained and specialized workers as a group." In fact, many scriveners suffered the ultimate indignity: physical labor! As Alsberg told a House of Representatives' committee, "This was the period during which one heard innumerable stories of skilled professional people and artists digging ditches, raking leaves, or tabulating street traffic."[26] Even for those writers belonging to communist front groups, solidarity with the workers of the world went only so far.

The enthusiasm of New Dealers and others for publicly supported artists was not universally shared in the world of arts and letters. In August 1934, Edward B. Rowan, former Assistant Technical Director of the then-defunct PWAP, solicited from prominent figures in that world their opinions of state-supported art. The journalist-essayist H. L. Mencken of the *Baltimore Sun*, the wit and slashing iconoclast who had been a major force in the promotion or discovery of numerous American writers, from Theodore Dreiser to Ruth Suckow, replied:

> I find myself in considerable doubt that any genuine "creative writers" are in need of government aid. As a matter of fact, the market for good writing is excellent at the moment, and no man or woman who can actually do it is in difficulties. My fear is that if you begin to offer subsidies to writers they will all go to quacks.
>
> What precisely do you propose to do in this direction? I'd like to hear your plans a bit more in detail. After twenty years of active magazine editing I am naturally widely acquainted among American authors. I can't recall a single one who really needs public assistance—that is, not one of any talent whatsoever. A great many pretenders, of course, are doing badly, but I can't see that it would be of any public benefit to encourage them in their bad work.[27]

FERA underwent an acronym transplant when its mission and related relief efforts were reconstituted under the Works Progress Administration (WPA), conjured up by executive order following passage of the Emergency Relief Appropriation Act of 1935. The act, which became law on April 8, authorized the President to spend $4.88 billion "to provide relief, work relief and to increase employment" in the Depression-wracked nation. A total of $300 million was to be dedicated to "assistance for educational, professional, and clerical persons."[28]

With almost thirteen million Americans, or one-quarter of the workforce, unemployed, the Brain Trust of the New Deal hit on a blunt solution: create government jobs. Though the agency would be a prime target of ridicule by fiscal conservatives, the more waggish of whom would rechristen it We Putter Along, We Piddle Around, or various other WPA combinations suggesting sloth, wastefulness, and indolence, over its eight-year life the WPA would make work for over eight million Americans. A small but inordinately examined number of these were men and women of arts and letters who found work with the division of the WPA known as Federal Project Number One, or Federal One, consisting of the WPA's Federal Art, Music, Theatre, Historical Records, and—most glamorously, at least in retrospect—Writers' Projects. At its peak on June 30, 1936, the WPA's arts and letters divisions would employ 44,797 persons of widely varying talents.[29]

Federal Project Number One was birthed on August 2, 1935. Its purpose, according to its official annunciation, was the sponsorship of "nation-wide projects intending to employ persons now on relief who are qualified in the fields of Art, Music, Drama, and Writing."[30] It marked a dramatic break with the American tradition of a separation of art and state.

Harry Hopkins, who had made the transition from supervising FERA to directing the WPA, said of artists, "Hell, they've got to eat just like other people."[31] There is much folksy truth in this remark. Then again Hopkins most famously said—or is said to have said; there is some evidence that the remark is apocryphal, or just approximate—in reference to FDR's political strategy, that it was "tax and tax, spend and spend, elect and elect," so we are not exactly quoting words of wisdom from the Sermon on the Mount.

The WPA, like government jobs programs of later years (for instance the Comprehensive Employment and Training Act, or CETA, of the 1970s), was a bonanza of patronage jobs. The party-in-power—in the WPA's case, the Democrats—behaved as a party in power is expected to behave: it rewarded its friends and sought to maximize its votes at the next election. Yet Federal One, because it touched on art and literature and high culture, has become enrobed, after the fact, in raiment of splendor.

For instance, rather breathlessly, Nick Taylor, author of a colon-clotted history of the WPA titled *American-Made: The Enduring Legacy of the WPA: When FDR Put the Nation to Work*, writes that "The WPA's Federal One. . . . freed the arts from their need to please commercial tastes and elite patrons."[32] It sounded like a socialist cultural paradise. Not even Federal One's most ecstatic boosters ordinarily dared to claim *that* much, but the retrospective halo surrounding the WPA's cultural projects grows more numinous with each passing year.

The poet W. H. Auden called the WPA's arts project

> one of the noblest and most absurd undertakings ever attempted by any state. Noblest because no other state has ever cared whether its artists as a group lived or died; other governments have hired certain individual artists to glorify their operations and have even granted a small pension from time to time for some artist with fame or influence, but to consider, in a time of general distress, starving artists as artists and not simply as paupers is unique to the Roosevelt Administration. Yet absurd, because a state can only function bureaucratically and impersonally—it has to assume that every member of a class is equivalent or comparable to every other member—but every artist, good or bad, is a member of a class of one.[33]

The men and women who ran Federal One were indisputably classes of one. Jacob Baker, an engineer cum publisher cum philosophical anarchist who had run FERA, was the assistant WPA administrator who handpicked the project directors, though by 1936 he was gone.

Baker had been an advocate of a decentralized federal writing and arts project, and the centralizers were ascendant. Anything Boise and Jefferson City and Columbus could do, Washington could do better! In retrospect, Jacob Baker ought to have known that anarchists seldom find government work possible, let alone rewarding.

As for the folks in charge, Hallie Flanagan, who took the theater position, was the director of the Vassar Experimental Theater and had been a Grinnell College classmate of Harry Hopkins. Nikolai Sokoloff, the Kiev-born music project director, had been conductor of the Cleveland Symphony Orchestra. Holger Cahill, director of the arts project, was an Iceland-born writer and arts administrator who had served as acting director of New York City's Museum of Modern Art (an entity that was to pop up again and again in the intersection of art and Big Government) and from 1929 until 1942 advised Abby Aldrich Rockefeller in the assemblage of her extensive folk art collection.[34] But none of these left a legacy, for better and for worse, as enduring as Henry Alsberg.

The Federal Writers' Project

Henry Alsberg, captain of the writers' division of Federal One (official title: National Director of the Federal Writers' Project), was a writer and theatrical producer whose associations included *The Nation*, the *New York Evening Post*, and the *New York World*. Alsberg had a privileged and prosperous upbringing. He studied at Columbia University and Harvard, but wanted to make sure that no one mistook him for a Babbitt-ish drone. He "refused to be photographed for the [Columbia] senior yearbook of 1900," not out of shyness but rather a sense of superiority.[35] Henry wanted all to know that he was not like everybody else! In 1926, he smugly wrote in a publication of that same Columbia Class of 1900 that "It's very difficult to say very much, as I am so completely out of touch with the point of view of the majority of them. They are leading the normal life of the average American middle-class citizen. I am more or less in revolt against everything they would hold most sacred, and advocate causes that would be abhorrent to all their habits and fixed beliefs."[36]

My, aren't we avant-garde!

Alsberg once said that his role was "saving the world from reactionaries."[37] He was not, however, averse to taking a paycheck from those same reactionaries.

Henry Alsberg was in many ways a failed writer. Though he worked as an editor and correspondent for various publications, he never wrote the novel he intended to write. As one puzzled colleague later said, "Henry Alsberg. . . . was a very odd duck. I don't know why in the devil he was the Director of the Writers' Project anyway, because he isn't a writer."[38]

He became a federal bureaucrat, not exactly the career destination of a radical in revolt. Jerre Mangione, in his entertaining and opinionated account of the FWP, describes his friend and coworker Alsberg as amiable enough but a lousy administrator, in fact "someone who could barely administer himself," a man "reluctant to make decisions" and in the "habit of leaving projects unfinished." He subjected subordinates to "suffocatingly long monologues" though he was, for the most part, popular with his staff.[39] He was, in short, a well-meaning bore and self-styled intellectual who thought himself better than the dullard taxpayers who supplied his salary. (Mangione, who later achieved prominence as a novelist and University of Pennsylvania professor, was the national coordinating editor of the FWP for most of its existence. He was also the uncle of jazz musicians Chuck and Gap Mangione.)

Alsberg seemed blithely unconcerned about the potential for mischief in a federal arts program. "For the first time in the history of the United States," he boasted to the *Saturday Review of Literature* in January 1936, "writers are working for the government as writers," just as "shipbuilders and other craftsmen" had labored for Uncle Sam in their professional capacities. Many of these writers, he said with writerly hyperbole, were "destitute" and "fighting off starvation."[40] The challenge for Washington was to find literary work for these penurious penmen without enlisting them in projects that would compromise their principles. Since the toilers spent no more than thirty hours per week in federal employ, there was sufficient time outside of their FWP labor to undertake their own writing projects.

Novels, poetry, and imaginative literature were not deemed to be proper subjects for FWP employees. While there was always the chance that a subsidized bard might produce the *Moby Dick* of the twentieth century, it was infinitely likelier that from his pen would flow a virtual effluent of mediocrity, and quite probably proletarian-themed mediocrity at that.

From several sources came the suggestion that the FWP should occupy itself with the production of guides to the forty-eight states. New Dealer Katherine Kellock, a "compulsive talker" and idea generator who was married to Harold Kellock, a Houdini biographer, had suggested to an aide to Jacob Baker that "The thing you have to do for writers is to put them to work writing Baedekers," a term borrowed from the popular travel guides by the German publisher.[41] (The American Baedeker, published in 1909, was rather out of date.) The idea made its way up the bureaucratic food chain, and the result was the American Guide series on which the FWP's reputation would come to rest. The American Guide series was to provide wholesome and salutary work to writers who revealed and celebrated the flora, fauna, history, cities, towns, and tourist attractions of the forty-eight states.

Typical of the worldview of some New Dealers, the original idea was for "writers, editors, historians, research workers, art critics, architects, archeologists, map draftsmen, geologists, and other professional workers" to prepare a single "American Guide."[42] Mercifully, this massive and unwieldy project gave way to the preparation of guides to each of the states, as well as numerous and sundry smaller volumes on historical, local, regional, social, and geographic subjects. These included works on subjects ranging from Death Valley to New England to the place names of South Dakota, studies of such episodes as the 1938 hurricane that devastated New England, and hundreds of pamphlets covering small towns from Romney, West Virginia, to Pittsburg, Kansas.

By the summer of 1935, the Federal Writers' Project was in business. Its primary goal was the production of the state guides. (A competing idea for a series of regional surveys of America was scrapped as insufficiently attentive to state distinctions). The FWP solemnly and foolishly pledged to finish these guides in six months, a timetable so absurdly impracticable that not even the starriest-eyed New Dealer believed it.

This unmeetable goal was made even more distant by Alsberg's centralist philosophy and demand that every jot and tittle of every guide receive the approval of the Washington headquarters. (He relented a couple of years into the project and loosened the reins, slightly, by appointing regional directors.)

The project was quickly enveloped in a romantic haze, though those who actually participated often recall the frustrations of navigating the bureaucratic haze. The enduring image, in its folksiest version, is of "Writers in libraries, writers bumping over dusty roads in Model A Fords, hungry authors, young writers with ambitious off-time projects, talented writers past their creative prime and preferring FWP work to home-relief, hacks with meaningless pasts (in literary terms) and hopeless futures," combining to produce volumes of intermittent brilliance, occasional triteness, and some lasting, though debatable, value.[43]

Washington dictated the template: the state guides were to begin with a history of the state and its people, covering their physical, cultural, and topographical aspects; continue with an accounting of the state's cities and their characteristics; and conclude with a highway tour of the state, annotated with tidbits and factoids and amusing asides. Part One was where the best writers had an opportunity to display their literary bona fides; Part Two was a meld of history and boosterism; and Part Three was akin to a tour book.

Yet the heavy thumbprint of Washington, DC, was never far from the page. State editors, after compiling their lists of which cities to highlight in Part Two, had to run them by the national headquarters, a humbling and frustrating step, for who knows Indiana better: a collection of Hoosier editors and writers or New Deal appointees on the Potomac? In the case of Indiana, the Washington staff rejected the inclusion of six cities, among them Madison (which is today famous for its architecture) and French Lick (the resort site that would produce basketballer Larry Bird, the legendary "Hick from French Lick").[44]

Directions from Washington were often obtuse or wrongheaded. "The mimeographed material that kept pouring into the office was written by urban-minded editors with urban areas in mind," said Ethel Schlasinger, who as a lass of just twenty years was named director of the North Dakota project.[45]

Ray Allen Billington, director of the Massachusetts project (and a eulogist, if a clear-eyed eulogist, of the program), recalled of his experience: "All reason and order seemed to have fled as writers converted reams of copy paper into the manuscripts that would justify their continued employment, as each day's mail from Washington brought orders that contradicted those of the day before."[46] The tug between the ideological centralizers and the more populist decentralizers that characterized other New Deal initiatives was perhaps even more marked in the FWP. Billington also wondered if the collectivist spirit of the project wasn't contrary to the pursuit of excellence. "[W]as the spark of genius dimmed by the meddling of too many blue pencils?" he asked, and in contrasting the limpid prose of Conrad Aiken's description of Deerfield, Massachusetts, with the serviceable account of Amherst in the same state guide—an account that was the result of several contributors—he answered, "cooperative writing dims the spark that glows in the words of the true author."[47]

State editors and writers fought back with the only weapons they had: words. James Thompson of the Oklahoma project, who would in later years gain fame as the hard-boiled *noir* novelist Jim Thompson, complained to FWP functionary Benjamin A. Botkin:

> We feel that in the matters of rewriting and editing, the efforts of the State office thus far virtually have been wasted. We think we would have saved time, money, and the lowering of morale by simply forwarding the source material to Washington and allowing it to be put in final form there. The Guide Book—to which we have chiefly devoted our time—is not ours. There is hardly a sentence in it that has not been changed from one to a dozen times. . . . We have come to know how the six hundred must have felt when they marched into the valley of death. All of our literary training may have taught us that interest and originality should never be sacrificed for brevity and simplicity, but we have learned to follow orders no matter how wrong we know them to be. We have not developed our talents; we have simply become cogs in a machine, the like of which is not to be found in private industry.[48]

It is worth noting that Jim Thompson, who compares the FWP bureaucracy unfavorably with private industry, was a member of the Communist Party. But he was an artist before he was a party man.

J. M. Scammell, a field supervisor in the western states, reported the pervasive belief within his jurisdiction that "the peculiarities of their states are not appreciated." He was sympathetic with the locals, noting that "There is a certain strong pride in state and individuality here in the West. . . . [Ross] Santee once told me that his aim was to make his guide actually *smell* of Arizona. [Byron] Crane complained that his predecessors in Montana were not Montanans and did not know the state; and that his aim was to make the Guide reek of Montana. . . . [T]here is everywhere apparent a discontent against criticism which they claim tends to emasculate this individuality and rob the tours and essays of color."[49]

These charges run contrary to the rosy myths in which the WPA state guides are encased, but who are you going to believe: top-notch writers like Jim Thompson and Ross Santee, men who were *there,* or New Deal eulogists?

(In defense of the Washington office—sort of—John Cheever, the postwar chronicler of WASP life who toiled, to his embarrassment, in the FWP headquarters as an editor, said that he loathed "twisting into order the sentences written by some incredibly lazy bastards."[50] Cheever despised the project and did not like to speak of his work thereon in later years.)

One might assume that censorship would not be an overly salient issue in the production of state guides. Tourism is seldom controversial. Guide writers were careful not to say that Barstow, California, was a pit, or that Ma's Motor Lodge was a cesspool. But the patronage of the federal government ensured that clashes were inevitable.

"The central office exercised control over all state copy," writes Monty Noam Penkower. The degree of this control varied depending on the personalities and competence of those involved. But even with the best-written guides, Washington exerted "autocratic power," as Idaho's Vardis Fisher complained.[51] And state governors, legislators, and even chambers of commerce got in on the act, too, objecting to material that seemed one-sided, partisan (if the partisanship was that of one's opponents), or insufficiently appreciative of the glories of the state.

The interference from the Washington office moved Miriam Allen deFord, a California writer of mystery and science fiction stories employed by the Golden State's project, to doggerel:

> I think that I have never tried
> A job as painful as the guide.
> A guide which changes every day
> Because our betters feel that way.[52]

At its acme in April 1936, the FWP employed 6,471 writers and researchers and clerks and photographers and secretaries and editors and mapmakers of all sorts, from the unquestionably talented (Vardis Fisher, Richard Wright, Conrad Aiken, Arna Bontemps, Kenneth Rexroth, Ralph Ellison, Saul Bellow, Loren Eiseley, Weldon Kees, Zora Neale Hurston, Nelson Algren) to the hopelessly purple. Many of the luminous names on this list worked for the feds only for a brief time, leaving as soon as they found work in the private sector, though in fairness to the FWP, they, as much as the deadwood, may be called alums. (The presence of talented African American writers such as Wright, Ellison, and Hurston might suggest that the FWP was a godsend to black writers, though in fact the number of them working on the FWP at any one time was about one hundred, or perhaps 2 percent of the workforce.)[53]

Field supervisors were sent out from Washington, the epicenter of editorial wisdom, to corral the yokels into artistry, or at least competence. The infighting and backbiting and prodigious feats of fact-collecting and editing and bottle-draining (as well as shirking and sniping) are entertainingly recounted in Jerre Mangione's *The Dream and the Deal*. The offices of the four-headed Federal One (the fifth head, the Historical Records Survey, was at first under the FWP) were in the spacious if down-rent confines of the Old Auditorium, a former performing arts venue more recently "utilized mainly for prize fights and dog shows."[54] Headquarters were soon removed to the mansion at 1500 I Street NW formerly occupied by Evalyn Walsh McLean, whose family holdings included the *Washington Post* and the Hope diamond. These surroundings, which featured "ornate chandeliers, silken walls, and Greek statues," were more satisfactory, adjudged the administrators.[55] (The arts project was later moved to the Ouray Building at 805 G Street NW, a handsome Italianate structure that could not compete with the McLean Mansion in the ornate chandelier department. Hallie Flanagan complained that the Ouray Building's stolidity and lack of flash induced "dull brown thoughts" in those who worked within. It's easy, it seems, to get used to taxpayer-supplied luxury.)[56]

State WPA administrators were sometimes recalcitrant in their dealings with the FWP. They resented the feds appointing state writers' project directors. Turf was disputed. The panjandrums in DC preferred that state directors have at least some reportorial, editorial, or novelistic experience; the state WPA honchos, who tended to be political appointees, lobbied for cronies and hacks and timeservers to fill these positions. Though Henry Alsberg tried to put able persons in the state posts, he sometimes ran up against the powers-that-be: the state WPA bosses. Patronage, it turns out, often trumps aesthetics.

The WPA requirement that 90 percent of the employees of its various programs, including Federal One, be certified via a means test as worthy of relief, chafed at the pride of many potential dolesmen. This act of abasement was just too much for many writers (and other out-of-work Americans). There was a stigma attached to relief; proud men and women were none too eager to forfeit their dignity for a government paycheck. (Lobbying by the FWP and writers' associations succeeded in reducing the on-relief portion of the workforce to 75 percent, though by 1937, when the project's appropriations were cut by a quarter, it was restored to close to 90 percent. These changes were greeted by a June 1937 strike in New York City. Writers as strikers were not quite as fearsome to the powers-that-be as, say, longshoremen. Instead of sabotage and violence, the writers tended toward long manifestos and tears.)

A not inconsiderable number of talented but unemployed writers refused to go on relief, thus depriving the FWP of their talents. They were just as needful of a monthly salary as the next down-and-outer, but they had inherited the stubborn American aversion to accepting government welfare. Private charity some of them might take, but a check from Washington? Never.

Jerre Mangione notes that in many parts of the country, "the hostility of the citizenry toward the WPA and the Writers' Project was often an obstacle." Outside the major cities, especially, the WPA was viewed as a wasteful generator of make-work at best, and a socialist scheme at worst. Folks did not want to be interviewed by representatives of the government, which made field work difficult. Agnes Wright Spring, who directed the Wyoming project, encountered so much resistance that she used her affiliation with the *Wyoming Stockman Farmer* in order to allay suspicions.[57]

It proved quite impossible to keep politics out of what was, after all, a political creation. Chicago Mayor Richard Daley's immortal motto "Jobs for the Boys" was no less an operating principle with some sections of the Federal Writers' Project than it was for ward-heelers in the Windy City.

William C. Fitzgerald, a supervisor in the Boston office of the Bay State project, recalled an office filled by "senior creeps who passed themselves off as writers when really they couldn't have conceived decently indecent graffiti. They were simply drones, misfits, happiest when engaged in some petty conspiracy and at their sourest when one ventured to note mistakes of spelling, grammar, in such copy as they turned in—if, indeed, they submitted any at all."[58]

The political hacks who infested the machinery of the state writers' projects gummed up the works in various ways. They padded payrolls with untalented cronies; they were indifferent to the quality of the work done; and they interfered in sundry matters. For instance, Matthew Murray, the director in Missouri, a state in which the corrupt Pendergast machine of Kansas City held sway, rejected a profile of Missouri's famed painter Thomas Hart Benton, saying, "I wouldn't hang him on my shithouse wall. Why don't you write about our beautiful roads instead? Now there's something really worth writing about."[59] The Missouri office was a fetid mixture of corruption and incompetence. Another director in the Show-Me State, Geraldine Parker, was so grossly inept that her staff went on strike demanding her ouster. (The Kansas City FWP office, a Pendergast outpost, "served as a gambling center for horse races, and film for the guide was used for pornography," according to Monty Noam Penkower.)[60]

Indiana: A Guide to the Hoosier State, which wasn't published until 1941, was the product of a staff of three hundred.[61] (By comparison, the South Dakota guide resulted from the labor of twenty-eight persons.) The Indiana state guide was the major undertaking of that state's writers' project, though a series of localized publications also found home between covers. The Indianans conducted interviews with old-timers, pored through yellowing newspapers, and drove the highways and backroads of the Hoosier State.

The director of the Indiana Writers' Project was Ross Lockridge, a popular historian whose son, Ross Lockridge Jr., would go on to write the best-seller *Raintree County* (1948), one of the most notable—and certainly one of the longest—Indiana novels. Lockridge was an independent spirit who had his own ideas about the project. He wanted his writers to spend less time compiling the state guide and more time helping local historians, keepers of pioneer cemeteries, and small newspapers. Independence, alas, was not a trait especially prized by federal administrators, so Lockridge—like 75 percent of the original state administrators—was shown the door.[62]

Writing is not a skill that lends itself to nine-to-five discipline or clock-punching. Yet most FWP employees had to sign in and sign out, for "the WPA's model for hourly employment was drawn from the routinized world of industry," as Bruce I. Bustard, a curator at the National Archives and Records Administration, wrote in *A New Deal for the Arts.*[63]

The government dole can breed docility. John T. Frederick, a Northwestern professor who directed the Illinois writing project, recalled that "a good 80 percent of the workers were so dependent on their monthly checks and so grateful for them that they would do nothing that could conceivably endanger them."[64] The problem, in Illinois at least, was not the radicalism of the FWP writers but rather their meekness and pliability. (As Frederick's example indicates, state directors were permitted to retain outside jobs.)

Robert West Howard, assistant director of the New York State project, sighed, "As far as local politicians were concerned, the Writers' Project was the place where you dumped the bastard you didn't know what to do with."[65] Writers being writers, there were also dipsomaniacs aplenty. Temperance was not among the job's requisites.

Almost as damaging to auctorial egos as the requirement that one be on relief was the anonymity that shrouded the FWP writers. Unlike, for instance, the painters or actors on the Federal One payroll, the writers did not affix their names to their work. In a few instances, for example that of Vardis Fisher and Idaho, word got out that a particularly strong effort was the work of one man or woman. But in the vast majority of cases, the writer labored without credit. On the other hand, he or she generally put in thirty hours a week, leaving time for outside writing projects.

By most accounts, the best state FWP director was Idaho's Vardis Fisher, a novelist whose own politics were intensely hostile toward the New Deal. Fisher produced the first and possibly best of the state guides, despite working with a small rag-tag staff with an inordinate number of useless and even unbalanced employees. (An enemy of Fisher tried to "pack the Project staff with former inmates of mental institutions."[66])

In the judgment of historian Ronald W. Taber in the *Pacific Northwest Quarterly*, the relative handful of Idaho FWP employees "published more creditable material than any state except perhaps New York."[67] The crown jewel was *Idaho: A Guide in Word and Picture*, first out of the gate and still the most praised of the guides. The dynamo behind this guide was Vardis Fisher. Born to a Mormon family in Idaho, Fisher had been educated at the Universities of Utah and Chicago. He was an established novelist when he accepted the offer to head the Idaho Writers' Project. Part of the lure was the $2,300 salary, which was more than a moderately successful but hardly best-selling novelist would make in an average year. Still, his salary was among the lowest of any state director, and the average monthly wage for Idaho Writers' Project employees was $69, or more than 30 percent below the wage in New York City.

Fisher recounted that upon his appointment, the director of another state project wired him, "Congratulations on your new position. Don't take it seriously. It is not intended that we should achieve anything but only that we should put the jobless to work so they will vote for Roosevelt. Take it philosophically and if they send you a telegram from Washington 150 words long, send them one 300 words long or call them long distance collect."[68]

The conscientious Fisher ignored this advice. Working with ten employees in a cramped Boise office, he supplemented his skeleton staff the old-fashioned way: with volunteers from high schools, librarians, teachers, service organizations, women's clubs, journalists, small-town politicians, professors, and others. The ringleader of this Gem State circus was Vardis Fisher, for as he wrote to Henry Alsberg, "The only writer on the project here is the State Director. . . . Idaho is not, of course, a state of unemployed writers." As Kenneth Larson, who had served as supervisor of Idaho's Historical Records Survey, told Ronald W. Taber in 1967, "The huge success that the Idaho Writers' Project became was. . . . almost a one-man job. Vardis Fisher deserves the credit. He did almost all the creative work himself. He was indefatigable in his efforts. The real goals of accomplishment were established by Fisher himself and not by the Federal Government."[69]

Interviewed in 1968 by Jerre Mangione, Fisher said, "By telephone and letter Alsberg told me repeatedly that for Idaho to be first among the forty-eight states would be dreadful embarrassment." Fisher, contumacious and independent as ever, added, "I thought the national office so incompetent and cynical and political that I cared nothing about its embarrassment."[70]

Henry Alsberg wanted the Washington, DC guide to be first published—an apt piece of symbolism, since the nation's capital was preeminent in the new political dispensation. Idaho, Alsberg believed, should be released much further down the line. It was such an unimportant state. Alsberg and the national headquarters tried all manner of delaying tactics, forcing on Fisher picayune edits and revisions in a crude attempt to derail the Gem State book.

A mountain of requests were dumped on Fisher. He had written his tour of the state from south to north; Alsberg told him to change it from north to south—a problem, since "at least 80 percent of the traffic [in Idaho] was south to north." Business and local government leaders went to bat for Fisher, protesting "[s]illy and arbitrary rules such as this." Alsberg, though praising Fisher for the literary quality of his manuscript, kept up the delaying tactics. The Washington office demanded the insertion of factually inaccurate statements about the Idaho batholith and a bridge near Arco, Idaho; Fisher, patience exhausted, set them straight and refused to make the changes. Nitpicking edits for punctuation and style seemed like gratuitous insults to Fisher. But he persevered, and in September 1936, less than a year after Fisher started the work, he contracted with Idaho's Caxton Printers to bring out the guide.[71]

Fighting Fisher to the last ditch, Alsberg even sent his associate director, George Cronyn, to Idaho in a bid to derail the project long enough to enable the DC guide to slip in under the wire. He brought with him a list of two thousand corrections demanded by the Washington office.[72] Cronyn spent much of his time with Fisher getting drunk and railing against the profusion of potatoes in the text. But Fisher pushed on. Idaho won the race.

Though he eventually had a staff of about twenty, Fisher wrote almost all of the Idaho guide himself (374 of its 405 pages) in a herculean effort to "bring honor to this small segment of a nationwide boondoggle."[73] The book, published in January 1937, was genuine literature—and it was achieved by one man, Vardis Fisher, over the most strenuous objections of the Federal Writers' Project. Fisher's name appears nowhere in the book. His prodigious accomplishment, though anonymous, seemed to run counter to the collectivist ethos of Federal One, although given the stubborn individuality of many artists, regardless of their professed political views, the question of whether or not artistic endeavors are ever really collectivist is problematic.

The rave reviews poured in. Bernard DeVoto in the *Saturday Review of Literature* called the Idaho guide an "almost unalloyed triumph." Even Alsberg wrote Fisher that it was a "swell book"—not exactly rhapsodic praise—though he complained to Ellen S. Woodward of the WPA that Fisher was "obstinate in his insistence on doing things his own way."

As for Vardis Fisher, when interviewed thirty years later he was proud of his work but dubious of the philosophy behind the FWP, saying, "Subsidized art becomes propaganda in support of the government in power."[74]

The guide to the nation's capital, *Washington: City and Capital,* was published in April 1937. Weighing in at 1,141 pages, its publication was fouled up by the Government Printing Office, which "had botched the publishing job by using a coated paper for what was supposed to be a handy volume."[75]

Although the massive Washington, DC, guide, naturally, was printed at the federal government's expense, the FWP's intention was that its books find commercial publishers. The Idaho guide was brought out by Caxton, a small but respected publishing house in Idaho. The letter of the law would seem to suggest that the books had to be published by the Government Printing Office, but most were brought out by commercial publishers such as Houghton Mifflin or Viking or Hastings House; others (for instance both Dakotas) relied on subvention from the state legislature. In some cases, sponsors—public agencies, local governments, private interests—agreed to buy the first two thousand copies of a book, which made it a far more attractive proposition to commercial publishers. Royalties went not to the authors of the volumes but to the project.

The state guides were ultimately issued by a total of fifteen publishers. Many of the FWP's smaller endeavors, the guides to cities, towns, or regions, were published by small local presses. The last of the state guides, that of Oklahoma, appeared at the end of 1941. The longest state guide was New York (782 pages) and the briefest was North Dakota (371 pages).

There was no apparent correlation between the number of writers on a state guide and the book's length. South Dakota, with just 28 workers, produced a guide of 180,000 words, a considerably higher worker-word ratio than such states as Ohio (281 workers, 187,000 words) and Pennsylvania (340 workers, 188,000 words).[76]

The dispersion of FWP monies to the 48 states irked New York City-based writers, who believed that they resided in the cultural capital of the world, and why should clodhoppers in the Dakotas or the Rockies share in the bounty? George Creel, who became famous during World War I for overseeing the Committee on Public Information, whose "Four Minute Men" were empowered by the federal government to burst into theaters and deliver war-propaganda speeches to captive patrons, derided "the stupid arrangement by which each state has been given a certain amount of money regardless of whether the state has writers or not." After all, said Creel, "writers are largely grouped in various centers."[77]

A residency requirement of two years was designed to ensure that the West Virginia project, for instance, hired actual West Virginians rather than Manhattanites who bought a bus ticket to Morgantown the previous week. Or, to strain credulity, that West Virginia writers didn't trickle into Manhattan and "steal" jobs from the locals. Still, this chafed, especially those who wanted to buy a bus ticket to or from Morgantown or the Port Authority and become a writing expat. Nevertheless, as Monty Noam Penkower writes, "probably half of the project's actual writers would come from New York City, Chicago, Boston, Philadelphia, and Los Angeles."[78]

Wages varied, with New York City writers being paid twice as much or more as those who worked in some Southern cities. For instance, New York City FWP employees received up to $103.50 per month, while those in Mississippi made just $39. Surely this was no reflection on the relative merits of literature in these two places, unless you believe that Henry Alsberg was superior to William Faulkner. This would seem a gross violation of egalitarian principles, but then some egalitarians are more equal than others. (Interestingly, Faulkner's younger brother, John, wrote a novel mocking the WPA. "This God damned WPA is ruining the whole country," wrote the lesser-known of the brothers Faulkner in *Men Working* (1941). "You can't get a man to stay with you long enough to make a crop and when you do get one he's been leaning on one of those WPA shovels so long about all he's good for is to stand in a watermelon patch for a scarecrow."[79] William Faulkner had something of the same attitude, though he expressed it in less homely phrases. The citizen, he said in 1940, "mustn't accept gratuity from the state. He mustn't let the state buy him by pensions or relief or dole or grants of any sort"—including cash for writers.[80])

There were four WPA salary levels: Professional, Skilled, Intermediate, and Unskilled. Though some of those who have read through the lesser works of the FWP may quibble, none of its employees was classified as Unskilled. Wages were pegged to classification as well as an employee's geographic region and city. The vast disparity between New York City and Mississippi suggests that the storied legislative skills of Southern warhorse politicos, the Foghorn Leghorns of the national legislature, were rather less than impressive than those of the land of Tammany Hall.

The New York City Writers' Project was turbulent, ideological, riven by intense factionalism. Its office was in the Port Authority, a dreary building that reeked of mind-numbing jobbery. New York City was also the focal point of the Stalinist-Trotskyite battle within the FWP, though both Stalinists and Trotskyites seemed quite indifferent to the fact that writers in Alabama, whatever their politics, were being paid far less than were those in New York. The politics of "fairness" stopped, it seems, at the Hudson's edge.

Despite or because of its large staff, its *extremely self-confident* staff, its eternally argumentative staff, its staff belonging to numerous unions and splinter groups, and its revolving door of directors, the New York City project lagged. Two years into the project, the New York City guide was nowhere to be seen. Little Idaho, with its skeleton staff, had far outpaced New York City, not only in quantity but in literary quality as well. (Mangione contrasts the "deeply dedicated" writers of the Midwestern states with "the cynicism and chaos" rampant in the New York City project.[81]) The vicious political infighting in the New York City project was an outgrowth of the sectarian leftism that ran rampant in certain sectors of Federal One. We will touch on this later in the chapter, but while Gotham was the center of the FWP's most sustained political infighting, it was not the only battlefield.

The Massachusetts Writers' Project, and specifically its state guide, was in the political crossfire, too. Conrad Aiken's much-praised essay on the literary culture of the state was balanced, after protests by project leftists, by a Marxist-inflected interpretation of the same subject. Some conservatives objected to the relative importance the authors of the guide gave to the Boston Tea Party (a grand total of nine lines in 675 pages) and the Sacco and Vanzetti cause célèbre (forty-one lines).[82] This illustrated nicely the pitfalls of government sponsorship of intellectual endeavor. Whether a writer devotes forty-one lines or forty-one pages to Sacco and Vanzetti—and whether he or she believes them to be martyrs or murderers—is, or should be, up to the writer. But when the state is underwriting the writer, his opinions must be vetted by agents of the state. The writer's freedom is severely constricted. Yes, he receives a paycheck—but the cost is higher than a writer of conscience should be able to bear.[83]

Former Massachusetts Governor Joseph E. Ely (D) denounced the state guide, saying that "they ought to take the books to Boston Common, pile them in a heap, set a match and have a bonfire."[84] Thus were Bostonians treated to the spectacle of the state's erstwhile highest elected official demanding the public burning of books whose composition had been funded by the federal government—an auto-da-fé pitting levels of government against each other, with the citizenry as bystander.

A contrary point of view was taken by Lawrence Estavan, one-time reporter for the *San Francisco Chronicle*, in his introduction to "Material Gathered," a mimeographed collection of creative works by participants in the San Francisco writers' project. Estavan, as Jerre Mangione relates, proposed "the establishment of federal magazines for creative writers in every locality capable of supporting them." Federal subsidy was superior to commercial publishing, argued Estavan, because commercial publishers are guided by the "real or fancied fear that their readers would be offended, their circulation would drop, their advertisers would withdraw their support." By contrast, "A federal magazine need have no such qualms. It could say things that need to be said. It would be financed by the whole people and the people would make it possible to hear their writers without fear."[85]

The credulousness of this passage is jaw-dropping. The Massachusetts dispute did not register with Estavan. Is the central government really the best guarantor of free and wide-ranging expression? Moreover, would a single government publisher be superior to the hundreds, even thousands, of commercial publishers? Surely not every commercial publisher responds to the same pressures in the same way.

Rivalling the Federal Writers' Project for controversy was the Federal Theatre Project (FTP), which was situated in New York City-based political disputation. But before we take a seat at that show, let us very briefly consider the relatively uncontroversial aspects of Federal One: the less ideologically charged Federal Music and Art Projects and the Historical Records Survey.

Art, Music, and Historical Records

Philanthropy had made the works of Old Masters and American painters alike more accessible than ever before in the years before the Depression. Art museum budgets rose from $15 million in 1910 to $58 million in 1930, though to the more populist-minded artists, this was hardly reason for exultation. Thomas Hart Benton, the Missouri muralist, harrumphed, "If it were left to me, I wouldn't have any museums. Museums don't buy enough of my paintings in an average year to pay for my boy's music lessons. Who looks at paintings in a museum? I'd rather sell mine to saloons, bawdy houses, Kiwanis and Rotary Clubs, Chambers of Commerce—even women's clubs. People go to saloons, but never to museums."[86]

Benton had faith in the ability of ordinary people to not only appreciate but also purchase works of art outside the channels of government and museums. (It should be pointed out that in our time museums, many with vast storehouses of unexhibited paintings, would survive just fine without any government subsidies, as the bulk of their acquisition funds come from private sources.)[87]

Yet by the mid-1930s the market for art, especially art by those not yet established in the field, had largely dried up. The Federal Art Project was intended to bridge the gap between American artists and their dwindling clientele. The output of the FAP in terms of sheer numbers is impressive. The Federal Art Project employed about 5,000 artists who "created some 108,000 easel paintings, 17,700 sculptures, 11,200 print designs, and 2,500 murals."[88] Even at the state level, the numbers are often impressively large. In Illinois, for instance, the FAP produced almost 5,000 easel paintings, almost 500 sculptures, and over 200 murals.[89]

About half of those employed by the FAP worked in the fine arts (murals, sculpture, painting, graphic arts); under a third were occupied in the practical or applied arts (posters, photography, arts and crafts, dioramas, models), and researching of the landmark Index of American Design, which explored "the evolution of native arts and crafts"[90]; a fifth were in such educational services as art galleries and teachings, and the remainder were in supervisory capacities.[91] As with the other divisions of Federal One, refractory artists resisted what they viewed as government employment. The painter Edward Hopper, who was hard up for money in the early 1930s, refused even to consider an association with the FAP because, as his biographer Gail Levin writes, he "believed that government funding would merely encourage artistic mediocrity and he condemned Roosevelt and all his works."[92]

Unlike later government-subsidized art, little of the work done under FAP auspices was abstract or experimental; much was in the American Scene genre of local life, whether urban-industrial or rural-agrarian. Some was quite good: even the most obstinate critics conceded that the project did occasionally employ artists of real talent. The quality varied enormously, from enduring to ephemeral, though the New Deal arts projects that are remembered most fondly—the murals that ornament hundreds of post offices across America—were not painted under the aegis of the Federal Art Project but rather the Treasury Department's Section of Painting and Sculpture. As with the PWAP, which had also been under Treasury, the post office muralists were selected in competitions.

The FAP, argued historian Victoria Grieve in *The Federal Art Project and the Creation of Middlebrow Culture*, had a populist bent that "championed broad access to the fine arts, widespread education, and the redefinition of art as a commodity available to all Americans."[93] It was, by and large, unfriendly to abstract art, though abstraction would get its revenge little more than a decade later, when the cultural arm of the nascent national security state began promoting self-consciously avant-garde works as the art of freedom. But unlike the Cold War art, the paintings and murals produced under the Federal Art Project were being paid for upfront, without any subterfuge, by the federal government, which was, certainly in theory and partially in practice, responsive to public pressures. A huge white canvas on which a subsidized artist threw a bucket of red paint might have spelled bad publicity, to which FAP director Holger Cahill had a sensible aversion.

Like the Federal Writers' and Theatre Projects, the Federal Art Project was geographically lopsided, which is to say it was Gotham-centric. As historian Richard D. McKinzie wrote in *A New Deal for Artists*, "What did astound some individuals was the extent to which New

York City overshadowed other cities as a cultural center. New York, in December 1937, employed 44.5 percent of all FAP artists." And although "[a]s many people lived in the Dakotas and Texas as in New York City . . . during the FAP's first year not one artist examined the life or permeated the culture of the three states."[94] This is astonishing. Texas, in the 1930s, was the home to a thriving regional art scene, exemplified by the "Dallas Nine" and associated Lone Star artists, some of whom had received commissions from the PWAP.[95] The disparity between New York City and Texas was not measured in quality or innovation but rather in success at accessing public monies. Some places—those with the loudest and glibbest claimants to federal funds—had much better pipelines to Washington than others did.

While the FAP disproportionately assisted New York City artists, some of its supporters sang a populist tune. For instance, Maury Maverick, the leftist Democratic congressman from Texas, framed the issue as one of plutocrats versus The People in a 1936 speech: "Mr. Mellon goes over to Europe and spends $100,000 on one picture. He goes over there and buys a picture painted four hundred years ago and he brings it back to this country and uses this $100,000 picture for the edification of the US people. My only comment is that I have no objection to foreign masters: they are all right. But on the other hand, the WPA spends something like $150,000 to $200,000 to put several thousand living native artists to work and save them from starvation."[96] Maverick's casual dismissal of the Old Masters—or "foreign masters," in his nativist locution—may have made art curators wince, but that kind of language has a real populist resonance. Too bad that in the year he made this rousing oration, not a single artist from his home state was on the FAP payroll.

***

The Federal Music Project ran into far less controversy than did the writers' or theatre projects, perhaps because music, though a universal language, is difficult to ideologize. Like the art and theatre projects, the music division could also show more immediate results than could the writers' project. A concert, play, or painting can be prepared in considerably less time than can a guide to Minnesota. And as was the case with actors and playwrights, the streets of New York were filled with out-of-work cornetists. The American Federation of Musicians reported that almost three-quarters of "formerly employed musicians" were music-jobless from 1929 to 1934.[97]

Project director Nikolai Sokoloff had a haughty reputation and was no fan of vernacular or popular American music. To compare the merits of swing music to classical, he sniffed, was "like comparing the funny papers to the work of a painter." He was impatient with those of modest talent, and denied that the Music Project was for "every Tom, Dick, or Harry who has no musical ability."[98] Yet Sokoloff did take music into public places and to audiences that were unused to melodies. The FMP provided work for about 7,000 musicians and claimed to have sponsored 225,000 performances of "symphonies, the grand old choral works, operas, and operettas, the madrigals, ballads, and folk songs of other centuries, as well as vital works of American composers," as Sokoloff told a House committee.[99] Like other elements of Federal One, the Music Project was New York City-focused, a bias that was greatly enhanced by Sokoloff's contempt for folk music forms emanating from exotic locales such as Texas and Kentucky. It did, however, extend its reach far enough inland to support thirty-four symphony orchestras in such far-flung cities as Grand Rapids, Omaha, Hartford, San Bernardino, Jacksonville, Providence, and Dallas. And its more adventurous employees recorded music of the Mississippi delta, the Texas-Mexico border, the Kentucky hills, the California missions, and the Sooner settlers.

Putting border ballads, cowboy songs, and blues on vinyl constituted a genuine cultural contribution by the FMP and was the tuneful equivalent of the Historical Records Survey, the least New York City-based initiative of the New Deal's art projects.

Federal One's Historical Records Survey (HRS) was not, strictly speaking, a subsidy to artists or writers, though as its director, Dr. Luther H. Evans, said, "its cultural value and its administrative requirements are so closely similar to those of the other projects that it is logically linked up with them."[100] The HRS consisted of several parts, the most ambitious of which was, in those predigitized days, a "comprehensive listing and description of the archives" of the 3,066 counties of the United States.[101] The 4,400 researchers employed at the project's peak were unable to complete the gargantuan task, though they did at least some work in most counties, and more or less met their goal in several hundred of those counties.

The truly enduring project of the Historical Records Survey, though, was folkloric: its collection of oral histories from approximately 3,000 ex-slaves, which in spite of the inevitable complications and drawbacks (inexperienced interviewers, subjects who were looking back on events of seventy years earlier) has proved to be a valuable historical resource. (This was presaged by a similar FERA project in which African American college graduates had interviewed approximately 250 ex-slaves.)

WPA history projects also included collections of the folklore of the states and regions, which covered everything from animal stories to superstitions to Indian tales and accounts of pioneer life to industrial legends. These were sometimes published as books or pamphlets and, especially in the South, made a real contribution. But reams and reams of this material molder in boxes and basements, awaiting eager scholars who may never show up.

In letting ordinary people tell their own stories without a partisan writer to shape the ideological slant, the FWP's Historical Records Survey, Folklore Unit, and Social-Ethnic Studies Unit represented the populist, as opposed to the Marxist, aspect of the project. These antithetical tendencies would meet head on in the flaming comet (or wet fizzling firecracker, depending on one's point of view) known as the Federal Theatre Project.

Federal Theatre Project

Hallie Flanagan, the former Harry Hopkins classmate (at Grinnell College in Iowa) who helmed the FTP, told Congress in February 1936 that "The Federal Theatre Project should only do such plays as the government can stand proudly behind in a planned theatrical program, national in scope, regional in emphasis, and American in democratic attitude. We are not so much concerned with finding individual hit shows, as with the development of a comprehensive dramatic program which will educate theatergoers and thus prove beneficial to the theatre industry."[102]

This sounded good, though execution did not always match theory. Under the Federal Theatre Project, unemployed thespians, directors, designers, playwrights, and stage hands were put to work in touring as well as community troupes putting on shows for adults, children, those who lived within walking distance of Broadway as well as—much less frequently—folks in distant hollers and hamlets. Hallie Flanagan boasted that the FTP worked "closely with psychologists and educators planning plays for children," and one can almost see the mouths of a thousand schoolkids yawning wide in anticipation of deathly dull didactic theater.[103]

The FTP had special theater units for African Americans as well as Spanish and Yiddish speakers. The project assigned city directors to

New York City, Chicago, and Los Angeles, and regional directors to the West, Midwest, East, and South.

Tickets were either cut-rate (from a nickel to $1.10) or, in the cases of shows for children, the underprivileged, and those resident in prisons, hospitals, and homes for the aged, free. The project had a heavily Manhattan-centric bias, a cause of some vexation to the commercial theater industry of Broadway, which did not relish the prospect of subsidized competition. Advertising was strictly limited, though the New York papers gave the shows plenty of free press. Contra the myth that the FTP drew an audience of the bedraggled, the down-and-out, and the poor but plucky, even its ardent admirer Jane de Hart Mathews concedes that "audiences seem to have been predominantly middle class, even in Harlem, despite a conscientious effort to attract low-income groups."[104] The people who paid market prices for commercial theater were, by and large, the same people who were paying cut-rate prices for the Federal Theatre. The FTP was not so much elevating the taste of those unfamiliar with drama as it was providing employment to playwrights, actors, directors, and stage crew.

There was no shortage of actors; Actors' Equity estimated that New York City was home to 5,000 out-of-work players, and by coincidence, that was close to the number of persons employed by the New York division of the Federal Theatre Project in all capacities.[105]

Acting is, even in the flushest of times, a sporadic vocation. Unless one latches onto a hit show or regular ensemble work, it's feast or famine. In the last Roaring Twenties' theatrical season of 1928–29, for instance, one study found that 79 percent of the members of Actors' Equity worked fewer than nine weeks in the year, and 40 percent were employed in their chosen field for under three and a half weeks.[106] Steady work it's not.

Given the abundance of out-of-work actors, the FTP had a somewhat easier time than other Federal One projects in barring the hopelessly untalented. Hallie Flanagan had emphasized that the FTP "is designed to reemploy only such members of the theatrical profession as are skilled enough to have a reasonable chance of making a living in the theatre later."[107] Hopeless hams and stumbling sots were not Flanagan's ideal workforce.

Yet relief, and not art, was the primary goal of the project.

The average number of persons employed by the Federal Theatre Project throughout its 1935–39 lifetime was ten thousand.[108] At its peak, the project employed nearly thirteen thousand. They were not evenly distributed among the forty-eight states.

In 1938, Hallie Flanagan testified before the House Committee on Patents that 8,739 persons in 22 states were then employed by the FTP. About 46 percent—4,011—were with the New York project.[109] In 1939, Federal One officials admitted to the hostile Upstate New York Republican Congressman John Taber that of the 8,145 people then employed by the 21 extant projects of the FTP, over 3,500 worked for the New York City theater outfit and the other 4,600 were spread over the remaining 20 cities.[110] As William F. McDonald wrote in *Federal Relief Administration and the Arts* (1969), his weighty Rockefeller Foundation-sponsored bureaucratic history of Federal One, "the Federal Theater Project became, to all intents and purposes, the New York City Theater Project," a development confirmed when in March 1937 Hallie Flanagan moved her headquarters from Washington to Manhattan.[111]

In her memoir *Arena: The History of the Federal Theatre*, Hallie Flanagan enthused that "Government subsidy of the theatre brought the United States into the best historic theatre tradition and into the best contemporary theatre practice."[112] Flanagan, a native Midwesterner, understood that theater beyond New York City had to be based in, to spring up from, local and regional traditions and practices and not be imposed by a "New York conception of theatre" or by "ideas emanating from Washington."[113] This is easier said than done, however, when the industry is anchored in New York and the checks for your program are being cut exclusively in Washington.

That said, there were voices within the FTP urging a decentralization of the project. One of the most passionate belonged to E. C. Mabie, a dedicated regionalist teaching at the University of Iowa (a state that was a hotbed of the regionalist arts movement, with such prominent figures as Grant Wood, Marvin Cone, Jay Sigmund, and Clyde and Jewell Tull). Mabie believed that if American drama were to flower, it would have to "grow up out of the soil as an expression of the life of the people in many regions."[114] This was a classic regionalist sentiment, one often tied to decentralist politics. Hallie Flanagan, who as a native Midwesterner shared, to an extent, Mabie's enthusiasm for indigenous arts, appointed the Iowan as the FTP's Midwest regional director.

He didn't last long. By early 1936 Mabie had resigned, due to "endless red tape and state WPA officials with little interest in theatre."[115]

(Flanagan admitted to Mabie in a letter of August 1935 that the FTP was bound up in "miles of red tape."[116])

The stricture on relocating relief recipients under Federal One prevented a mass exodus of New York City actors to the provinces, for which the provinces probably said a small prayer of thanks to the god of bureaucracy. But the envisioned regional theaters never properly developed, and in time, as sympathetic historian Jane de Hart Mathews writes in *The Federal Theater, 1935–1939: Plays, Relief, Politics,* "state after state was left virtually untouched by Federal Theatre productions."[117]

The children's theater under the FTP was fairly noncontroversial. Shows were produced in schools and parks and hospitals and reformatories. The claim was made that the project, in all its aspects, reached as many as thirty million people, though this is almost certainly a case of bureaucratic decimal point-misplacing.

Politics was the bane of the FTP's adult theater, and some playwrights even tried to smuggle messages into their dramas for the little ones. Brooks Atkinson of the *New York Times* called one Children's Theatre production, *The Revolt of the Beavers,* "Marxism à la Mother Goose." Jane de Hart Mathews describes the play, written by Oscar Saul and Lou Lantz, as the story of "a country ruled by a cruel beaver chief who owned a 'busy wheel' on which bark was turned into food, clothing, and shelter. When Boss Chief not only refused the working beavers their share of the bark, but threatened to replace them with the jobless, barkless beavers, Oakleaf came to the rescue. Returning from exile—he had tried previously to organize a club for 'sad beavers to get glad'—Oakleaf disguised himself as a polar bear, organized both the working bears and the barkless beavers, and led them in revolt. The cruel beaver chief and his henchmen were sent into exile, and the beavers worked, shared, and lived happily ever after."[118] This infantile allegory bored children and outraged adults. No doubt the playwrights felt themselves quite heroic for taking federal funds in return for child-directed agitprop.

Didacticism was not disdained in the Federal Theatre Project. After all, First Lady Eleanor Roosevelt had said that "the time had come when Americans might consider the theatre, as it was considered abroad, a part of education."[119] Subjects of original FTP productions included the dangers of syphilis (*Spirochete*), the glories of public utilities (*Power*), and Southern injustices (*Turpentine*). The most famous of all FTP productions, Marc Blitzstein's musical *The Cradle Will Rock,* a sledgehammer-nuanced pro-union piece, was cancelled by project headquarters in June 1937 over concerns that its unsubtle leftist message strayed too far over the propaganda line. (The official explanation, contained in a letter to Hallie Flanagan from Ellen Woodward, who supervised the WPA's women's and professional worker relief projects, was that "no openings of new productions shall take place until after the beginning of the coming fiscal year, that is, July 1, 1937."[120] The musical was later staged by Orson Welles's Mercury Theatre Company and has occasionally been revived over the years, more as a curiosity piece than a classic.)

Many of the socially conscious plays produced under the FTP's auspices were of the "living newspaper" genre. They were, in a very real sense, taken directly from the headlines.[121] "Living newspaper" plays drew life from topical, sometimes controversial, subjects. Hallie Flanagan called them a "terse, cinematic, hard-hitting, dramatic form."[122] They were also as overtly political as anything ever to come out of Federal One.

Flanagan was won over to the living newspaper approach to theater by a trip to Russia. "She had seen Soviet propaganda and its revolution dramatized for audiences," writes Kelly Ronayne, and pronounced it "vital and important."[123] Ideally, every FTP show built on this model would end "with some sort of call for social action."[124] This call, you may be sure, never sounded limited-government, constitutional, or libertarian themes.

In fact, while guiding the Vassar Experimental Theatre, Flanagan had cowritten, with Margaret Ellen Clifford, a proto-living newspaper play titled *Can You Hear Their Voices?* Produced in 1931, the play consisted of vignettes portraying down-and-out Arkansas dirt farmers. According to Jane de Hart Matthews, at the conclusion of *Can You Hear Their Voices?*, the protagonist "sent his sons to Communist headquarters in the hope that they could 'make a better world.' A voice is heard saying to the audience: 'These boys are symbols of thousands of our people who are turning somewhere for leaders. Will it be to the educated minority? Can You Hear Their Voices?'"[125]

This sounds like agitprop above and beyond the call of duty, though it was denounced by Communist theater critics for muffling, or even excising, the explicitly pro-Communist theme of the source material, which was a story by Whittaker Chambers, who in later years would be most notable for his very public apostasy from Communism. In any case, and whether *Can You Hear Their Voices?* was Red theater or mushy watery liberalism, Hallie Flanagan viewed the stage as a proper place for political preachments.

Yet Flanagan and her coterie would deny that the FTP had any propagandistic purpose other than an anodyne commitment to democracy. Rather, it was intended to bring theater to the people and to provide employment for out-of-work writers, performers, directors, stagehands, ushers, seamstresses, business managers, ticket-sellers, and other supporting crew. The majority—perhaps 60 percent—were actors. Another 10–15 percent were stagehands and technicians; newspapermen and playwrights constituted 5–10 percent of the total; and the remaining 20 percent were a congeries of "ushers, cleaners, porters, seamstresses, box-office employees, business managers, bookers, and the necessary clerical staff."[126]

Hallie Flanagan's hope was to give work to unemployed stage actors and crew while also creating "theater enterprises of lasting value."[127] One complication: the more talented employees throughout Federal One would leave the program when they found work in commercial theater, with newspapers or book publishers or advertising agencies, or in other better-paying, more prestigious labors. Thus "through the sheer force of inertia" and incompetence did the project retain its less talented employees while its top shelf was denuded.[128]

Elmer Rice, in charge of the elephantine (by comparison with other regions) New York City FTP branch, hired pretty much anyone who called himself an actor, to Hallie Flanagan's chagrin. Rice was confident that the untalented could be discarded as easily as one might dismiss an also-ran at an audition, but as Flanagan later wrote, "Elmer underestimated, as I did at that time, the difficulty of eliminating from a project set up because of need, destitute men and women once they had been taken on."[129] In other words, once hired, never fired. To a professional like Rice, this was maddening.

Art and poverty have long been intertwined. The romantic sees the starving artist painting his masterpiece in his unfurnished garret; the realist sees an impecunious poet who is in greater need of nutrition than inspiration. There is no particular virtue in starvation; the best artists are not necessarily those with the most inadequate diets. And so as Barry B. Witham wrote in *The Federal Theatre Project: A Case Study*, the FTP "would always host a struggle between those who were 'right for the part' and those who qualified for relief."[130] Finding the golden mean—the starving actor who made a perfect Hamlet—was devilishly difficult.

George Jean Nathan, the sometimes acerbic critic, was, to put it mildly, skeptical of the talents of those employed by the project.

Huffing that the FTP had done "next to nothing to exonerate its existence," with the possible exception of the Living Newspaper, he unloaded this verbal fusillade:

> [A]t least three-quarters of the younger people who have been living off it are spongers and grafters and no more deserving of charity from this particular source than they are deserving of Civil War pensions or Congressional dispensations of *pate de foie gras*. They have clearly demonstrated that they have nothing to give to the theatre—whether in the way of playwriting, producing, acting or scene painting—beyond a puissant and understandable itch to shine in easy and romantic jobs. With no faintest competence whatsoever, and infinitely better suited to humbler and more prosaic work, they are simply stagestruck and theatre struck loafers, and the Federal Theatre Project recklessly affords them the opportunity to pleasure their fatuous whim.

Nathan followed the skein to what he thought its logical conclusion: "If the present governmental waste of money keeps up, it probably will not be long before we shall analogously have a Federal Movie Fans Project, to provide relief for the countless morons who are destitute of quarters with which to obtain autographed photographs of their favorite screen players, to say nothing of a Federal Night Club Project, to vouchsafe succor to Americans who want to dance the rumba and haven't any money left after paying taxes to pay the corollary minimum food and booze check."[131] (This is a good sample of Nathan's humor; he was the man who minted the timeless aphorism, "I drink to make my friends amusing.")

Few critics were quite as caustic as Nathan, though his stylish scorn is a healthy antidote to the often adulatory accounts of the FTP by those in political accord with its mission. Nathan was seconded by the acclaimed Shakespearean actor Otis Skinner, who in 1938 exclaimed, "Good God! You can't legislate genius. . . . What has this federal theatre done? It's simply enabling a lot of unworthy people to make a livelihood in the theatre in which they could not exist otherwise."[132]

The project had more than its share of missteps, not all of them political in nature, though sometimes there was less to the story than met the eye. In Minnesota, for instance, the state's theatre project was effectively killed by a front-page story in the December 13, 1935, edition of the *Minneapolis Journal* which read: "Ruby Bae, Put Out of Job by Police, Becomes Federal Fan Dancer No. 1." It seems that one Ruby Bae, an ecdysiast, to use the term coined by H.L. Mencken, had been arrested by the Minneapolis vice squad for "cavorting about Coffee Dan's night club in the nude." The authorities had "fined her $50 for disorderly conduct and closed the club, putting Ruby and her two fans on the official unemployment list." As an artist on relief, Miss Bae promptly applied to the nascent Minneapolis branch of the Federal Theatre Project, which signed her up as a dancer. The *Journal* reported that she would soon be strutting her stuff for the bug-eyed boys in northern Minnesota Civilian Conservation Corps camps. In fact, Ruby was to go on the federal dole as a tap dancer, properly clothed. But the story created a mini-tempest and led to an abrupt end for the Minnesota Theatre Project.[133]

Ruby Bae aside, the begetters of the FTP proudly declared their devotion to unfettered speech. Harry Hopkins, speaking at an FTP kickoff at the University of Iowa, proclaimed: "I am asked whether a theatre subsidized by the government can be kept free from censorship, and I say, yes, it is going to be kept free from censorship. What we want is a free, adult, uncensored theatre."[134] This was, as we shall see, problematic. And the obverse of the censorship coin—propaganda—seemed never to be out of circulation.

To the extent that the politically oriented original plays of the FTP had a common theme, it was an almost childlike faith in the benevolence of government in all its works. In *Spirochete,* a kind of public service announcement against the spread of syphilis, the audience is instructed that "The people and the State must do" their part in combating this scourge by enacting new social-welfare laws.[135] *Spirochete* presents doctors as "heroic figures struggling against public ignorance," in Barry B. Witham's account, and the "closest thing to a villain in the piece. . . . is a capitalist system that does not prize the worker, only the amount of labor a worker can produce."[136] In an FTP play about the plight of the farmer, *Triple-A Plowed Under,* the noble husbandman is the bulwark of the US effort in the First World War. Agricultural production is not honored as the reification of the agrarian ideal or as a means of providing sustenance to the hungry but instead for its usefulness to the military and the central state: "Every bushel of barley is a barrel of bullets."[137]

In *Power,* a glorification of the Tennessee Valley Authority and the concept of government ownership of utilities, a young girl has this dazzling exchange with her father on the subject of a private utility company.

Girl: Daddy, who is the government?
Father: The government is you and me, I guess—the people.
Girl: Do all people need electricity?
Father: Yes.
Girl: And does the company own what all the people want?
Father: That's right!
Girl: Gee, Daddy: The people are awfully dumb.[138]

In one of *Power*'s must-be-seen-to-be-believed scenes, "photographs of hydroelectric dams flash dramatically in the background" while "a group of farmers and workers march on stage and sing 'The TVA Song,'" which goes like this:

All up and down the valley
They heard the great alarm;
The government means business
It's working like a charm.
Oh, see them boys a' comin'
Their government they trust,
Just hear their hammers ringin'
They'll build that dam or bust.[139]

Could there have been a dry eye in the house after this moment of sublimity?

Brooks Atkinson of the *New York Times* called *Power* "the most indignant and militant proletarian drama of the season. . . . staged with government funds."[140] There is a chasm of meaning between those ellipses.

For his part, Harry Hopkins was moved to frankness after seeing *Power*. He exclaimed to the cast and crew, "Now let's get one thing clear: you will take a lot of criticism on this play. People will say it's propaganda. Well, I say what of it? It's propaganda to educate the consumer who's paying for power."[141] A righteous cause excuses everything.

Power was so over the top that even mainstream newspapers rebuked it. The Seattle production thereof, in which a cast of two hundred put on eight performances, was castigated by both the *Post-Intelligencer* ("Propaganda for public ownership. Private utilities are assailed, satirized, ridiculed, exposed, attacked, and condemned") and the *Seattle Times* ("That Old Debbil, the Power Trust, is the villain and the TVA is the hero in as fine a piece of overdone propaganda as ever trod the boards. . . . The play has the subtlety of a sledgehammer and the restraint of a groundswell").[142]

In his study of Seattle's experience with the FTP, University of Washington drama professor Barry B. Witham marvels that "Even a cursory reading of *Power* today is startling in the degree to which the private sector is hounded and vilified. Electric power is repeatedly represented in the play as a right of all citizens, like the air we breathe. The consumer is depicted as frail, ignorant and, often, an easy mark for the machinations of private enterprise," which is portrayed as the domain of mustache-twirling villains straight out of an 1890s melodrama.[143] All that's missing is a damsel in distress tied to the railroad tracks while a train marked CRUEL CAPITALISM hurtles along its homicidal way.

But then as Harry Hopkins asked, what of it? Federally sponsored propaganda in the service of a cause of which one approves is appropriate and just, and only the most hidebound reactionary or fanged defender of the oligarchy would protest.

Other FTP plays defended the WPA. Talk about not biting the hand that feeds you; this was a case of rolling over on one's back and eagerly licking that hand. In the Theatre Project's *Sing for Your Supper*, tuneful WPA workers warble:

> When you look at things today
> Like Boulder Dam and TVA
> And all those playgrounds where kids can play
> We did it—by leaning on a shovel![144]

This may be trenchant analysis or embarrassing didacticism, depending on one's political and aesthetic preferences. Reading the lyrics, without benefit of seeing the performance, these plays can be downright embarrassing in their obviousness. Even the admiring critic Charles R. Walker called the FTP's living newspapers "open propaganda, openly arrived at."[145] Whether it was a fit subject for federal government sponsorship is another question.

In *One-Third of a Nation*, its title taken from President Roosevelt's second inaugural address ("I see one-third of a nation ill-housed, ill-clad, ill-nourished"), the problems of slum housing are examined with an eye to stricter regulation of housing stock in America. Again, it was a dramatization of a plank in the urban liberal political platform.

Triple-A Plowed Under, *Power*, and *One-Third of a Nation* were produced primarily in New York City, though they did receive productions in other FTP outposts, with the scripts sometimes adapted to local conditions in an effort to bring theater to that great wilderness beyond the Hudson.

Hallie Flanagan tried to spread the wealth of the FTP, saying in retrospect that "we were reluctant to spend all the money in congested areas like New York City," but the relative scarcity of theaters and professional actors in the South, Midwest, the Plains, and the Rockies presented a challenge. (Casts were "augment[ed] . . . when necessary from New York or Los Angeles."[146]) Flanagan noted that the best FTP production in the South, *Altars of Steel*, was by a Birmingham, Alabama, playwright and concerned the steel industry of that state. It was an enormous hit in Atlanta. By contrast, few Atlantans attended a production of New York City FTP director Elmer Rice's play *The Adding Machine*, but then the play's director, who was not a Southerner, admitted to Flanagan that he never even bothered to get to know Atlanta. Surely the city had nothing to offer sophisticates like him. (Amusingly, there was no Federal Theatre in Washington, DC, because, Hallie Flanagan explained, a survey of the city revealed "no dramatic talent." The surveyors had obviously skipped the daily display of histrionics on the House and Senate floors.)[147]

In her study of the FTP, Professor Ronayne concludes, approvingly, that "the Federal Theatre Project aimed to educate its public on the importance of a new social welfare state," which would take greater responsibility for the sheltering, the health, the livelihoods, and the intellectual development of its citizens. "Although at the outset the FTP was not intended to be a political organ of the New Deal, once put into practice much of its content featured themes that were close to the hearts of New Dealers."[148]

In that spirit, Hallie Flanagan saw her project not simply as providing stop-gap employment for jobless actors and playwrights and stagehands; rather, she declared with a certain grandiosity, "these activities represent a new frontier in America, a frontier against disease, dirt, poverty, illiteracy, unemployment, despair, and at the same time against selfishness, special privilege, and social apathy." This was a considerably expanded portfolio from that which had been handed to her by Harry Hopkins. And just how government, let alone theater, might eradicate *dirt* is a mystery.

Although its advocates liked to imply, then and now, that the FTP's (or Federal One's) critics were philistines, boorish oafs incapable of appreciating anything more challenging than an Edgar Guest rhyme or a Currier and Ives print, in fact many of them argued from first principles.

For instance, Mildred Seydell of the *Atlanta Georgian*, taking on Hallie Flanagan's theater of propaganda, wrote, "I believe in free speech and if private interests wish to put forward their grievances against present-day American institutions, I for one might criticize them but would not say that the authorities should stop them. But when tax money is used for propaganda for the purpose of putting on plays that cause controversy and that give birth to hate, I think it is high time for complaint."[149]

Ms. Seydell would deny that she was calling for censorship. To refuse to subsidize is not the same as to ban or prohibit. The distinction is relevant and helps to illuminate one of the murkier episodes of the Federal Theatre Project. The FTP could flay cartoon capitalists all it wanted, but when the project ran afoul of Rooseveltian policy preferences, it was reined in. Such was the case with the very first "living newspaper" play, *Ethiopia*, which concerned the Italian invasion of that African nation.

Ethiopia was an hour-long show which was scheduled to go up on the stage of the Biltmore on West 47th Street. Admission was a quarter. The playwrights were Morris Watson and Arthur Arent, though the research team numbered about seventy-five. Cast, crew, and assorted FTP wage-drawers on the play numbered over three hundred. This was no backyard hay-bales-for-seats production.

Word leaked out that *Ethiopia* might possibly offend Italy's fascist duce, Benito Mussolini. When the White House got wind of this "living newspaper," inquiries were made. Hallie Flanagan assured the authorities that Mussolini was depicted "sympathetically and with power," as Susan Quinn notes in her history of the FTP, *Furious Improvisation: How the WPA and a Cast of Thousands Made High Art Out of Desperate Times*.[150] Flanagan's obsequiousness toward power was not enough. Jacob Baker, who received her letter due to Harry Hopkins's travels, was unsympathetic. Eleanor Roosevelt, though friendly to the project, was not helpful. A new rule was promulgated: no depiction of foreign heads of state was permitted without the approval of the State Department. A dress rehearsal of *Ethiopia* was staged for the New York critics, but the show's planned run was cancelled. *Ethiopia* was shelved without ever receiving a public performance.

The episode was a crucible for its participants, especially Elmer Rice, the director of the New York City Federal Theatre Project, who had envisioned an FTP that was "uncensored politically and morally."[151]

Rice had won the Pulitzer Prize for his 1929 play *Tenement* and was among New York City's most prominent dramatists. He was also a politically active socialist who had supported the Communist Party ticket in 1932. Rice joined the FTP out of a belief that it represented "public interest" theater. He denied that it was, as he characterized critics' conception of the project, a "super-boondoggle, a sinecure for the faithful, an attempt to supplant the professional theatre by the amateur and a plot to overthrow the government of the United States."[152] Instead, Rice said in a speech at New York's Town Hall Club, "the WPA movement marks the first time that the Government has recognized the importance of art and is the entering wedge for the new theater. Rugged individualism is now a museum piece, and the finish of the commercial theater predicted by me for two decades is now in sight and inevitable."

Finding a more spectacularly wrong prophecy than the Communist Rice's prediction that commercial theater was deader than a doornail with no hope of resurrection would be hard. Indeed, as Harrison Grey Fiske pointed out, no sooner had the words slipped from Rice's mouth than events were repudiating them: "While the Federal Theater in New York was spending hundreds of thousands of dollars on a dozen paltry productions, the 'archaic system' brought forward, without fuss and feathers, a number of creditable plays that met with hearty approval.... among these were *Victoria Regina, Pride and Prejudice, Ethan Frome, Winterset, First Lady, Call it a Day, Love on the Dole, Parnell, Boy Meets Girl,* besides revivals of *Romeo and Juliet, Ghosts, Saint Joan, Cyrano de Bergerac,* and Gilbert and Sulllivan operas."[153]

In the case of *Ethiopia*, though, Elmer Rice showed his mettle. Standing on principle, he fired off a telegram to Harry Hopkins informing him that "if you support [Jacob] Baker's decision there is nothing for me to do except regretfully tender my resignation."[154] The resignation was accepted. Elmer Rice, the communist-supporting collector of Old Masters paintings, had taken a stand against censorship. He fired a parting shot, asserting that he would not be "the servant of a government which plays the shabby game of partisan politics at the expense of freedom and the principles of democracy."[155] So much for Harry Hopkins's promise of "a free, adult, uncensored theatre." Elmer Rice had complained of "arbitrary and inflexible regulations.... chair-warmers [and] petty bureaucrats jealous of their brief authority," and FTP figures in "relatively high places who are, perhaps, more interested in the future of the Democratic Party than in the future of the theatre."[156] For his part, Rice chose the latter. He chose art over politics.

Hallie Flanagan chose to stay on. She now understood that the art created under Federal One would be subject to restrictions. Specifically, it could not contradict the New Deal or the administration's foreign policy. As long as the plays and living newspapers behaved, and did not color outside the lines, they would be permitted to go on.

Though in retrospect *Ethiopia* has been rendered as an open and shut case of censorship, its source of financing complicates matters. In a contemporaneous account, Harrison Gray Fiske in the *Saturday Evening Post* called *Ethiopia* "a blatant left-wing contraption" and argued that the administration had no choice but to interfere, as "a Government-subsidized enterprise, naturally, could not be permitted flagrantly to irritate or offend the heads of friendly nations," especially at a time of mounting international tension.[157] Had *Ethiopia* been staged at one of New York's numerous commercial or off-Broadway theaters, there would have been no question of the impropriety of shutting it down. But he who takes the king's shilling cannot dissent from the king's foreign policy.

A California production of one of Elmer Rice's political plays, *Judgement Day*, was cancelled when in early 1938 the California Federal Theatre came under the supervision of Lieutenant Colonel Donald H. Connolly, who looked askance at didactic theater—or at least at those specimens of didactic theater whose political bent he found objectionable. Hallie Flanagan pleaded with Harry Hopkins to "end this sort of petty dictatorship of the arts," which was a direct contradiction of the pledge Hopkins had made of a freewheeling and censorship-free federal theater.[158] To expect a federal program that was created by political persons and was staging productions with explicitly political messages—messages that were almost exclusively social democratic or socialist in content—to be free of the taint of political interference displays a level of naïveté, if not unreality, that is downright astonishing. Yet Flanagan was capable of self-satisfied smugness when proclaiming the FTP's bravery in taking on political subjects. "Giving apoplexy to people who consider it radical for a government-sponsored theatre to produce plays on subjects vitally concerning the governed is one function of the theatre," she asserted in August 1938.[159]

The complacency evident in such a remark harmonized with the overall gestalt of Federal One: its administrators were bringing culture to the deprived masses, and only the most benighted mossback or mean-spirited right-wing crazy could possibly object. The fact that not a single FTP production reflected the views of, for instance, anti-New Deal conservatives, was of no concern; after all, those people didn't write plays, or watch plays, or appreciate plays. They were rich and obdurate businessmen, hard-hearted; the least repugnant of the bunch were simply old fogeys professing an annoyingly quaint faith in the horse-and-buggy Constitution. The best thing to do was not argue with them—how can one argue with an unreasoning philistine?—but rather to wait them out. They were old, most were decrepit, and all of them would die sooner rather than later.

Flanagan herself came down hard on *Injunction Granted*, an FTP living newspaper production about labor struggles that was blatant agitprop. Brooks Atkinson of the *New York Times* wrote: "The Moscow stylization of writing and staging reduces the long struggle to adolescent gibberish. . . . You can recognize the workers by their honest virility. The capitalists you can recognize by their morning coats and cunning demeanor. . . . It bludgeons capital and the courts as if revolution were already accomplished. If it wants to give the Federal Theatre a bad name for political insurgence it has found the most effective method."[160]

Hallie Flanagan had ordered script alterations in the rehearsals for *Injunction Granted*. It was, she thought, "bad journalism and hysterical theater."[161] After viewing its opening night performance, Flanagan dashed off a note to director Joseph Losey and Morris Watson, supervisor of the Living Newspaper section, in which she called *Injunction Granted* "special pleading, biased, an editorial, not a news issue." It was "one-sided," she complained, and "Whatever my personal sympathies are I cannot, as custodian of federal funds, have such funds used as a party tool. That goes for the communist party as well as for the democratic party."[162] Flanagan suggested revising the play, perhaps having forgotten Harry Hopkins's pledge of no censorship.

Joseph Losey, the director and at various times a member of the Communist Party, refused to comply with Flanagan's requests. And after all, if the FTP really was committed to freedom of expression, why shouldn't Losey refuse? He was the director; shouldn't the final say in what goes into the show be his? Hallie Flanagan didn't think so. She was, once again, on the side of the censors. The FTP took a big public relations hit with *Injunction Granted* and its crude hectoring style. Losey was lost to the Federal Theatre Project, while Flanagan stayed on. Before the show went dark, it underwent limited revisions, though in the view of FTP skeptics it was still an extreme case of subsidized artists biting the hand that feeds them.

Reds Under Beds, or Trodding Boards?

Congressional red-baiters took aim at the FTP as they did at other elements of Federal One. Their avenue of attack was through the US House of Representatives' investigative body that became known, and notorious, as the Dies Committee. Rep. Martin Dies (D-TX), a New Deal supporter, along with Rep. Samuel Dickstein (D-NY), was the prime force behind the creation in 1938 of the House Committee Investigating Un-American Activities. (The opening of the Soviet archives after the fall of the USSR revealed that Dickstein was on the payroll of the NKVD, the forerunner of the KGB. This is a most inconvenient fact for some who believe that the history of American censorship and persecution of those with unpopular opinions is conterminous with the American Right.) Commonly known as the Dies Committee, HUAC (as it was later dubbed) was empowered to investigate—civil libertarians would say harass—dissenters on both left and right, especially putative communists and fascists. Dies had heard the stories of communist infiltration of the FWP and the FTP, so it became a plump target for his committee, which found, unsurprisingly, that there was a significant Communist presence in both projects, particularly in New York City. Even if their motives and methods were sometimes disreputable, congressional red-baiters were often far more accurate than their patronizing opponents in the art world conceded them to be. After all, the level of communist influence in the federal arts projects of the 1930s was not dominant, but it was significant. However, overheated language and occasional recklessness made the efforts of Dies and company less credible, especially among the intelligentsia. There were plenty of writers, painters, actors, musicians, and playwrights who despised the rabid and sectarian communists who could make life in Federal One so unpleasant, but these noncommunist artists did not, for the most part, wish to make common cause with what they regarded as know-nothing anticommunist politicians.

For an example of the latter, Rep. Joe Starnes, an Alabama Democrat, pricked up his ears when it was revealed during a Dies Committee hearing that Hallie Flanagan had used the phrase "a certain Marlowesque madness." "You are quoting from this Marlowe. Is he a Communist?" interrogated Starnes. Mrs. Flanagan explained that she was referring to Christopher Marlowe, whom he described as "the greatest dramatist in the period of Shakespeare, immediately preceding Shakespeare."[163] (Flanagan did turn a nice phrase before Dies and his committee investigating un-American activities when she told the members that "Since August 29, 1935, I have been concerned with combating un-American inactivity."[164])

Rep. J. Parnell Thomas (R-NJ), a committee stalwart, charged that "practically every play was clear unadulterated propaganda," a gross exaggeration that ignored the children's plays, the classical pieces (from *Julius Caesar* and *Macbeth* to *She Stoops to Conquer* and *The Importance of Being Earnest*), and the historical pageants that the FTP also put on.[165] He castigated the theater project because it "produces communistic plays" and "fosters New Deal propaganda."[166] For her part, Hallie Flanagan did not deny that propaganda was an element of federally subsidized theater, but she sought to turn that point to her advantage. Flanagan told the Dies Committee:

> I could not say that we never did a propaganda play. But I should like to go to the actual definition of "propaganda." Propaganda, after all, is education. It is education focused on certain things. For example, some of you gentlemen have doubtless seen *One-Third of a Nation*; and I certainly would not sit here and say that that was not a propaganda play. . . . I should like to say very truthfully that to the best of my knowledge we have never done a play which was propaganda for communism, but we have done plays which were propaganda for democracy, propaganda for better housing. . . .[167]

Propaganda that served the cause of the party in power, it seems, was permissible. Problems only intruded when propaganda might serve a party out the power, such as the Communists. That is what censorship was for.

Chairman Dies, whom historiography has condemned, not without cause, to the role of inquisitorial jackass, was in fact capable of asking sensible, even at times cogent, questions. Consider this exchange between Dies and Flanagan:

Chairman Dies: In other words, you believe it is correct to use the Federal Theater to educate people, audiences, along social or economic lines, is that correct?

Mrs. Flanagan: Among other things; yes. I have pointed out to the committee that only 10 percent of the plays that we do—

Chairman Dies: I understand. Do you not also think that since the Federal Theatre Project is an agency of the Government and that all of our people support it through their tax money, people of different classes, different races, different religions, some who are workers, some who are businessmen, don't you think that being true that no play should ever be produced which undertakes to portray the interests of one class to the disadvantage of another class, even though that might be accurate, even though factually there may be justification normally for that, yet because of the very fact that we are using taxpayers' money to produce plays, do you not think it is questionable whether it is right to produce plays that are biased in favor of one class against another?

Mrs. Flanagan: We are not doing plays to stir up class hatred.

Chairman Dies: Then this Federal Theatre is a very powerful vehicle of expression isn't it, and of propaganda, because as you say, it reaches 25,000,000 people. It therefore can be used or abused.

Mrs. Flanagan: Yes.

Chairman Dies: With serious consequences, can it not?

Mrs. Flanagan: Yes, sir.

Chairman Dies: And do you know of any way in which it could be more seriously abused than it would be to portray, as I said a few moments ago, one class, putting them at an advantage over another class?

Mrs. Flanagan: I have been giving a long list of illustrations of the fact that we do not so do.

Chairman Dies: What is the objective of the play, what impression is it designed to bring in the mind of the audience—take the play *Power*—that public ownership is a good thing?

Mrs. Flanagan: I think the first thing the play does is to make you understand more about power, where it comes from, and how it has evolved, about its whole historical use.

Chairman Dies: All right.

Mrs. Flanagan: I think it also does speak highly for the public ownership of power.

Chairman Dies: Let us just take that one instance. We will assume, for the sake of argument that maybe the public ownership of power is a desirable thing, but do you not think it improper that the Federal

Theatre, using the taxpayers' money, should present a play to the audience which champions one side of a controversy?

Mrs. Flanagan: No, Congressman Dies; I do not consider it improper. I have just said that I felt that in a small percentage of our plays, and pointed out that it is 10 percent that do hold a brief for a certain cause in accord with general forward-looking tendencies, and I say—

Chairman Dies: Who is to determine what is a forward-looking tendency?

Mrs. Flanagan: Why, our play policy board chooses these plays.

Chairman Dies: They are to determine the question as to what is a forward-looking tendency. They therefore would have the idea that public ownership of utilities was a forward-looking tendency?

Mrs. Flanagan: Also, with the idea, Congressman Dies, that first the play must be good, it must have the power to hold people in the audience.

Chairman Dies: I am assuming that, but we are confining ourselves to the proposition—take *Power*—you say that your policy board must first pass on this, isn't that right?

Mrs. Flanagan: Yes.

Chairman Dies: Then your policy board approves the question of public ownership of utilities. Then you think that because they approve the principle of public ownership of utilities, you believe it is proper that the Federal theaters shall exhibit a play in which it champions the right to public ownership, do you not?

Mrs. Flanagan: I think so.[168]

Hallie Flanagan has no objection to propagandistic plays as long as they are, to use her trite phrase, "forward-looking." That is to say, in accord with the general views of President Roosevelt and the New Dealers. Propaganda for causes that are not, in the eyes of a conventional liberal Democrat of the time, "forward-looking"—say, communism or laissez-faire or conservatism or agrarian populism—will not be subsidized. The FTP has, as a corporate whole, a point of view—and it will support plays that comport with that view and refuse to support plays that run afoul of it. This is thoroughly illiberal, but for the most part, the liberals of 1938 did not mind.

Earlier in the decade, in the first stages of the experiment in state-sponsored culture, an art journalist wondered, "Must art be C.W.A.'d into Rooseveltianism?"[169] Would public monies be available to artists who might satirize FDR or the New Deal? In the case of critics from the left, the answer was a qualified yes. But one searches in vain for New Deal-funded art that lacerates the President or his programs from a libertarian or conservative or even mildly Republican perspective. And there were many artists decidedly outside the Roosevelt camp, among them Pulitzer Prize-winning playwright Maxwell Anderson, poets Edgar Lee Masters, Robinson Jeffers, and E. E. Cummings, and essayists Edmund Wilson and Dwight Macdonald, to name just a few. Surely there were a significant number of unemployed writers and playwrights with similarly astringent views of the New Deal. Of course many FDR critics had a strong libertarian streak and would have refused federal subsidy even if offered.

The historian of Federal One, Jane de Hart Mathews, has called the project an example of "cultural democracy" for its effort to "integrate the artist into the mainstream of American life and make the arts both expressive of the spirit of a nation and accessible to its people," but it is a curious form of democracy which leaves a substantial portion of the population—to put it in its most bluntly political form, *Republicans*—almost entirely out of the picture.[170] Their political values were mocked, particularly by Living Newspapers and the most polemical elements of the FTP and FWP, and their exponents were unsubsidized (in part by choice: artists distrustful of the New Deal or resistant to the lure of the dole were unlikely to apply to Federal One), even though their tax dollars were welcomed by the program administrators.

The Dies Committee Report of January 3, 1939, was emphatic: "We are convinced that a rather large number of the employees on the Federal Theatre Project are either members of the Communist Party or are sympathetic with the Communist Party."[171] As for the Federal Writers' Project, Dies insisted that Federal One was "doing more to spread Communist propaganda than the Communist Party itself," and Dies Committee member Rep. Parnell Thomas opined that the FWP was "worse than the Federal Theatre Project and a hotbed of Communism." This was not at all true in, say, North Dakota or Texas or Vermont, but the New York City branches of Federal One were unquestionably populated with CP members. Testifying before the Dies Committee in 1938, Ralph De Sola, a zoologist and one-time party functionary active in the New York City FWP, estimated that more than one hundred of the approximately three hundred writers in the New York City project were members of the Communist Party.[172] This may have been an exaggeration, but De Sola was not weaving his story out of whole cloth.

Again, this points to the deal with the devil that subsidized writers make: Communist or Marxist writers were publishing frequently with the commercial presses and newspapers of all shapes and sizes, but once they sought federal sponsorship they placed themselves under federal supervision, if not surveillance.

For the most part, the institutional communist movement in the United States—as opposed to the often fractious, unruly, independent-minded artists who might call themselves communists but were far too free-spirited to sit through a single meeting, let alone to take orders from grim-faced commissars—eagerly advocated a government arts program. Much of the early agitation for writers and artists to become employees of the federal government came from the John Reed Club, a Marxist-inflected organization that was founded in 1929 by intellectuals associated with *New Masses*, the leftist journal. The club, named for the communist journalist later immortalized, and prettied up, by Warren Beatty in his film *Reds* (1981), affiliated with the Communist Party USA the next year. It would eventually consist of thirty chapters and in 1936 be absorbed by the Communist Party's American Artists' Congress, which agitated for culture to be defined as a public service and those who provide culture to be considered public servants—that is, when they weren't setting aside their brushes to "fight War, Fascism, and Reaction."[173]

New Masses and the John Reed Club were affiliated with the International Union of Revolutionary Writers (IURW) and the International Bureau of Revolutionary Artists (IBRA). The "magazine's allegiance to Soviet Russia," notes Marist Professor Virginia Hagelstein Marquardt in the *Journal of Decorative and Propaganda Arts*, was evident not only in its polemical work but in its illustrations, which "typically contrasted hungry, unemployed, and brutalized workers in America with well-fed, productive workers in Russia."[174] It laid the Marxist-Leninism on a bit thick even for the taste of many on the Left. There was much talk of *proletarian art* and *revolutionary art*, so much so that in 1936, as part of the Communist Party's "Popular Front" strategy to forge a broad-based Left using patriotic symbolism instead of Soviet boilerplate, the John Reed Club melted into the American Artists' Congress "on the suggestion of Alexander Trachtenberg, Communist Party representative" at the club's national convention.[175]

So the charges by Republicans and others that Federal One was gainfully employing Communist artists and writers—propagandists, some of them—were hardly conjured out of thin air. The American Artists' Congress "essentially continued the objectives of the John Reed Club," writes Marquadt, in pursuing a revolutionary art with political content.[176]

Another CP front group, the Unemployed Writers Association (UWA), was positively indignant that intellectuals were not being subsidized by Washington. The UWA was born in January 1934 and rapidly attracted five hundred members. Its demands included a minimum salary of $30 a week for writers, who would be assigned various tasks (none glamorizing the tenets or personalities of capitalism, you may be sure), and the drawing up of a "national plan for all writers."[177] The totalitarian implications of the latter demand seem not to have bothered the UWA, but then neither did events in the Soviet Union. In any event, a "national plan for all writers" was likely to repel any writer worth his or her salt.

The UWA's secretary, Robert Whitcomb, wrote in February 1934:

> The unemployed writers of New York City do not intend to continue under the semi-starvation conditions meted out to them, particularly while painters of pictures, some of them, receive adequate treatment from the government. . . . If the government does not intend to formulate some policy regarding the class of intellectual known as a writer, who is trained for nothing else in the present economic emergency, then the writer must organize and conduct a fight to better his condition.[178]

These were important *and* importunate scribes! The prospect of writers organizing and fighting no doubt filled the authorities with something short of dread. Image-conscious, the Unemployed Writers Association changed its name to the Writers' Union. Alas, simply altering the name of one's organization does not magically produce jobs. Most of the unemployed writers were still unemployed, union or not.

Ray A. Billington, Massachusetts FWP director and staunch liberal, estimated that up to half of his writing staff consisted of communists or sympathizers. As one left-winger in New York City charged, "We'd fight, we'd stage riots and revolutions if they didn't hush us up. We're all taking hush money." Even Trotskyites have their price. Nevertheless, Communist-tinctured unions such as the Writers' Union and the Writers Alliance led occasional strikes demanding more government employment of writers, or at least writers with the correct political views. Jerre Mangione reports watching as the Writers' Union picketed the Port Authority Building in Manhattan on February 25, 1935, under the leadership of the writer Earl Conrad, who held aloft a signboard declaring "CHILDREN NEED BOOKS. WRITERS NEED A BREAK. WE DEMAND PROJECTS."[179]

The FTP and FWP were enlivened by frequent sniping between the Communists and the New Dealers. (Except in remote locations, Republicans were nowhere to be found.) And these internecine quarrels did not only afflict New York City. Jerre Mangione writes that in San Francisco, the "heavy infiltration of leftwing personnel" meant that a significant portion of the staff "were more intent on functioning as missionaries for Marxism than workers for the Project." Conrad Aiken, perhaps the most prestigious writer to accept a job with the FWP, quit the Massachusetts project less than half a year into his stint because he couldn't stand the "Commies" and "hopelessly incompetent, except for the photographers," among his coworkers.[180]

The "Commies" and "hopelessly incompetent" were distinct groups, though they were largely united by their desire to give Federal One a form of eternal life. Stuart Davis, the abstract artist who served as secretary of the American Artists' Congress, told FAP director Holger Cahill in 1937 that by Marxist lights, "the original intention of an emergency stop gap has been changed by social dialectic into its opposite," which in plain English meant that the project should be made permanent.[181]

A Bureau of Fine Arts?

Ought Federal One to be made permanent, or should its functions, at least, be transferred to a durable bureaucracy? So proposed its most fervent supporters.

In 1937, Rep. John Coffee (D-WA) and Senator Claude Pepper (D-FL) introduced companion legislation to establish a Bureau of Fine Arts. Their proposal would draw criticism from all segments of the artistic and political world outside a fairly narrow base of support. The Coffee-Pepper bills (the differences between them were minor; much smaller than between their caffeinated and condimentary eponyms) would have given Federal One a more or less permanent lease on life, though they did stipulate that those hired thereunder must be "competent."[182]

Coffee-Pepper, in the critical assessment of the Fine Arts Federation of New York, was a naked attempt to unionize, and thus sap the creative spirit from, American artists. "In essence the Coffee-Pepper bill is not a bill to create a Government Bureau of Fine Arts at all," declared the Fine Arts Federation, "but to create a Government Bureau of Labor in the Arts and for Permanent Relief to Artists." (Members of the Fine Arts Federation of New York included the National Academy of Design, the American Watercolor Society, the Society of American Artists, the National Sculptors' Society, and the New York chapters of the American Society of Landscape Architects, the American Artists Professional League, and other combinations of painters, artists, illustrators, and architects.)

The Federation was not, on principle, antagonistic to a federal role in the arts, though it allowed that perhaps "Government's best contribution to American art is to let it develop freely under its own native momentum which has carried it to its present preeminence in the art world." But Coffee-Pepper was neither wise activity nor masterly inactivity: it was, said the Federation, an appallingly objectionable "effort to organize artists into labor groups, affiliate them with labor as labor, not as art, and thus give art employment to the greatest possible number that can be loaded onto the Government, regardless of artistic talent or quality."[183] Coffee-Pepper would reduce the artist from proud independence to the subservient role of the dues-paying, clock-punching (and clock-watching) employee of a vast and faceless bureaucracy.

At the pinnacle of the Bureau of Fine Arts would sit a commissioner who was chosen by the President from a list of candidates submitted to him "by organizations representing the greatest number of artists employed in each of the arts under the Bureau." In practice, this would mean the major unions of performing artists. The commissioner's six assistants would be selected from a list similarly drawn up. Smaller, private organizations of artists would play no role in this process. Alarmingly, to the Fine Arts Federation of New York and others, there was no requirement that a commissioner or his assistants be working artists. They could be, say, union officials. Which is why the Fine Arts Federation denounced Coffee-Pepper as "organized labor control."[184]

The Fine Arts Federation concluded its pox on Coffee-Pepper: "It is obvious. . . . that the so-called Bureau of Fine Arts is projected as a labor union for a mass of artists who would otherwise be unemployed or in danger of unemployment. The aegis of the Government is invoked in order to create prestige, power, and security of employment, but the power is to be wielded by the members of the union, not the Government. . . . As a permanent set-up, rather than as emergency relief, the proposal introduces a certain totalitarian concept of Federal functions incompatible with the free enterprise which has heretofore been the particular genius of our democracy."[185]

The invocation of tyranny was not fanciful. The brutal suppression and manipulation of art in the Soviet Union and Nazi Germany were on almost every artist's mind by the late 1930s. Most were wary of all-powerful states, and distrustful of empty phrases and sloganeering. With an eye to the totalitarian states across the Atlantic, Peyton Boswell editorialized in *Art Digest*: "Let us hope the dictator who outlines our art projects for us in the future is a benevolent one. Let us hope he knows a thing or two about art. Let us hope he will be no over-enthusiastic admirer of Herr Hitler, that he will not consider it necessary to sterilize all perpetrators of modern art."[186]

This was not a case of unlettered peasants trying to burn down the art museum. Coffee-Pepper had proposed the nationalization and bureaucratization of American art. The Communist Party and its fronts were almost the only groups that did not lodge fundamental objections to these bills. Even Eleanor Roosevelt, who had taken a special interest in federal patronage of the arts, told Senator Pepper that while "Of course I am in favor of the idea of your bill," she worried about the "danger of censorship of the arts if they become a part of government."[187]

In the *Magazine of Art*, the director of the Worcester Art Museum, Francis Henry Taylor—who was later the director of the Metropolitan Museum of Art—called Coffee-Pepper "one of the most dangerous pieces of class legislation that an organized minority has ever succeeded in introducing into Congress." This "lotus of the American Renaissance" had flowered, wrote Taylor, warming to his vituperative task, in "the cesspool of art politics."[188]

Taylor was not opposed, on principle, to federal patronage of the arts. But the entity created by Coffee-Pepper—and Taylor reminded his readers that "[n]ew departments are easily created and almost never are dissolved"—was an out-and-out payoff to the unions. It was a jobs bill, and nothing more, that would guarantee employment in perpetuity to talentless hacks who wished to sup at the pork barrel forever more. Real artists who made the mistake of entering Bureau employment would find themselves at the mercy of shop foremen, clock-punching, and strikers. The whole shebang was nothing more than the project of "an organized minority who wish to entrench themselves against the day when there is no longer any Santa Claus."[189] A Bureau of Fine Arts would degrade that which it was ostensibly promoting.

At the *Baltimore Sun*, Gerald W. Johnson, writing, it seems, under the invective-laced influence of the *Sun*'s legendary H. L. Mencken, called Coffee-Pepper "a bill to saddle the taxpayers with the duty of providing a living permanently for all the sorry daubers, spavined dancers, ham actors, and radical scriveners who have lately luxuriated on the doles under the auspices of the FAP."[190] Along the same lines, though annunciated with loftier rhetoric, a New York City Democratic congressman, Rep. William I. Sirovich, proposed the establishment of a Federal Bureau of Fine Arts—a moniker uncomfortably close, for those artists of anarchic temperament, to the Federal Bureau of Investigation.

As chairman of the House Committee on Patents, Sirovich was able to schedule hearings on his proposal to create what he was then calling the Department of Science, Art and Literature. Sirovich's bill was a concatenation of "Whereases" that, if laid end to end, might have spanned the entirety of Broadway. It began by confidently asserting that a "broad interpretation" of the Constitution's Article 1, Section 8, granting the Congress the power to "promote the progress of science and useful arts by securing for limited times to authors and inventors the exclusive right to their respective writings and discoveries," coupled with a "close interpretation" of the preamble's invocation of the "general welfare," brought this new department well within the boundaries of constitutional propriety. Besides, modern contingencies "could not have been foreseen by the framers of the Constitution."

Next, Rep. Sirovich sounds that smugly self-satisfied note that has been played with such regularity by those who would transfer taxpayer monies to intellectuals. "[I]n the opinion of the best-informed men and women of the United States of America," goes his third "Whereas," "'man shall not live by bread alone' and. . . . there is more to life and living than the solely material things of existence."[191]

Having established that potential critics of this legislation must be low-browed cretins or money-grubbing materialists, Sirovich departs for the outer realms of the rhetorical empyrean. We read, in subsequent paragraphs, that:

> Whereas science and technology have joined hands with art to form a new trinity of life and have touched the commonplace with magic idealism. . . .
>
> Whereas radio has become the handmaiden in modern days of the muse of music, speeding her harmonies and melodies through the air. . . .

> Whereas the limitations of the olden stage have been removed by the motion picture, accompanied by sonancy, and the genius of dramatic authors and writers is no longer pent up in the Utica of confination to small stages and auditoriums but ranges the United States so that the lesser villages may now receive the same presentations as the major cities, and instead of fustian and buckram the backgrounds of film dramas are. . . . realistic. . . .[192]

These passages, which go on and on, are so overwritten as to make one believe that a useful Department of Science, Art and Literature would have as its first order of business the indictment of its author for offenses against the language.

The first witness at Rep. Sirovich's hearing was Burgess Meredith, acting president of Actors Equity and chairman of the National Advisory Board of the Federal Theatre Project, who was just beginning his long career as ham par excellence.

Meredith, after opining that "the job of Government . . . is to benefit as many people as possible," urged the committee to continue subsidizing theater à la the FTP, though he conceded that it "is probably unwise for the Government to enter into competition with commercial enterprises." He enthused that "The stage can be a magnificent means for helping propagandize for democracy in this country," and one can imagine the winces on the faces of the bill's supporters.[193]

Next up in the witness chair was Rockwell Kent, the great illustrator and vice president of the Bureau of Artists Guild. Kent was quite far to the left politically but he was an independent sort who lived in the Adirondack Mountains, far from the perfervid atmosphere of doctrinaire communism. He complained that the legislation had been drawn up in top-heavy fashion, with too much power vested in the Secretary of Science, Art and Literature and his three undersecretaries of each of the aforementioned branches. "I am against cultured people being chosen to administer the Fine Arts Department," Kent stated. "I am against grown-up people or children all over this country being told by any cultural group what they shall like."[194]

One Congressman, Wisconsin Democrat Thomas O'Malley, engaged Kent in a colloquy about how best to nurture artists:

O'Malley: Do you not think that perhaps it would be better for the artists to go their own way and gradually over the years to develop their talents, with the people gradually learning to appreciate, than permitting an institution for the development of the American arts to fall into the hands. . . . of Army officers, whose knowledge of trajectories is much more intimate than their knowledge of art?

Kent: Unfortunately the people are not gradually learning to appreciate art. Today in the usual art gallery they take a little catalogue and if they see some picture which they may like but cannot find in the catalogue, they are afraid to express themselves on it for fear of making a social blunder. There is no popular influence in art; there should be. . . . And as things stand today the masses of our people have no voice through art.

Rockwell Kent seems to have envisioned the role of the federal government as that of a populist tutor. Rep. O'Malley likened this to a "national Department of Education," which he said he opposed because "I have always felt that education should belong entirely to the home folks, and not be forced on them by any bureau far away from the National Capital."

Kent agreed, in a way. He pronounced himself "as much against the imposition of education by a bureaucracy as I am against the imposition of certain standards of art in a bureaucracy." But he added the caveat that "It must all be run democratically." Just how this was to be done was left unexplored.[195]

Another leftist artist, the novelist of Southern squalor Erskine Caldwell, vice president of the League of American Writers, a Communist Party front group, also wound up bantering for most of his testimony with the puckish and quick-drawing Rep. O'Malley.

"Mr. Caldwell," began Rep. O'Malley cheerfully, "is not everybody a writer?"

"No," replied Caldwell.

"Who would decide who was the writer to be subsidized?" O'Malley pressed. "Personally, I have never met anyone who did not think he could write. I have been in the advertising agency business for the past 15 years, and I never had an employee who did not have somewhere in the back of his head the 'great novel,' which if he had the time and a subsidy to enable him to go off somewhere in a cabin, he was sure he could produce."

Caldwell, not sure what to make of this line of questioning from a Democrat from the most progressive of states, responds that a writer's output "is the best means of determining his qualifications as a writer."

"Well, who would do the determining?" asks O'Malley.

"The public," says Caldwell, which is another way of saying "the market," which is emphatically what Caldwell did *not* want to say.

But there are fine books that the public does not buy, points out O'Malley. Even the university presses pass on worthy works.

This is why we need a Bureau of Fine Arts, says Caldwell: to subsidize "scientific tracts and intellectual works that appeal to a select public."

Now we're getting somewhere, thinks O'Malley. But who decides which books are to be published by the government?

A man whose "qualifications are established by the writers' organizations," offers Caldwell—organizations such as the League of American Writers.

"Would you get into politics here?" asks O'Malley.

"I hardly think so, in our organizations," Caldwell primly replies.

This was rich, given that Earl Browder, general secretary of the Communist Party USA, was the keynote speaker at the League's founding conference, but O'Malley let it pass. He wanted to know how the federal government could possibly distinguish among the claims for support by numberless writers and would-be writers.

"Do you not think that if we should subsidize writers in order to accomplish the weeding-out process," he queried Caldwell, "we should, in fairness, also subsidize everyone who felt he was an inventor?" (This hearing was held, recall, under the auspices of the House Committee on Patents.)

Caldwell disclaimed any knowledge of the world of tinkerers and inventors. O'Malley continued: "If a department to subsidize writers is set up, someone must be qualified to decide who is a writer and who is not. And, when we do that, we thereby establish a dictatorship of letters; we do not let the letters and arts find themselves; we do not let the artist, or the writer, prove to the world, on his own account, that he is entitled to recognition and acceptance."

Did you not write your best-selling novel *Tobacco Road* on your own, without government subvention, Rep. O'Malley asked Erskine Caldwell. The author allowed that he had, although he had also received a $500 advance from the publisher.

"In other words, the publisher gambled on the possibility of your producing a success that would net him some financial return?"

"That is the way it turned out," answered Caldwell.

"Do you think there is any moral or constitutional right, for instance, for the Government to gamble with the taxpayers' money upon that same basis?"

Caldwell here gave a glimpse of his true desideratum. "Well, I would consider it a salaried basis, not as a subsidy to gamble on, but as a permanent salary. I would think, as a writer engaged in writing, he should be paid a weekly or a monthly salary, rather than a lump sum of $500."

A nation of writers paid from the public treasury? O'Malley was dumbfounded.

"You would keep them on a salary whether they had produced or not produced?"

"Yes," said Caldwell, adding that he was confident that the words would flow if given encouragement by regular paychecks.

O'Malley adduced the romantic image of the starving artist. "If a man or a woman is an artist," he said, "he will show it under any condition."

"If he is not forced back into the bread line and to live on an empty stomach," shot back Caldwell. "He cannot write on an empty stomach. He has to go out and, while writing, do something else to live on."

"Of course, the best works I have always believed came as a result of an empty stomach," said O'Malley, perhaps with a touch of sententiousness.

"That is a very nice legend," replied Caldwell, "but actually it is not very true; because I have tried it myself and I found myself going around begging meals of people, instead of writing."

After a California Democrat led a brief detour into the economics of motion picture making, the redoubtable Thomas O'Malley was back for one more exchange with Erskine Caldwell about what O'Malley viewed as the inevitable politicization of a national writers' program. Would not the Secretary of Science, Art and Literature use his position to promote aesthetic or ideological allies and punish, or at least refrain from assisting, those working within other traditions or antitraditions?

"You would think, then," began Rep. O'Malley, "that you can find some member of human society who would not endeavor to forward his own ideas and his own little pet hobbies?"

Yes, allowed Caldwell. As long as this secretary were "surrounded by a competent advisory committee," selected from such groups as, oh, say, the League of American Writers, then "that possible danger would be eliminated."

"I wish I could believe, as you do, that some man could be found who would not use all this as a medium for his own pet ideas and as a source of propaganda, as is done in human society the world over," concluded Rep. O'Malley.[196]

No such skepticism was evident when Frank Gillmore, executive director of the 25,000-member Associated Actors and Artists of America, occupied the chair. The quadruple A was the umbrella under which the various performers' unions, among them Actors Equity and the Screen Actors Guild, conjoined.

Gillmore, the founder and former president of Actors' Equity, presented to the committee a brief, written by counsel Paul N. Turner, that bespoke a childlike faith in a benevolent national government whose stretch and goodness seemingly knew no limits. This paean to the Great Benignant Father in Washington included such observations as:

—"In Government hands we may hope for a more complete organization and coordination of effort in the art world," for "[w]e lack today a central bureau for survey, planning, direction, and experiment." (A "central bureau" in charge of experimentation is an oxymoron that not even the most cynical Soviet minister would dare propose.)

—"Of necessity our National Government is more and more entering into our private lives. The aim is to give us better and happier living."[197] (That a substantial body of persons believed that the intrusion of national government into "private lives" was for the sole and express purpose of spreading happiness and joy is cause for marveling. One of Frank Gillmore's two silent screen credits was for his role in *The Fairy and the Waif*; one suspects that even the fairy and waif would have rolled their eyes at the naïveté of this assertion.)

Other witnesses were more frankly self-serving. William Fineberg, representing the Musicians' Union of Greater New York, endorsed making "the present WPA arts and music projects permanent in many of their aspects." He added a forensic flourish—"Why cannot we foster a national symphony orchestra, why cannot we have a national opera company, why cannot we have a national academy of painting, why cannot we have a national theater?"—but the gist of his message was Jobs for the Boys.[198]

The enthusiasm of Fineberg, Gillmore, and the other union representatives for Rep. Sirovich's bill only served to emphasize a basic objection of many artists to this and the Coffee-Pepper legislation: behind the high-falutin gaseous bombast of art and culture and edification, they were seen as power plays by organized labor. This was the contention of Arthur F. Brinckerhoff, president of the Fine Arts Federation of New York.

Brinckerhoff professed his federation's support for relief efforts to aid out-of-work artists, but these should be temporary, not permanent. The Fine Arts Federation of New York was unalterably opposed to any national bureau or department to oversee the nation's artistic life, and it expressed that opposition forthrightly:

> [The Federation] completely dissents. . . . from the claim to be implied from these bills that these forms of Government control of art and artists will be healthy for American art or will in the long run have a cultural effect. On the contrary, the federation believes that these forms of control will in the long run substitute journeyman standards of art for truly artistic standards, mediocre common standards in place of the highest individual standards, regimentation of art work in place of individual talent, and personal and political pull in the award of art jobs in place of free and open competition. This is to sterilize the soil in which art grows and reduce art to the level of either mass employment or political patronage.[199]

The debate over the Sirovich and Coffee-Pepper bills revealed variant attitudes toward the cult of the "expert" and the idea that by vesting decision-making authority in a hierophantic class of professionals we can remove politics, personal feelings, axe-grinding, unfairness, preferential treatment, prejudice, and indeed all manner of bias from the decisions. Panels of certified experts and respected professionals, the assumption went, would invariably prefer and select those artists or writers who were, in some never defined way, objectively the best of the lot.

Rep. Fritz Lanham (D-TX)—a colorful chap, an amateur magician who had written musical comedies and toured with a stage company as a young man[200]—engaged in this illuminating exchange about a government-funded national theater with witness Lawrence Langner, the director of the Theatre Guild of New York:

Rep. Lanham: And do you think there is no fear, by reason of the fact the Federal Theater necessarily would partake somewhat of the nature of a political group, that there would not be the writing and presentation of propaganda plays advocating some political idea, or something that whatever administration might be in power at the time might wish to force into the minds of the people, and there might also not be a tendency for propaganda for foreign doctrines hostile to the spirit of our American ideals and institutions to creep into some of these plays? Do you not think that is much more likely to be avoided under private philanthropy in carrying out purposes of this kind, than under Federal patronage and subsidy?

Mr. Langner: No, sir. I think in your Federal Theater there should be embodied in this bill, if it goes into that much detail, the idea of play selection boards, or a board, on which people drawn from universities, as deans of universities, would be placed; it should be a board selected without any political bias.[201]

The ingenuousness of such an assertion boggles the mind, though Mr. Langner seems to have been quite sincere—perhaps more sincere than Erskine Caldwell, who had assured the committee that the Secretary of Science, Art and Literature would be above politics and petty concerns if only he was selected with input from such groups as the League of American Writers. Nevertheless, this faith in the ability of credentialed experts to rise above politics and deliver Solomonic verdicts on aesthetic questions is a consistent theme of the era.

The Sirovich bill hit the House floor in June 1938, and the resultant hilarity made national news.

Rep. Dewey Jackson Short (R-MO), identified in press accounts as a preacher from the Ozarks, mocked the Federal Bureau of Fine Arts with a vigorous song and dance. The good congressman actually tap-danced on the House floor and swayed balletically between his satirical thrusts. "Of course all we need to do with 12 million people out of work is to teach toe dancing so we can restore prosperity to the poor American farmer or the wage earner."

Expressing his love of Chopin, Wagner, and Beethoven, Rep. Short confessed that "God knows I have never enjoyed even Puccini on an empty stomach. I can't see how anybody could enjoy Mendelssohn with the seat of his pants out."

Rep. Sirovich's resolution was tabled, 195–35. Its sponsor was sent into paroxysms. "For twelve years I have denounced Communism, Nazism, and Fascism. The only way to overcome it is to create a department of fine arts."

Huh?

At one point Sirovich declared, "You can't regiment drama, the plastic arts, and literature in a democracy." To which statement a voice rang from the gallery, "Why?" bringing down the house, and House, in gales of laughter.[202] Sirovich depicted the battle as between sophisticates like himself and ignorant hicks, presumably like Rep. Short, though what the press accounts did not say about Short, the "Ozarks preacher," is that he was a professor of ethics and philosophy who had studied at, among other institutions, Harvard and Oxford. Just one of those minor details that sometimes get overlooked.

While Sirovich stacked cliché on cliché, his critics jested, though underneath the mockery there was a sharp point. Rep. James Willis Taylor (R-TN) wondered why we should cage "these terpsichoreans, thespians, and people in one gigantic bureaucracy." His colleague Melvin Maas (R-MN) asked, "What protection is there for Charlie McCarthy?"[203]

Even Hallie Flanagan considered Sirovich's plan to be "indefinite and grandiose."[204] (With greater specificity but no greater luck, Flanagan proposed, in 1939, to make a revamped FTP a permanent program, funded by a tax on movie and theater tickets.) But under questioning from the House Committee on Patents, Flanagan did envision a positive role for a Bureau of Fine Arts: "I feel we could bring about a situation whereby, when you go into the theater which says 'Federal theater,' you can fairly expect the same excellence that you would expect from anything stamped with the Government Bureau of Standards."[205]

Yes, nothing says unbridled genius quite like a government approval stamp!

The Sirovich bill's greatest service was in prompting discussion of a question that had been pushed to the side by the exigency of relief and the distraction of political brawling over Federal One, and that is: Why do artists create? Is it the expression of some inner drive, the barbaric yawp of the individual, a desire to praise god or nature or one of god's or nature's creatures that the artist finds fetching? Is it the need to put food on the table and pay the mortgage? Is it the craving for fame or honor or recognition? Is it some combination of all of these motivations?

The drive, however sputtering, for a permanent federal arts program sparked debate over the source of art, and the ways in which society and government might encourage or discourage it. Playwright Channing Pollock said, "The true artist doesn't want to be encouraged. He is an internal combustion engine. For every great artist produced by spoon-feeding, I'll show you 500 who found their own nourishment."[206]

Enough of cossetted, coddled, fragile and frangible artistes who fold their tents at the first sign of adversity. Pollock spoke for the bold, the hardy, those who weathered storms and would slap paint on canvas or words on paper come hell or high water.

Juliana Force, director of the Whitney Museum and the first New York City director of the Federal Art Project, had become convinced that putting artists on the government payroll was simply subsidizing mediocrity. "The Government," she told the New York *Sun*, "now gives any man who says he can paint $18 or $21 a week. The basements of our public buildings are littered with the results. Friends of the Project argue that they have found four or five good artists among the thousands helped, but I believe these would have been discovered anyway. You can't keep a real painter from painting."[207]

Mrs. Force was hardly a libertarian proponent of letting the marketplace sort out the artistic wheat from the chaff. She called on the federal government to purchase works by contemporary American artists for inclusion in what she believed should be an American wing in every American art museum, and she praised the Treasury Department's Edward Bruce for his department's commissioning of talented sculptors and muralists to create art for federal buildings. But she denied that indiscriminate support of artists would produce anything other than a surfeit of bad art.

Yet others viewed artists as an interest group that merited its own place at the federal table (or trough, depending on your point of view). Marc Connelly, the Pulitzer Prize-winning playwright (*The Green Pastures*), Algonquin Round Table wit, and president of the Authors' League of America, forerunner of today's Authors Guild, spoke for his organization when he expressed the hope that "the United States may well recognize that the important contributions to its culture made by the creative, artistic elements of the population are as equally worthy of consideration as the agricultural or business interests."[208]

One can envision that under this dispensation writers and artists would have their own lobbies, issue their own set of demands, perhaps rent space on K Street and employ ex-members of Congress to buttonhole their former colleagues in pursuit of favorable legislative treatment. We were spared tariffs on foreign novels and production quotas for poets, though half a century later, when President Reagan proposed halving the budget of the National Endowment for the Arts, the uproar from certain quarters was such that one might have thought the ethanol or synthetic fuels lobby had been under a budget-cutting assault.

All Things Must End

The Dies Committee didn't finish off Federal One. The war did. The old chestnut that with the end of the 1930s "Dr. New Deal retired and Dr. Win the War took over" largely explains the demise of the federal arts projects. Their purpose had never really been the promotion of the arts but, rather, relief for the unemployed and the destitute. Encouraging an American artistic renaissance, as Federal One's most fervent believers desired, was not a compatible goal with providing a steady paycheck for unemployed persons who called themselves artists. As *Fortune* magazine conceded in a 1937 article lauding the program, "it was clear enough at the outset that the whole 5,500 relief painters and sculptors were not going to turn into Cezannes or Donatellos once they got a brush or a chisel in their hands and a hot plate of soup under their belts."[209]

In April 1939, the Works Progress Administration became the Work Projects Administration, a minor nomenclatorial change that signified a major diminution of the WPA. The vast domain of Depression-era relief was shrinking. The nontheater elements of Federal One would henceforth require local sponsorship, and the FTP was slated for a quiet expiry. The fact that it was singled out for abolition suggests the narrowness of its geographic base—New York City, despite Hallie Flanagan's theoretical support of regional theater—and the cumulative effect of the assaults on the projects as heavy-handed polemical art. The Federal Writers' Project probably had a more significant communist presence than did the Federal Theatre Project, but the FWP had become best known for its guidebooks, which were, in the main, nonpartisan and well-written surveys of the states and cities and regions of the entire United States. That Idaho was first out of the gate in its production of a state guide may have embarrassed Henry Alsberg and the FWP bureaucracy in Washington, but it also demonstrated the wide reach of the writers' project, in contrast to the concentrated provincialism of Hallie Flanagan's project. (And the irony is that Flanagan was a native Midwesterner and Alsberg a dyed-in-the-wool New Yorker.)

In June 1939, FTP partisans made a last-ditch effort to save federally subsidized theater. As if validating the wildest claims of the red-baiters, a prominent champion of saving the FTP was Rep. Vito Marcantonio, an Italian American congressman from Harlem who was an ally of the Communist Party USA and probably the closest thing to a genuine communist ever to serve in the Congress.

An attempt to restore funding for the FTP failed in the House by a vote of 192–56. Supporters enlisted various celebrities (Tyrone Power, Raymond Massey, Orson Welles, Walter Winchell) to lobby the Senate for another chance. For instance, flamboyant actress Tallulah Bankhead tried to coax support from her populist Democratic uncle, and US Senator from Alabama, John H. Bankhead II, but the senator rebuffed his niece's overtures to ride to the rescue of the New York City theatrical community, since the "city fellers in Congress never vote to do anything for the farmers."[210] The Senate retained the FTP within Federal One and provided it with an appropriation, but the reprieve was fleeting. Funding for the FTP was dropped by the House-Senate conference committee charged with ironing out differences between the respective chambers' bills.

The curtain closed on the Federal Theatre Project on June 30, 1939. Relief was going out of style; war was coming on. Those elements of Federal One outside the theater project were headed for a slower death. In order to survive, they would have to obtain state or local government supervision and funding equal to 25 percent of their budgets—no easy task in hard times.

Federal Writers' Project administrators tried to rouse their constituency to action in lobbying for life extension. Commercial publishers and the American Hotel Association praised the guide books; an organization calling itself the Federal Arts Sponsoring Committee protested the contemplated abolition of the project.

FWP Director Alsberg, hearing the wolf at the door, wrote Brain Truster Benjamin Cohen suggesting that Federal One be spun off from the WPA and given permanent status. But then Alsberg, according to his former subaltern Mangione, was given to "a relentless optimism streaked with naïveté."[211]

As military spending threatened to crowd out spending on government employment programs, and Federal One looked to be a goner, proponents of the FWP sought "some spectacular and newsworthy means of demonstrating to Congress that the nation's leading intellectuals were opposed to the abolition of Federal One." The plan they hit upon? "[A] march to Washington by the most prominent figures in the world of arts and letters." The sheer improbability of organizing such a march, let alone persuading sedentary and solitary writers and artists to do anything as gauche and physical as march on Washington, would have daunted most people, but when one's livelihood is at risk, men and women are capable of extraordinary feats. So Jerre Mangione led a delegation to the home of writer Heywood Broun in Stamford, Connecticut, to ask Mr. Broun to lead the charge. Broun deftly deflected the request, opining that Alexander Woolcott, who unlike Broun was not considered a leftist, was their man. Woolcott, a man of prodigious girth, was unlikely to lead a march to anything much further away than his own refrigerator, but the Mangione delegation gave it a shot. It was in vain, as the vain Woolcott launched into a nasty attack on one member of the delegation, a playwright: "I remember you. You were the perpetrator of an awful play I once had to review."[212]

There would be no march on Washington. The Washington staff of what was now called the Writers' Program was halved. Henry Alsberg was forced out of the directorship, a victim of his own lack of administrative and political skills. Alsberg was succeeded in 1939 by a Michigan newspaperman named John Newsome, who had directed the Wolverine State's writers' project. Newsome's was a winding-down operation. The salad days were over. The FWP did secure enough local pledges in all but two states to endure into 1940, its major activity being to finish the uncompleted state guides as well as various local studies. As of January 1940, the remnant of what had been the FWP still had 3,654 people on the federal payroll, and by year's end that figure was 3,667. In November 1941, a month before Pearl Harbor, the program employed 2,200 writers and others, down from its peak of 6,686 in April 1936.[213]

Prefiguring the Bill Clinton-Rahm Emanuel dictum to never let a good crisis go to waste, honchos of the FWP/Writers' Program sought to attach the project to the coming war effort. Katherine Kellock, the compulsive talker who is credited with conceiving the idea of the guidebooks, wrote in 1940, "Books like these are needed as never before if Americans are to understand their heritage and the culture they are now called on to defend."

As Monty Noam Penkower notes, "The Writers' Program shifted its work to war themes." Its books were distributed to military bases. Guides to military installations and histories on martial themes were churned out. By early 1942, the vestiges of the FWP had been renamed the Writers' Unit of the War Services Subdivision. Its job was to "build morale": that is to say, its job was propaganda on behalf of the war effort.[214] The writers' project had turned into that which its most cogent early critics had warned against: a mere propaganda arm of the federal government which employed writers to glorify the activities of the state.

A sympathetic newspaper in Jacksonville, Florida, took up for the Writers' Program as a weapon of the war: "In this hour—when all available manpower and industry are being mobilized for the national defense program—we should remember that an American takes pride in his community, state, and nation only after he has acquired a broad knowledge of their democratic values, and has seen how he as an individual fits into the American tradition. By providing such knowledge the WPA Writers' Project is making a definite, though indirect, contribution to the nation's defense program."[215] Indirect contributions were not enough, though. Washington needed men and materiel, not essays. Writers were about to go off the dole. The other surviving elements of Federal One also took on a martial hue. Artists "produced posters urging increased industrial production, designed camp insignias, and drew charts showing the silhouettes of aircraft."[216] Musicians and bands played at military bases and piped out the airs of war.

Federal One limped on into early 1943, a shadow of its former self, sputtering, in some cases frantically attempting to refit itself for military garb. It survived over these last years and months only by reorienting its remaining activities toward serving military needs. By June 30, 1943, even the ghost was gone. All that was left was the subsequent nostalgia-tinted memories of that golden moment when the federal government was run by enlightened men who understood the importance of culture and the imperative of taxpayer support thereof—or at least that is how the FWP, FTP, and Federal One in general are depicted in most of the literature, scholarly and popular, covering the era.

The savings from shuttering Federal One, and the writers' project in particular, were very modest. Over the period 1935–43 the FWP had cost $25.7 million, or not even 1 percent of the total WPA expenditure of about $3 billion.[217] While the WPA employed as many as two million persons at any one time, the FWP peak of approximately 6,500 was less than half of 1 percent of that whole. In approximately 300 books, 700 pamphlets, and hundreds of articles or leaflets, project writers committed twelve million words to print.[218]

Even its fiercest critics did not claim that the Federal Writers' Project was bankrupting the Treasury. They did, however, deny that it was nurturing arts and letters in the Republic. They insisted that it was welfare for intellectuals (or at least that is how a significant number of its beneficiaries viewed themselves) or, in less lofty terms, white-collar welfare. Harry Hopkins, who correctly observed that even artists and eggheads gotta eat, would not have wholly disagreed.

Despite the headaches, the Stalinists, the hacks, and the dullards, Jerre Mangione, from his central perch at the FWP headquarters in Washington, found it "an exhilarating time."[219] Unquestionably, the project brought together some talented writers exploring fertile fields within an ideological matrix that historian Jerrold Hirsch, in *Portrait of America: A Cultural History of the Federal Writers' Project* (2003), called "romantic nationalist, pluralistic, and cosmopolitan."[220] The critic Lewis Mumford, nobody's idea of a flag-waving jingo, deemed the guides "the finest contribution to American patriotism that has been made in our generation. . . . The Guides are indispensable toward creating that new sense of the regional setting and regional history, without which we cannot have an informed. . . . body of citizens."[221] John Steinbeck, in *Travels with Charley*, opined that the American Guide series constituted "the most comprehensive account of the United States ever got together."[222]

At its best, the FWP interpreted, sympathetically but not entirely uncritically, the numerous and fascinating tiles of the American mosaic. As one of its most thoughtful figures, Midwest regional director John T. Frederick, founding editor of *The Midland: A Magazine of the American Middle West*, explained to a conference in Chicago: "It seems to me possible for us to make a real contribution to a new attitude for the home town, on the part of the coming generation. And I think that is a tremendously important thing to do. If we can, in dealing with Galena or Dubuque, or any small city of the middle west, help people who are living there, and growing up there to see that they have something in their own home town that is special and intrinsically worthy, not something to get away from, but something to foster and appreciate, I think that is a pretty good job for us to try to do."[223]

A very worthy sentiment, to be sure, though by the time Frederick uttered these words in 1936, the regionalist literary movement was well under way, with novelists and poets from Iowa to Florida turning their attentions to matters in their own home regions, whether historical or contemporary—and this was all being done without the slightest goad from the central government. *The Midland*, which did a good deal to nurture regional writing in the Middle West, had been started in 1915 without any alms from Washington. No less than H. L. Mencken, then the most influential critic in America, called *The Midland* "probably the most important literary magazine ever published in America."[224] No one would ever say that of any product of the Federal Writers' Project. Yet Frederick would no doubt point out that *The Midland* could not survive the Depression, and that this economic cataclysm had so altered economic circumstances that federal assistance was now a requisite.

Not even the most dogmatic Rooseveltian could say with a straight face that Federal One's politics were neutral. It was a creation of the New Deal, and it never bit the hand that fed it. The WPA's arts and letters projects, as one sympathetic historian writes, "celebrated the social and economic progress made under President Roosevelt and promoted his programs. It emphasized what America had gained through the New Deal and contrasted these advances with what they saw as the misery and poverty of earlier years."[225] The American Guides, as Daniel M. Fox observed in "The Achievement of the Federal Writers' Project," showered with praise "the New Deal improvements and experiments," though to varying degrees, and generally hailed the Roosevelt administration as wise and far-seeing and a necessary corrective to what is sometimes depicted as the dog-eat-dog world of laissez-faire.[226]

WPA art extolled the Civilian Conservation Corps and the Resettlement Administration, while WPA theatre praised rural electrification and the TVA. It's what a later generation of marketers would call *synergy*.

"Did the project have any literary or historical value?" wrote Vardis Fisher in response to a question in 1968. "Of course, but not much in proportion to the money spent."[227] Inevitably, if you pay enough writers and painters and actors to practice their craft, some fine work (as well as considerable dross) will result. The multitalented Jacques Barzun, asked in 1950 to assess the output of New Deal cultural programs, remarked that "all the WPA proves is that from a huge grouping of American artists a sizable amount of good work can be obtained."[228]

George Biddle, the upper-class artist and FDR friend who had planted the ideational seed of muralists working for plumbers' wages and turning out timeless works of art, exulted of Federal One that "For the first time in our history the Federal Government has recognized that it has the same obligation to keep an artist alive during the depression as to keep a farmer or carpenter alive."[229] Previous generations of Americans might have thought that the artist, like the farmer and the carpenter, shared in that obligation.

The "other people's money" syndrome was on display throughout the lifetime of Federal One. Harry Hopkins was saluted by *Fortune* as the Maecenas of modern America. He "rivals Andrew Mellon as an art patron and far surpasses him as a patron of living artists," having spent, as of 1937, $46 million on the arts. "Aside from the totalitarian states in which all art is a state perquisite—usually under the shadow of the Ministry of Propaganda—Hopkins spends more on art than any official of any government," gushed *Fortune*.[230] This profligacy was a self-evidently good thing, in *Fortune*'s telling, and bore no resemblance whatsoever to the expenditure of money on the arts by those totalitarians who conscripted artists into the service of the state. One need not be a cynic to note that while Mellon spent his own fortune on art treasures, Hopkins spent only other people's money. And whereas the art collected by the Mellon family came to constitute the heart of the National Gallery of Art and other museums, the works executed under the administration of Harry Hopkins have proved rather less durable.

Hallie Flanagan, looking back on the Federal Theatre Project, concluded with much self-satisfaction that the "federal projects were America's protest against a too thin-blooded culture."[231] Thin-blooded? Hemingway, Faulkner, Cather, Fitzgerald, Winslow Homer, Eakins, Grant Wood, Charles Ives, Scott Joplin, Ben Hecht, Anita Loos, D. W. Griffith, Buster Keaton. . . . just for starters. This is the thin blood that needed to be thickened by Henry Alsberg, Hallie Flanagan, Harry Hopkins, & Co.? Only a vampire could consider the rich, complex, multifarious American and regional cultures that had developed by the mid-1930s to be thin, diluted, watery, anemic.

One panegyrist of Federal One writes that in the 1930s, "most of this nation's citizens subsisted on the aesthetically deficient pap served up as entertainment—a later generation would call it *kitsch*."[232] Really? The blues? Country music? The golden age of the *Saturday Evening Post* and the American short story? And all of these entertainments accessible to people of very modest means? *Pap*? And beyond this, in the kitsch-ville of the West Coast, the 1930s—the decade of the Depression—were possibly the most artistically fertile era in the history of American cinema.

But as we will see, the claim that American culture is insubstantial (or, to switch imagery, arid) and that only the infusion of federal dollars can elevate it to a station commensurate with the standing of the United States in the world is one that will recur every time the question of government-sponsored culture comes up.[233]

Notes

1. James Madison, *Notes of Debates in the Federal Convention of 1787 Reported by James Madison*, with an introduction by Adrienne Koch (Athens, OH: Ohio University Press, 1966/1840).
2. John Trumbull, *Dictionary of American Biography*, Vol. 19, 29.
3. John Trumbull, *Letters Proposing a Plan for the Permanent Encouragement of the Fine Arts By the National Government, Addressed to The President of the United States* (New York: Olana Gallery, 1973/1827), 3.
4. Ibid., 3–4.
5. Ibid., 6.
6. Ibid., 6–7.

7. See James T. Bennett, *The Doomsday Lobby: Hype and Panic from Sputniks, Martians, and Marauding Meteors* (New York: Springer, 2010), 9–12.
8. John Quincy Adams, "First Annual Message," December 6, 1825, accessed October 9, 2015, http://millercenter.org/president/jqadams/speeches/speech-3514.
9. Ray Allen Billington, "Government and the Arts: The W.P.A. Experience," *American Quarterly* 13, no. 4 (Winter 1961): 467.
10. William J. Barber, "'Sweet are the Uses of Adversity': Federal Patronage of the Arts in the Great Depression," in *Economic Engagements with Art*, eds. Neil De Marchi and Craufurd D.W. Goodwin (Durham, NC: Duke University Press, 1999), 236.
11. Victoria M. Grieve, "'Work That Satisfies the Creative Instinct': Eleanor Roosevelt and the Arts and Crafts," *Winterthur Portfolio* 42, no. 2/3 (Summer/Autumn 2008): 176–7.
12. Bruce I. Bustard, *A New Deal for the Arts* (Washington, DC: National Archives and Records Administration in Association with the University of Washington Press, 1997), 5–6.
13. William F. McDonald, *Federal Relief Administration and the Arts* (Columbus: Ohio State University Press, 1969), 363.
14. Jonathan Harris, *Federal Art and National Culture: The Politics of Identity in New Deal America* (Cambridge: Cambridge University Press, 1995), 25.
15. Jerre Mangione, *The Dream and the Deal: The Federal Writers' Project, 1935–1943* (Boston, MA: Little, Brown, 1972), 33.
16. Richard D. McKinzie, *The New Deal for Artists* (Princeton, NJ: Princeton University Press, 1973), 25.
17. William Hauptman, "The Suppression of Art in the McCarthy Decade," *Artforum* 12, no. 4 (October 1973): 51–52.
18. Jane de Hart Mathews, "Art and Politics in Cold War America," *American Historical Review* 81, no. 4 (October 1976): 767.
19. McKinzie, *The New Deal for Artists*, 27.
20. Bustard, *A New Deal for the Arts*, 27.
21. Tyler Cowen, *Good and Plenty: The Creative Successes of American Arts Funding* (Princeton, NJ: Princeton University Press, 2006), 70.
22. McDonald, *Federal Relief Administration and the Arts*, 363.
23. Garnett McCoy, "Poverty, Politics, and Artists, 1930–1945," *Art in America* 54, no. 4 (1965): 96.
24. Monty Noam Penkower, *The Federal Writers' Project: A Study in Government Patronage of the Arts* (Urbana: University of Illinois Press, 1977), 7.
25. Ibid., 16.
26. "Department of Science, Art and Literature," *Hearings before the Committee on Patents, U.S. House of Representatives*, 75th Congress, 3rd Session, February 7–11, 1938 (Washington, DC: Government Printing Office, 1938), 131.
27. Bustard, *A New Deal for the Arts*, 6.
28. Emergency Relief Appropriation Act of 1935, accessed October 9, 2015, http://www.fofweb.com/History.
29. McDonald, *Federal Relief Administration and the Arts*, 215.
30. Ibid., 129.
31. Mangione, *The Dream and the Deal*, 11.

32. Nick Taylor, *American-Made: The Enduring Legacy of the WPA: When FDR Put the Nation to Work* (New York: Bantam, 2008), 247.
33. W. H. Auden, Introduction to Anzia Yezierska, *Red Ribbon on a White Horse* (New York: Scribner's, 1950), 17.
34. Victoria Grieve, *The Federal Art Project and the Creation of Middlebrow Culture* (Urbana: University of Illinois Press, 2009), 47–48.
35. Penkower, *The Federal Writers' Project*, 18.
36. Mangione, *The Dream and the Deal*, 56.
37. Jerrold Hirsch, *Portrait of America: A Cultural History of the Federal Writers' Project* (Chapel Hill: University of North Carolina Press, 2003), 26.
38. Penkower, *The Federal Writers' Project*, 28.
39. Mangione, *The Dream and the Deal*, 57, 59.
40. Henry G. Alsberg, "Writers and the Government," *Saturday Review of Literature*, January 4, 1936, 9.
41. Mangione, *The Dream and the Deal*, 63, 46.
42. Ibid., 47.
43. Daniel M. Fox, "The Achievement of the Federal Writers' Project," *American Quarterly* 13, no. 1 (Spring 1961): 3.
44. George T. Blakey, *Creating a Hoosier Self-Portrait: The Federal Writers' Project in Indiana, 1935–1942* (Bloomington: Indiana University Press, 2005), 64.
45. Mangione, *The Dream and the Deal*, 88.
46. Billington, "Government and the Arts," 470.
47. Ibid., 473–4.
48. McDonald, *Federal Relief Administration and the Arts*, 744–5.
49. Ibid., 745.
50. "John Cheever: Reluctant New Dealer on the Way to Fame," The New England Historical Society, accessed October 9, 2015, http://www.newenglandhistoricalsociety.com/john-cheever-reluctant-new-dealer.
51. Penkower, *The Federal Writers' Project*, 96, 98.
52. Blair Bolles, "The Federal Writers' Project," *Saturday Review of Literature* (July 9, 1938): 3.
53. African American percentage from Penkower, *The Federal Writers' Project*, 67; payroll number from Bolles, "The Federal Writers' Project," 4.
54. Mangione, *The Dream and the Deal*, 70.
55. Penkower, *The Federal Writers' Project*, 37.
56. Jane de Hart Matthews, *The Federal Theatre, 1935–1939: Plays, Relief, and Politics* (Princeton, NJ: Princeton University Press, 1967), 158.
57. Mangione, *The Dream and the Deal*, 117.
58. Ibid., 106.
59. Ibid., 195.
60. Penkower, *The Federal Writers' Project*, 162.
61. Blakey, *Creating a Hoosier Self-Portrait*, 2.
62. Ibid., 46.
63. Bustard, *A New Deal for the Arts*, 14.
64. Mangione, *The Dream and the Deal*, 84.
65. Ibid., 151.
66. Ibid., 79.

67. Ronald W. Taber, "Vardis Fisher and the 'Idaho Guide,'" *Pacific Northwest Quarterly* 59, no. 2 (April 1968): 68.
68. Penkower, *The Federal Writers' Project*, 40.
69. Taber, "Vardis Fisher and the 'Idaho Guide,'" 71.
70. Mangione, *The Dream and the Deal*, 191.
71. Taber, "Vardis Fisher and the 'Idaho Guide,'" 72–74.
72. Ibid., 74.
73. Ibid., 71; Mangione, *The Dream and the Deal*, 203.
74. Taber, "Vardis Fisher and the 'Idaho Guide,'" 74–75.
75. Bolles, "The Federal Writers' Project," 4.
76. McDonald, *Federal Relief Administration and the Arts*, 736.
77. Mangione, *The Dream and the Deal*, 98–99.
78. Penkower, *The Federal Writers' Project*, 58.
79. Elmo Howell, "William Faulkner and the New Deal," *Midwest Quarterly* 5 (July 1964): 323; see John Faulkner, *Men Working* (New York: Harcourt, Brace and Company, 1941).
80. Howell, "William Faulkner and the New Deal," 324.
81. Mangione, *The Dream and the Deal*, 237.
82. Billington, "Government and the Arts," 477.
83. The *Detroit Free Press* editorialized of the Massachusetts matter that the administration was using the guides to "slip over quite a lot of propaganda against American institutions." Penkower, *The Federal Writers' Project*, 103.
84. Billington, "Government and the Arts," 478.
85. Mangione, *The Dream and the Deal*, 242.
86. McKinzie, *The New Deal for Artists*, 5, 3.
87. Ernest van den Haag, "Should the Government Subsidize the Arts?" *Policy Review* 13 (September 1979): 71.
88. Bustard, *A New Deal for the Arts*, 9.
89. Peggy Boyer Long, "The Case for Public Support of the Arts Is Pretty Much What it Was Nearly Seven Decades Ago," *Illinois Issues*, December 2002, accessed October 9, 2015, http://illinoisissues-archive.uis.edu/editor/public.html.
90. Billington, "Government and the Arts," 469.
91. "Department of Science, Art and Literature," *Hearings before the Committee on Patents*, U.S. House of Representatives, 113.
92. Gail Levin, *Edward Hopper: An Intimate Biography* (Berkeley: University of California Press, 1998/1995), 271.
93. Grieve, *The Federal Art Project and the Creation of Middlebrow Culture*, 83.
94. McKinzie, *The New Deal for Artists*, 93–94.
95. "Dallas Nine," Texas State Historical Association, accessed October 9, 2015, http://www.tshaonline.org/handbook/online/articles/kjd01.
96. Charles Harrison and Paul Wood, eds., *Art in Theory: 1900–1990* (Cambridge, MA: Blackwell Publishers, 1993), 133.
97. McDonald, *Federal Relief Administration and the Arts*, 587.
98. Taylor, *American-Made: The Enduring Legacy of the WPA*, 284–5.
99. Bustard, *A New Deal for the Arts*, 9; "Department of Science, Art and Literature," *Hearings before the Committee on Patents*, U.S. House of Representatives, 121.
100. Ibid., 143.

101. Ibid., 145.
102. Ronayne, *Stages of Modernity*, 3.
103. "Department of Science, Art and Literature," *Hearings before the Committee on Patents*, U.S. House of Representatives, 93.
104. Jane de Hart Mathews, "Arts and the People: The New Deal Quest for a Cultural Democracy," *Journal of American History* 62, no. 2 (September 1975): 330.
105. Hallie Flanagan, *Arena: The History of the Federal Theatre* (New York: Benjamin Blom, 1940), 20, 57.
106. McDonald, *Federal Relief Administration and the Arts*, 484.
107. Ibid., 510.
108. Paul Sporn, *Against Itself: The Federal Theater and Writers' Projects in the Midwest* (Detroit: Wayne State University Press, 1995), 41.
109. "Department of Science, Art and Literature," *Hearings before the Committee on Patents*, U.S. House of Representatives, 91.
110. McKinzie, *The New Deal for Artists*, 161.
111. McDonald, *Federal Relief Administration and the Arts*, 509. For a brief take on McDonald's tome by the preeminent classical liberal historian of his age, see Arthur A. Ekirch's review of *Federal Relief Administration and the Arts* in the *American Historical Review* 75, no. 4 (April 1970): 1204–5.
112. Flanagan, *Arena*, 21.
113. Ibid., 23.
114. Mathews, *The Federal Theatre, 1935–1939*, 30.
115. "E.C. Mabie, the W.P.A. and the U.I. Theatre," accessed October 9, 2015, http://www.lib.uiowa.edu/exhibits/previous/mabie.
116. Mathews, *The Federal Theatre, 1935–1939*, 34.
117. Ibid., 179.
118. Ibid., 116.
119. Ronayne, *Stages of Modernity*, 58.
120. Mathews, *The Federal Theatre, 1935–1939*, 123.
121. In *Stages of Modernity*, based on her doctoral dissertation, Kelly K. Ronayne examines several of these socially conscious plays.
122. "Department of Science, Art and Literature," *Hearings before the Committee on Patents*, U.S. House of Representatives, 93.
123. Ronayne, *Stages of Modernity*, 40; Harrison Grey Fiske, "The Federal Doom-Boggle," *Saturday Evening Post*, August 1, 1936, 23.
124. Ronayne, *Stages of Modernity*, 40.
125. Mathews, *The Federal Theatre, 1935–1939*, 21.
126. Fiske, "The Federal Doom-Boggle," 70.
127. Ibid., 68.
128. Billington, "Government and the Arts," 472.
129. Flanagan, *Arena*, 54.
130. Barry B. Witham, *The Federal Theatre Project: A Case Study* (Cambridge: Cambridge University Press, 2003), 3.
131. George Jean Nathan, "A Government in Greasepaint," *Newsweek*, July 3, 1937. Barry B. Witham tells of Florence James, director of the Seattle production of *Power*, and her difficulty in dealing with the vaudevillians in the cast, "many of them out-of-work old-timers with little understanding of modern theatre." James recalled, "One of them came to me one day and asked what

mug I wanted him to use. I did not know what he was talking about. He then explained to me that he had 46 mugs and wanted me to see them so I could tell him which one. I explained to him that he should memorize his lines and say them, and the mug he wore every day would be just fine." Witham, *The Federal Theatre Project*, 84.

132. Grieve, *The Federal Art Project and the Creation of Middlebrow Culture*, 169.
133. Anne Ursu, "The Red Curtain," *City Pages*, August 12, 1998, accessed October 9, 2015, http://www.citypages.com/1998-08-12/arts/the-red-curtain.
134. Flanagan, *Arena*, 28.
135. Ronayne, *Stages of Modernity*, 61.
136. Witham, *The Federal Theatre Project*, 119.
137. Ronayne, *Stages of Modernity*, 42.
138. Ibid., 46.
139. Bustard, *A New Deal for the Arts*, 80.
140. Mathews, *The Federal Theatre, 1935–1939*, 114.
141. Flanagan, *Arena*, 185.
142. Ibid., 306–7; Witham, *The Federal Theatre Project*, 86.
143. Ibid., 80.
144. Bustard, *A New Deal for the Arts*, 81.
145. Charles R. Walker, "Theater on the Left," *The Nation*, June 24, 1939.
146. Flanagan, *Arena*, 81–82.
147. Ibid., 90, 256.
148. Ronayne, *Stages of Modernity*, 63, 80.
149. Ibid., 67.
150. Susan Quinn, *Furious Improvisation: How the WPA and a Cast of Thousands Made High Art out of Desperate Times* (New York: Walker & Company, ebook 2011/2008), unpaginated ebook.
151. Fiske, "The Federal Doom-Boggle," 68.
152. Quinn, *Furious Improvisation.*
153. Fiske, "The Federal Doom-Boggle," 69, 71.
154. Quinn, *Furious Improvisation.*
155. Flanagan, *Arena*, 66.
156. Fiske, "The Federal Doom-Boggle," 70.
157. Ibid.
158. Mathews, *The Federal Theatre, 1935–1939*, 165.
159. Ibid., 177.
160. Quinn, *Furious Improvisation.*
161. Flanagan, *Arena*, 72.
162. Mathews, *The Federal Theatre, 1935–1939*, 110–11.
163. Flanagan, *Arena*, 342.
164. Kate Dossett, "Gender and the Dies Committee Hearings on the Federal Theatre Project," *Journal of American Studies* 47 (November 2013): 1006.
165. Flanagan, *Arena*, 337.
166. Dossett, "Gender and the Dies Committee Hearings on the Federal Theatre Project," 1009.
167. "Hallie Flanagan," accessed October 9, 2015, http://newdeal.feri.org/nchs/huac04.htm.
168. Ibid.
169. McKinzie, *The New Deal for Artists*, 21.

170. Mathews, "Arts and the People," 316.
171. Flanagan, *Arena*, 347.
172. Penkower, *The Federal Writers' Project*, 194–96.
173. Grieve, *The Federal Art Project and the Creation of Middlebrow Culture*, 91.
174. Virginia Hagelstein Marquardt, "'New Masses' and John Reed Club Artists, 1926–1936: Evolution of Ideology, Subject Matter, and Style," *Journal of Decorative and Propaganda Arts* 12 (Spring 1989): 68.
175. Ibid., 72.
176. Ibid., 73.
177. Penkower, *The Federal Writers' Project*, 12.
178. Mangione, *The Dream and the Deal*, 36.
179. Ibid., 85, 159, 37–38.
180. Ibid., 134, 105.
181. McKinzie, *The New Deal for Artists*, 98.
182. Grieve, *The Federal Art Project and the Creation of Middlebrow Culture*, 166.
183. "Department of Science, Art and Literature," *Hearings before the Committee on Patents*, U.S. House of Representatives, 78–79.
184. Ibid., 79.
185. Ibid., 80; see also "Federal Bureau of Arts Opposed," *New York Times*, February 13, 1938.
186. Grieve, *The Federal Art Project and the Creation of Middlebrow Culture*, 166–7.
187. Grieve, "'Work That Satisfies the Creative Instinct,'" 179.
188. Francis Henry Taylor, "Pork Barrel Renaissance," *Magazine of Art* 31 (March 1938): 157.
189. Ibid., 186–7.
190. Grieve, *The Federal Art Project and the Creation of Middlebrow Culture*, 169.
191. "Department of Science, Art and Literature," *Hearings before the Committee on Patents*, U.S. House of Representatives, 1.
192. Ibid., 2.
193. Ibid., 3, 8.
194. Ibid., 16.
195. Ibid., 19.
196. *passim*, 39–44.
197. Ibid., 49.
198. Ibid., 55.
199. Ibid., 72.
200. "Lanham, Frederick Garland," *The Handbook of Texas*, Texas State Historical Association, accessed October 12, 2015, http://www.tshaonline.org/handbook/online/articles/fla33.
201. "Department of Science, Art and Literature," *Hearings before the Committee on Patents*, U.S. House of Representatives, 193.
202. "Federal Arts Bill Crushed With Ridicule," *St. Petersburg Times*, June 16, 1938.
203. "Congress Has Good Laugh on Fine Arts Bureau Bill," Lawrence (KS) *Daily Journal-World*, June 16, 1938.
204. Flanagan, *Arena*, 326.

205. "Department of Science, Art and Literature," *Hearings before the Committee on Patents*, U.S. House of Representatives, 105–6.
206. "Art and Appetite," Hagerstown (MD) *Daily Mail*, June 4, 1938.
207. "Mrs. Force Attacks WPA Project Art," *Art Digest* 15 (May 1, 1941): 9.
208. "Department of Science, Art and Literature," *Hearings before the Committee on Patents*, U.S. House of Representatives, 215.
209. "Unemployed Arts," *Fortune* (May 1937): 113.
210. Mathews, *The Federal Theatre, 1935–1939*, 284.
211. Mangione, *The Dream and the Deal*, 6.
212. Ibid., 17–18, 20.
213. Penkower, *The Federal Writers' Project*, 223; Mangione, *The Dream and the Deal*, 9.
214. Penkower, *The Federal Writers' Project*, 230, 234.
215. Hirsch, *Portrait of America*, 221.
216. Bustard, *A New Deal for the Arts*, 126.
217. Mangione, *The Dream and the Deal*, 369.
218. Blakey, *Creating a Hoosier Self-Portrait*, 20; Robert A. Rosenstone, "The Federal (Mostly Non-) Writers' Project," *Reviews in American History* 6, no. 3 (September 1978): 400.
219. Mangione, *The Dream and the Deal*, 223.
220. Hirsch, *Portrait of America*, 28.
221. Fox, "The Achievement of the Federal Writers' Project," 19.
222. John Steinbeck, *Travels with Charley in Search of America* (New York: Penguin, 2002/1962), 103.
223. Hirsch, *Portrait of America*, 37.
224. Sargent Bush Jr., "The Achievement of John T. Frederick," *Books at Iowa* 14, April 1971, accessed October 12, 2015, http://www.lib.uiowa.edu/scua/bai/bush.htm.
225. Bustard, *A New Deal for the Arts*, 71.
226. Fox, "The Achievement of the Federal Writers' Project," 7.
227. Penkower, *The Federal Writers' Project*, 247.
228. McKinzie, *The New Deal for Artists*, 176.
229. Howard E. Wooden, "The Neglected Generation of American Realist Painters: 1930–1948," Wichita Art Museum, 2009, accessed October 12, 2015, http://www.tfaoi.com/aa/8aa/8aa327.htm.
230. "Unemployed Arts," 117.
231. Flanagan, *Arena*, 231.
232. Mathews, "Arts and the People," 321.
233. As the American newspaper industry collapsed in the early twenty-first century, Mark Pinsky in *The New Republic* called for a revived Federal Writers' Project to hire "dislocated 'old media' journalists from newspapers, radio and television" and put them to work, under federal auspices, "documenting the ground-level impact of the Great Recession; chronicling the transition to a green economy; or capturing the experiences of the thousands of immigrants who are changing the American complexion." The ideological slant of each of these stories isn't hard to decipher. Pinsky suggested that the "new FWP" could be administered as "an individual grant program through community colleges and universities" in order to

"minimize bureaucracy and overhead." In other words, cut out the middleman, which means more money for the writers—something which writers of every era would heartily endorse. Mark Pinsky, "Write Now," *The New Republic*, December 8, 2008, accessed October 12, 2015, www.newrepublic.com/article/politics/write-now.

Part Two

Weaponizing Art—and Intellectuals

US Representative Jacob Javits (R-NY) had proposed the creation of a National Theater and Academy and a National Opera and Ballet in 1948–49. These institutions would inordinately benefit Javits's home city, though he was, of course, above such petty political calculations.[1] Instead, Javits promoted culture as an element of national defense. "[I]f we do not want to fight the Russians with the atom bomb, then we have got to defeat their effort with two other weapons—economic and cultural. . . . but in the cultural field we have not even touched it."[2]

One wonders just how acquainted Javits was with the "cultural field" on which he imagined the United States was losing so badly to the Russians. The late 1940s and early 1950s were a fecund time for American arts and culture. Or were Steinbeck and Faulkner, John Ford and Howard Hawks, Aaron Copland and Duke Ellington, Robert Frost and Frank Lloyd Wright, Martha Graham and Andrew Wyeth, mere pikers compared to what American culture might be if only Washington took a stronger hand at the helm?

The arts were to be a weapon—a tony weapon, to be sure, but a weapon nonetheless—in the Cold War. Senator Herbert Lehman (D-NY) explained in 1954: "I believe that the fine arts, in their broadest sense, provide one of the most effective ways of transmitting to the peoples of the world the true essence of democracy. We can help destroy the Communist myth by encouraging cultural interchange of representative American artists with others in the free world."[3]

That the arts were the cultural expression of the American soul was a debatable, if plausible, supposition; that the US government was the political expression of that soul was perhaps a less tenable argument. That therefore the US government ought to underwrite the arts and brandish them to the other nations of the world as evidence that the unaligned nations of the world ought to side with the West rather than the Soviet bloc was a syllogism of shaky foundation. But it went largely unchallenged among Cold War liberals. Whatever uncertainty they may have felt about the United States as the world's supreme military power was eased by the thought that the same government that was manufacturing nuclear weapons and engaging in fitful games of nuclear brinksmanship was also sending modernist paintings to European galleries. The cultural Cold War gave the military Cold War a tincture of sophistication.

Gary O. Larson, in his valuable study, *The Reluctant Patron: The United States Government and the Arts, 1943–1965*, quotes Senator James E. Murray (D-MT) making the point even more explicitly (and crassly): "We are presently engaged in the greatest sales campaign in history; we are striving to convince hundreds of millions of people around the world that the American way of life is superior to the slave existence that the totalitarian aggressors would thrust on them. And our very existence as free men may well depend on the success of our sales effort."[4]

This is inartfully phrased; it shouldn't have been *that* difficult to convince men and women that "the American way of life" was better than "a slave existence." And the huckster tone of Senator Murray's statement would send shivers down the spine of the Biddles and Flanagans and other prophets of government-supported culture. A sales campaign? That was for the Babbitts or, at best, the men in the gray flannel suits. This was *art*. It did not need to be sold. In fact, to those who understood the artist as a special being, a man apart, commerce was a sullying, if sometimes, unfortunately, necessary, element of the artist's life.

The effort to found a National Theater, which was bandied about during the years of the Federal Theatre Project but didn't really achieve its very modest apex until after the Second World War, shows the extent to which the arts had become part of the arsenal of democracy.

Proponents of a national theater disagreed on exactly what this meant. Would it be a palatial edifice in which the classic dramatic works would be performed? Would it limit its repertoire to American playwrights? Would it be a repertory company or would it feature entirely new casts for each play? Where would it be housed? (The tug of war between Manhattan and Washington, DC, would have been something to see. As for Chicago, Tacoma, Fargo, Chattanooga. . . . to have even suggested such places would have provoked hearty laughter.)

A second matter that almost everyone involved agreed on was that its purpose had nothing to do with relief. The poverty or joblessness of a playwright, director, or performer would have no bearing whatsoever on his employability with the National Theater.

Nepotism was another question altogether. As Wilella Waldorf, columnist for *Theatre* magazine, half-joked in 1945, "One of the major arguments against a National Theater has always been the cynical prediction that at least half the acting company would, of necessity, be made up of Congressmen's relatives, with periodic disturbances to be counted on every time the rumor went around that an assistant property man's third cousin had been glimpsed at a Communist rally."[5] Martin Dies and his allies kept that prophesy from being entirely farcical.

Senator Elbert D. Thomas, a Utah Democrat who had been born into a theatrical family, contended in 1946, "Under the test of war, the American theatre proved its universal power to move and unify. . . . The people of the theatre, realizing the tremendous part they played in total mobilization for war, are now endeavoring through the National Theatre movement, to be of equal service in contributing to the national well-being, happiness and cultural enrichment during peacetime."

Senator Thomas was explicit in regarding theater as an instrument of the state: either as a unifier of the state's subjects or in a tutorial role, instructing the public in the tenets of the regime. The arts, Thomas understood, "had a very real utility, and could serve as an attractive means that might be productively exploited to achieve targeted ends," writes Charlotte M. Canning in her monograph "'In the Interest of the State': A Cold War National Theatre for the United States."[6] Senator Thomas, the leading political force behind a National Theatre, was no crude manipulator of art for politics' sake, but he seemed possessed of a pure faith that such an institution would provide nothing but uplift and edification. The worries of others, including playwrights, that a troupe, an ensemble, a dramatic company, that was selected and underwritten by Uncle Sam might veer into politicized theater seems not to have troubled Senator Thomas.

In the early Cold War era, the idea's partisans sought to piggyback on national defense. "By 1950," writes Charlotte M. Canning, "no argument for a national theatre would omit a reference to the international, and international need made a national theatre all the more urgent."[7] The intellectuals of the nonaligned nations and the Eastern bloc, it was asserted, would gravitate westward if they saw such a tangible commitment of the US government to its own intellectuals.

The American National Theatre and Academy (ANTA) was the prime institutional backer of a national theater. Its secretary, Rosamund Gilder, was a key figure in the founding of the International Theatre Institute (ITI), a performing arts entity affiliated with the United Nations Educational Scientific, and Cultural Organization. Both ANTA and the US branch of the ITI were persistent advocates of a national theatre for the United States. They were also the recipient of funds from the Fairfield Foundation, which as we shall see shortly, was a front group set up by the Central Intelligence Agency (CIA) to fund American cultural organizations thought to be useful in the Cold War.

If the dream of a national theater never quite materialized, at least the National Endowment for the Arts would in the mid-1960s assume some of the burden of underwriting nonprofit theater. But other disciplines found the Cold War to be a boon—and none more so than that avant-garde school of painting known as Abstract Expressionism.

Abstract Expressionism: It's the Bomb

The diplomats of the State Department had long prided themselves on being cultured. They knew which fork to use on which victual, they read novels that were not part of the Book of the Month Club, and they professed to understand abstract art. So in 1946 the State Department launched a cultural offensive that was to be picked up and carried on, eventually, by the Central Intelligence Agency and associated clandestine organizations. The aim? Proving to the world that Americans were not grubby materialists and knuckle-dragging philistines. The weapon of choice? Modern art. The means? Secret subsidization of such art—and, collaterally, artists.

The idea was to send art, particularly art of an avant-garde nature, out across the globe, as part of the US campaign to convince the nations of the world to side with Washington in the postwar, soon to be Cold War, era. This initiative experienced its first of many stubbed toes in 1946, when the State Department, under the supervision of its resident art maven, Joseph Leroy Davidson, an art historian and former curator at the Walker Art Center in Minneapolis, organized "Advancing American Art," a traveling exhibit of three discrete shows featuring 117 works by 69 American artists. Most of these artists were of modernist bent, and among them were such notables as Georgia O'Keeffe, Adolph Gottlieb, and Ben Shahn. These works were not on loan from museums; they were purchased by the State Department on a budget of a bit less than $50,000.

The purpose, as Assistant Secretary of State for Public Affairs William Benton testified in 1947, was to prove to the world that Americans are not a "materialistic, money-mad race without interest in art and without appreciation of artists or music."[8] Mr. Benton, the man so disdainful of materialism, first gained prominence as one of America's top advertising men as a partner in Benton & Bowles. He was part of the team that gave America the ad campaigns for Maxwell House coffee, Post Toasties, Hellmann's mayonnaise, and Palmolive beauty products.[9] But he appreciated art and music.

Before its worldwide tour, which was to include stops in Paris, Prague, Budapest, Havana, Port-au-Prince, and other strategically or politically important sites, the exhibit went on display at the Metropolitan Museum of Art in October 1946. Critical opinion cleaved along predictable lines; New York City critics and the middlebrow Manhattan press praised the work, while populists in the media, for instance the Hearst chain's *New York Journal-American*, mocked the exhibit with glee. Underneath a photo of one somewhat inscrutable piece, the *Journal-American* ran the caption: "This is a t-u-r-k-e-y. A t-u-r-k-e-y is a b-i-r-d. It is an impressionist turkey, by Everett Spruce, an abstract turkey, maybe, or even a cubistic turkey. It is not good for eating. Is it good painting? The State Department says, yes."[10] (Ironically, artist Everett Spruce was a well-regarded "Lone Star regionalist" and long-time professor of art at the University of Texas. As a somewhat naturalistic interpreter of the Southwestern United States, his art was anything but abstract.)[11]

This kind of rambunctious low-browism drove the Manhattan art world crazy. One perplexed congressman lamented, "I am just a dumb American who pays taxes for this kind of trash."[12] Even the President of the United States got into the act. Harry Truman, in a letter leaked to the press, called the works on display "merely the vaporings of half-baked lazy people." Then again, Truman may be said to have lacked proper appreciation for nonrepresentative art. Of the Japanese-American Yasuo Kuniyoshi's painting "Circus Girl Resting," with its zaftig title character sitting next to an incongruous bowl of fruit, Truman told a press conference, "If that's art, then I'm a Hottentot!"[13] Just imagine if Truman had seen Jackson Pollock's "One: Number 31, 1950," with its reticulate veins and lines and drips on a canvas.

The American Artists Professional League (AAPL) damned the exhibit for its arrant bias in favor of abstraction and modernism, whose advocates, believed many AAPL members, were pursuing "a monopoly in museums and. . . . criticism and galleries."[14] These were hardly the ravings of paranoids; the most influential museums, critics, and galleries in the postwar era unquestionably promoted modernism and disdained traditionalist artists. If this had occurred within a free marketplace of art and ideas, one might trust time and shifting opinion to ratify or reverse the critical consensus. But the AAPL detected, in such activities as "Advancing American Art," the coercive hand of the federal government. Surely a policy of laissez-faire was the best means of protecting the freedom and integrity of American artists from government repression or manipulation. If the modernists were to be lauded and subsidized by the State Department, would their elevation by domestic agencies not follow closely behind?

AAPL national vice president Albert Reid charged that Leroy Davidson's selections for "Advancing American Art" were not "indigenous to our soil."[15] They represented foreign traditions, not American ones, and were an attempt by the federal government to alter the shape of the American art world. In the crude words of Rep. George Dondero (R-MI), these were "foreign art manglers."[16]

As Gary O. Larson notes in *The Reluctant Patron: The United States Government and the Arts, 1943–1965*, the AAPL enlisted the National Academy of Design, the Salmagundi Club, the Society of Illustrators, Allied Artists, the Fine Arts Federation, and the Municipal Art Society in its campaign to halt "Advancing American Art."[17] The State Department gave in. Secretary of State George C. Marshall sent down the word: "no more taxpayers' money for modern art."[18] The show was recalled.

After the cancellation of "Advancing American Art," the State Department sold off the artwork therein, which included works by Arshile Gorky, Adolph Gottlieb, and Ben Shahn, as "surplus government property" for a grand total of $5,544.[19] The reason for this pittance was not a lack of interest in the works, but rather a federal regulation mandating the sale of surplus art to public institutions at a whopping 95 percent discount.

The State Department's promotion of modern art was no one-time fluke. It presaged a concerted effort on the part of the contemporary art establishment and the cultural mandarins of US foreign policy to use the burgeoning New York-bred art form of Abstract Expressionism as a weapon in the nascent Cold War with the Soviet Union.

Abstract Expressionism, whose leading lights included Jackson Pollock, Willem de Kooning, Mark Rothko, and Robert Motherwell, among many others, was closely tied to New York's Museum of Modern Art (MOMA). The term was a broad rubric which gathered painters bound by a nonobjective, abstract style and a belief that "the authenticity or value of work lay in its directness and immediacy of expression," as a MOMA essayist put it.[20] The value and meaning of such work is of course outside the purview of this book, but its intimate connection with the federal government is not. (Frances Stonor Saunders notes that most of the Abstract Expressionists "had worked for the Federal Arts Project under Roosevelt's New Deal, producing subsidized art for the government and getting involved in left-wing politics."[21])

Its fanciers touted Abstract Expressionism with the messianic fervor which often attaches to avant-garde movements. Its lack of easily identifiable subject matter seemed revolutionary, and to certain of its apostles it was individualism incarnate. Those who wished to use the US government to subsidize and disseminate Abstract Expressionist works argued that its very abstruseness—the incomprehensibility of its subject matter—made it a totalitarian's worst nightmare, since it could be not manipulated for political ends. It was free form, without form, formless, even. It was the expression of the artist's soul, his or her genius, and could not be packaged in service of any political cause.

Except the cause of the West.[22]

The institutional vessel for the federal government's promotion of modern art was the Museum of Modern Art, which had been cofounded by Abby Aldrich Rockefeller in 1929 and was, to a large extent, the family museum. Nelson Rockefeller served at various times as its president, as did other members of the family. Perhaps the most deeply embarrassing story within the colorful and often fractious history of contemporary art is the way that MOMA worked hand in glove with the CIA to promote modern art. To many partisans, it's downright mortifying! Amusingly, one historian has located criticism of federal aid to modern art in "the psychological sources of antiradicalism," as though being critical of a school of art that was heavily promoted by the Rockefellers and the CIA is somehow "antiradical." Then again, this historian praises Nelson Rockefeller as one of the "more enlightened anticommunists."[23]

Art historian Eva Cockcroft has detailed the MOMA-CIA connections in "Abstract Expressionism, Weapon of the Cold War." Even before the agency's birth, MOMA had become "the latest and strangest recruit in Uncle Sam's defense line-up," as a 1941 Central Press story had it. The museum executed thirty-eight contracts for the supply of artwork, much of it shipped for exhibition in Latin America, an area of special interest for Nelson Rockefeller. After the war, the Museum's division of international programs, headed by Porter A. McCrary, who had worked for Nelson in the US Office of Inter-American Affairs, set out to "let it be known especially in Europe that America was not the cultural backwater that the Russians. . . . were trying to demonstrate that it was," as Russell Lynes wrote in his history of MOMA.[24] The Museum undertook exhibits of modern American art in Paris, London, Tokyo, and elsewhere, and acted as a kind of ambassador of American art on the international scene.

This would be routine and unobjectionable to all but a modernist-hating fringe were it not for the fact that MOMA was intimately involved with the Central Intelligence Agency in promoting Abstract Expressionists—the first time that the US government had sanctioned a particular school of art as somehow representative of the country's strengths and character. (The Federal Art Project, while it contained significant factions of Americana and social realist painters, was never under the thumb of a single artistic tendency.)

August Heckscher, chairman of the board of MOMA's International Council, and later a central figure in the creation of the National Endowment for the Arts, saw the museum as a key front in the battle against communism: "We know that where tyranny takes over, whether under Fascism or Communism, modern art is destroyed and exiled."[25]

Tom Braden was the linchpin. As a Dartmouth student, the Iowa-born Braden had caught the eye of Dartmouth trustee Nelson Rockefeller, who invited him to edit the newsletter of the Rockefeller Center. This was the start of a relationship not without an element of, perhaps, over-familiarity. After serving in the Office of Strategic Services in the Second World War, Braden came home and reentered the Rockefeller orbit. He would be the executive secretary of MOMA in 1948–49, just before signing on with the CIA. (His wife, Joan, was a personal secretary to Rockefeller and occasionally hinted, with varying degrees of coyness, that the notoriously nonmonogamous Rockefeller was more than just a boss.)

Whatever the exact nature of the relationship between Nelson Rockefeller and the Bradens, Tom Braden and Rockefeller's family museum cooperated in promoting Rockefeller's favorite artists and style of art around the world, courtesy of the US taxpayer and without the input of the busybodies of the US Congress, whose sanction was bypassed. MOMA and the CIA sent Abstract Expressionist works abroad in a series of international shows and exhibits.

Braden became a self-styled defender of "creativity," which he saw as under attack in the postwar world. Though Braden himself was not an artist, the boy from Iowa crafted for himself an image of suavity and derring-do. A trench-coated smoker of unfiltered Camels, his face handsome and leathery like a bookish Marlboro man, Braden had a dream: "We wanted all the people who were writers, who were musicians, who were artists, and all the people who follow those people—people like you and me who go to concerts or visit art galleries—to demonstrate that the West and the United States was devoted to freedom of expression and to intellectual achievement without any rigid barriers as to what you must write and what you must say and what you must do and what you must paint—which was what was going on in the Soviet Union."[26] The idea was to contrast the free, unfettered, unconstrained, often unruly intellectual and artistic life of the West with the regimented, strictly regulated life of the intellectual and the artist in the Communist bloc. The fact that this contrast was to be highlighted by government monies secretly funneled to intellectuals and artists and institutions said to embody the spirit of the free West was not, to Braden, a complicating factor.

Modern art of the sort that filled MOMA was Braden's particular interest, and he insisted that it bore a "peculiar relationship to democratic government and to private enterprise." As for MOMA, Braden's son Nicholas, in a friendly interview with journalist John Meroney for *Playboy*, would later say, not entirely in jest, that his father told him that "MOMA was a front for the CIA."[27]

The Perfect Villain

As if stepping out of central casting in response to a call for a Middle American yahoo who combined histrionics, bombast, and manic anticommunism, and who would make a perfect foil for advocates of government aid to modern art, Rep. George Dondero (R-MI), an attorney from Royal Oak, Michigan, and proto-McCarthyite Republican congressman bumbled onto the stage.

Dondero was no dummy—contrary to the assumptions of the art cognoscenti, a failure to appreciate Abstract Expressionism is not evidence of a mental defect—but he overstated his case so absurdly, and cast his net so widely, that he covered his name in ridicule. His

August 16, 1949, speech on the House floor, delicately titled "Modern art shackled to communism," encapsulates his political-aesthetic principles. Rep. Dondero declaimed:

> [A]rt is considered a weapon of communism, and the Communist doctrinaire names the artist as a soldier of the revolution. It is a weapon in the hands of a soldier in the revolution against our form of government, and against any government or system other than communism. . . .
>
> So-called modern or contemporary art in our own beloved country contains all the isms of depravity, decadence, and destruction.
>
> What are these isms that are the very foundation of so-called modern art?. . . . I call the roll of infamy without claim that my list is all-inclusive: dadaism, futurism, constructionism, suprematism, cubism, expressionism, surrealism, and abstractionism. All these isms are of foreign origin, and truly should have no place in American art. While not all are media of social or political protest, all are instruments and weapons of destruction. . . .
>
> Cubism aims to destroy by designed disorder.
> Futurism aims to destroy by the machine myth. . . .
> Dadaism aims to destroy by ridicule.
> Expressionism aims to destroy by aping the primitive and insane. . . .
> Abstractionism aims to destroy by the creation of brainstorms.
> Surrealism aims to destroy by the denial of reason. . . .
>
> The evidence of evil design is everywhere, only the roll call of the art contortionists is different. The question is, what have we, the plain American people, done to deserve this sore affliction that has been visited on us so direly; who has brought down this curse on us; who has let into our homeland this horde of germ-carrying art vermin?. . . .
>
> We are now face to face with the intolerable situation, where public schools, colleges, and universities, art and technical schools, invaded by a horde of foreign art manglers, are selling to our young men and women a subversive doctrine of "isms," Communist-inspired and Communist-connected which have one common, boasted goal—the destruction of our cultural tradition and priceless heritage. . . . Communist art, aided and abetted by misguided Americans, is stabbing our glorious American art in the back with murderous intent.[28]

To borrow from the board game Clue, the Communist did it with an abstract canvas in the art gallery.

This is not the sort of rhetoric designed to endear its speaker to the arts crowd. Dondero had his fans—he may be said to have spoken for anyone who ever wandered into the modern art wing of a museum, pondered a blank white canvas containing a single blue dot, and muttered, "My kid could do better than this"—but among the intelligentsia, he was a crude joke. Moreover, he had "no background in art or art criticism," as one observer sniffed, the implication being that he ought to have shut up and let those knowledgeable about art do the criticizing.[29] A good point. . . . up to the point where taxpayer funds are expended, which is where Dondero, as a representative of his Michigan constituents, had a perfect right, even a responsibility, to weigh in.

Dondero's rhetoric was so over-the-top and under-the-gutter that a conspiratorial mind might assume he was an agent provocateur, planted on the Republican Right by witty and mischievous Dadaists. He dehumanized his targets with such Stalinist/Trotyskite locutions as "human art termites" and the aforementioned "germ-carrying art vermin."[30] He was no fool—the International Fine Arts Council, the American Artists Professional League, and the Painters and Sculptors Club of Los Angeles honored him for his defense of what they regarded as artistic verities—but his verbal excesses have ensured him a posthumous bad reputation.

Jacob Javits, then a US representative, later a US senator, challenged Dondero. "The very point which distinguishes our form of free expression from communism is the fact that modern art can live and flourish here without state authority or censorship and be accepted by Americans who think well of it."[31]

Few outside the most humid of fever swamps would disagree with Javits, though his affirmation of free expression elides one point: modern art was at that very moment receiving the sanction of state authority—and in a mostly clandestine, undemocratic manner. CIA expenditures on the promotion of this art were not subject to congressional approval or public scrutiny. (Curiously, one of the founding fathers of the New Deal arts project, George Biddle, who had convinced his old friend Franklin Roosevelt that muralists ought to find work with the federal government, condemned nonobjective art in 1947 as the product of "war neurosis, a dealer-rigged market, and snobbism."[32] He had no idea of the extent to which the market was being rigged by those other than dealers.)

Not all critics of federally subsidized art were redolent of philistinism. Jacques Barzun, the eminent scholar and historian, wrote in 1950 that even the best-intentioned government patronage "will breed red tape, investigations by the Civil Service Commission and the FBI, [and] queries whether a given style or statement of belief is not subversive. . . . We live in the Great Paper Age—we must never forget it—and paper means petty rules framed in advance of facts, as well as the substitution of verbal description for performance."[33] He was, in a sense, warning artists against the likes of Dondero at the same time he was taking the side of Dondero on the question of subsidy.

Congressman Dondero struck sophisticates as the most egregious of philistines: a Michigan moron who spoke only for other morons. The fact that he was an elected official in a representative government was a minor irritation easily gotten around. As Tom Braden explained, "We had a lot of trouble with Congressman Dondero. He couldn't stand modern art. He thought it was a travesty, he thought it was sinful, he thought it was ugly. He put up a heck of a fight about painting, and he made it very difficult to get Congress to go along with some of the things that we wanted to do—send art abroad, send symphonies abroad, publish magazines abroad, whatever. That's one of the reasons why it had to be done covertly; it had to be covert because it would have been turned down if it had been put to a vote in a democracy. In order to encourage openness we had to be secret."[34]

It is perhaps not surprising that those who shared Braden's Cold War liberal views would be ones who made famous the paradoxical assertion that they had to destroy a village—that is, Vietnam—in order to save it. Braden likened the US government to the enlightened popes who commissioned the Sistine Chapel: "I suppose that if it had been submitted to a vote of the Italian people there would have been many, many negative responses: 'It's naked,' or 'It isn't the way I imagined God,' or whatever. I don't think it would have gotten through the Italian parliament, if there had been a parliament at the time. . . . You have always to battle your own ignoramuses, or, to put it more politely, people who just don't understand."[35] That the man on whom the saccharine television series *Eight is Enough* was based saw himself taking up the lance on behalf of high culture and against the ignoramuses says a lot about him or about us. Pope Julius II gave patronage to Michelangelo; Tom Braden and the Truman-Eisenhower CIA played Maecenas to Jackson Pollock. History may judge who was the wiser.

An impatience with, if not downright contempt for, the Madisonian machinery of our constitutional government pervades the rationales for Washington's sub rosa subsidies of artists and intellectuals. The conceit is always of a piece with Tom Braden's complaint that elected representatives and the people who elect them *just don't understand.* "Does anyone really think that congressmen would foster a foreign tour by an artist who has or has had left-wing connections?"[36] Braden asked in defense of his deceptions. The answer is, quite possibly, no, though that does not answer the question of whether it is kosher to deceive the members of Congress and very possibly the artist himself, who may not know that his or her tour is being underwritten by a US intelligence agency.

As for the artists who benefitted from this federal intervention, David and Cecile Shapiro write, "Few are ever likely to argue about the purposes for which their paintings are exhibited just so long as they are in fact widely and regularly shown." The international exhibition of American Abstract Expressionists coincided with a revolutionary development in the world of art museums. No longer were museums regarded as the repositories of the works of dead masters; in the 1950s, "Museums backed up exhibitions of [Abstract Expressionist paintings] with massive purchases of work by living artists on a scale that had never before been approached."[37] Inflating the reputations of favored artists inflated the prices their artwork commanded.

This was not, of course, the primary intention of the cultural Cold Warriors. The size of Mark Rothko's bank account was irrelevant to them. CIA case officer Donald Jameson told Frances Stonor Saunders in 1995, "Regarding Abstract Expressionism, I'd love to be able to say that the CIA invented it just to see what happens in New York and downtown SoHo tomorrow!" But of course that was not the case. Jameson conceded that most of the artists whose works were supported by the agency were less than ferocious Cold Warriors. They were not informed directly of the connection, "because most of them were people who had very little respect for the government, in particular, and certainly none for the CIA. If you had to use people who considered themselves one way or another to be closer to Moscow than to Washington, well, so much the better perhaps."[38] Nevertheless, writes Hugh Wilford, "[T]here was a basic sympathy between many intelligence officers and modernist artists, based on such shared values as formalism, internationalism (or 'cosmopolitanism'), and elitism."[39]

The shibboleth of the hour was *freedom*, but as is often the case, that word meant vastly different things to different people. Just as Harry Truman and Senator Robert Taft, "Mr. Republican," contested the meaning of that protean word, so did artists and their explicators. And what were the elements of this "freedom" being advertised by the CIA's favored artists to the uncommitted artists and intellectuals of the world? It bore glancingly little resemblance to the Jeffersonian life, liberty, and pursuit of happiness conception, or the "negative liberty" of the classical liberals.

The chief theorist of Abstract Expressionism, the art critic Clement Greenberg, authored the noteworthy essay "Avant-Garde and Kitsch," in which he praised avant-garde culture as the product of "a superior consciousness of history" that had developed in the nineteenth century, more or less simultaneously with "scientific revolutionary thought in Europe."[40] "Kitsch," by contrast, he disparaged as phony culture, ersatz culture, culture that is consumed by workers and displaced peasants. As examples Greenberg adduces Hollywood movies, comics, Tin Pan Alley music, illustrations, pulp fiction—art that, not coincidentally, is of broad appeal and neither begs nor needs subvention from government or the rich. But it is not "true culture," insists Greenberg; it holds the lure of "enormous profits" and, in some forms, has a universal appeal that crowds out native cultures. Even in the early Soviet Union, when the Bolsheviks encouraged "avant-garde cinema, the Russian masses continued to prefer Hollywood movies."[41] Those stupid masses!

The Western bourgeois world, which had thrown artists into "the markets of capitalism," is, mercifully, passing. The fact that "[c]apitalism [is] in decline" is so obvious that, in Greenberg's conclusion, "it becomes necessary to quote Marx word for word. Today [he is writing in 1939, recall] we no longer look toward socialism for a new culture—as inevitably one will appear, once we do have socialism. Today we look to socialism *simply* for the preservation of whatever living culture we have right now."[42] Once socialism saved the day—which would have come as a shock to the British, the French, the Americans, and other non-Soviet allies in the coming world war—the new economy would provide workers and peasants with sufficient leisure time that they might, eventually, come to prefer Picasso to Clark Gable.

Greenberg's influential essay was published in the Trotskyite *Partisan Review. Partisan Review*, founded in 1934, was a project of the John Reed Club and thus of the Communist Party, though after a brief interruption in publication it reappeared in 1937 firmly "outside the Stalinist orbit."[43] Greenberg's ideas bear the stamp of "Leon Trotsky's theories of culture" and "can be considered the manifesto and program for the art movement known today as Abstract Expressionism," wrote David and Cecile Shapiro in "Abstract Expressionism: The Politics of Apolitical Painting."[44] The Shapiros connect the Abstract Expressionists' dismissal of the cold dead hand of the past with Trotsky's theory of permanent revolution.

Noting the disdain this brand of socialism held for the demotic taste of the masses, the Shapiros remark, "By making the enjoyment of recondite, hermetic art a cultural test, the avant-garde became attractive, a barrier to be overcome, for those with upwardly mobile aspirations. Who wants to be left standing outside the gardens of the elite?"[45] This description of the upwardly mobile striver for whom appreciation of difficult art is a marker of class fits Tom Braden to a T. No sunny landscapes or majestic mountains—the subjects one might find in a decidedly dernière-garde household—for him!

By the 1950s, the Abstract Expressionists had "effectively routed other stylistic and philosophic expressions in American painting." At decade's end, according to critic John Canaday in the *New York Times*, "an unknown artist trying to exhibit in New York couldn't find a gallery unless he was painting" in the regnant Abstract Expressionist style.[46] It has been a source of amusement to AE's critics, and a vexatious bother to its proselytes, that this rapid ascent to the top of the art world was facilitated, in part, by the covert actions of the US government, in particular the Central Intelligence Agency. In the words of David and Cecile Shapiro, "the lever that lifted Abstract Expressionism to the peak it achieved as the quasi-official art of the decade, suppressing other kinds of painting to a degree not heretofore conceivable in our society, was an arm of the United States government."[47]

Of course Abstract Expressionism was not given birth by the taxpayer, and it may well have achieved its overwhelmingly prominent place in the art world of the 1950s even if Tom Braden had collected Norman Rockwell and sputtered with incomprehension at the works of Robert Motherwell. But this art form and its practitioners were also supported by the federal government through a much wider campaign by which American and other Western intellectuals were subsidized by taxpayer monies secretly allotted—and here we meet the Congress for Cultural Freedom.

The Congress for Cultural Freedom

Once more, Tom Braden steps to the fore. The bureaucratic funnel for the CIA cultural subsidies was the agency's International Organizations Division (IOD), a Braden brainchild. With his aide Cord Meyer Jr., a "ruthless operator" who had achieved a national profile through his advocacy of one-world government with the United World Federalists, Braden took to distributing American taxpayers' money to intellectuals as well as artists via deceptive conduits.[48] (Braden passed the IOD off to Meyer in 1954, when he "'retired' from the CIA and moved to California to edit a newspaper purchased for him by Nelson Rockefeller," the Oceanside *Blade-Tribune*.[49] Braden hoped to use this to launch a political career, but unlike the world of espionage, a politician must seek public support. He never found it. How it must have rankled Braden, the former OSS officer who fancied himself a dashing man of international intrigue, to be played by the lumpish and doughy Dick Van Patten in *Eight is Enough*!)

In his telling, in 1950 Braden shared with CIA Deputy Director Allen Dulles his revolutionary idea: that the United States should fight the Soviet Union on the cultural battleground by secretly funding professors, students, artists, magazines, and intellectuals in America, Western Europe, and strategically significant places in the Third World, and among the so-called nonaligned nations.

Dulles loved the idea, but others in the agency did not. Frank Wisner, the CIA's Director of Policy Coordination, sided with one subordinate who told him, "Frank, this is just another one of those goddamned proposals for getting into everybody's hair."[50] Indeed, most of the panjandrums of the CIA agreed that Braden's plan was ill-conceived, but Dulles liked it, overruled the objections, and so was born the International Organizations Division.

Despite the mystery of espionage and the romance of subterfuge, creating dummy foundations through which to channel taxpayer money to intellectuals and artists was an easy play, according to Tom Braden. He explained, "We would go to somebody in New York who was a well-known rich person and we would say, 'We want to set up a foundation.' We would tell him what we were trying to do and pledge him to secrecy, and he would say, 'Of course I'll do it,' and then you would publish a letterhead and his name would be on it and there would be a foundation. It was really a pretty simple device."[51]

The CIA, which had a reputation as the most urbane and liberal element of the US defense complex, pursued with great vigor a policy of subsidizing the noncommunist left, or NCL (no bureaucratic act can be without its own acronym) through the 1950s and early 1960s. This was called the "long leash" policy: Subsidized intellectuals of the left were permitted to criticize US policies, which only went to emphasize the contrast with the Soviet Union, whose dissidents were in prisons or mental hospitals.

Hugh Wilford's *The Mighty Wurlitzer: How the CIA Played America* (2008) draws its title from an observation by Frank Wisner, the CIA's first chief of the Office of Policy Coordination, its propaganda arm, that the agency's front groups were like a "mighty Wurlitzer" organ that boomed out whatever tune the CIA wished to play.[52] This is not an image that suggests bold independence on the part of those subsidized, but then the stakes were such that conformity might be seen to be a virtue.

For in all the outrage over the eventual revelations of the CIA's sponsorship of intellectuals, often forgotten was the context of those early years of the Cold War, when the United States and the Soviet Union seemed to be facing off in a Manichean battle of good and evil, pitting a free society against a closed totalitarian one. No doubt many of those who accepted the king's shilling believed that doing the king's bidding in this instance was virtuous, even noble. We mustn't forget that.

The centerpiece of the cultural offensive, the prime middleman underwriting the work of intellectuals in the Cold War cause, was the Congress for Cultural Freedom. The Congress for Cultural Freedom (CCF), though professing to be a private organization, was in fact "the CIA's principal front operation in the cultural field."[53] Its inauguration was a grand affair in West Berlin over four days (June 26–29) in 1950 planned and supervised by men whom their radical erstwhile comrades would mockingly call "State Department socialists": Sidney Hook, James Burnham, Arthur Koestler, government-subsidized editor Melvin J. Lasky, CIA agent and AFL-CIO operative Irving Brown, and CIA agent Michael Josselson, an Estonian-born executive with Gimbel Brothers department stores who in the Second World War became a US Army intelligence officer. Josselson was named executive director of the Congress for Cultural Freedom in 1950 and would hold that post until his ignominious departure in 1967.

The Berlin conference was ostensibly sponsored by *Der Monat* (*The Month*), a magazine edited by American Melvin Lasky and the recipient of Marshall Plan funds from the US government. In fact, the cost of the congress (budgeted at $50,000) was picked up, secretly, by the State Department, the CIA, and its Office of Policy Coordination (OPC). (The OPC was something of a blueblood club within the CIA. As Hugh Wilford writes, CIA director Walter Bedell Smith, a bilious Indiana-bred soldier who had dropped out of Butler University, disdained the Ivy Leaguers of the Office of Policy Coordination, whose "MGs and Jaguars" contrasted with the "Chevrolets and Fords" of other employees in the CIA parking lot.[54])

The funds for the first congress came largely from the Marshall Plan. Although Marshall Plan monies had been appropriated by the

US Congress for the purpose of rebuilding Western Europe, they were a "slush fund" for the CIA, as former agency officer Lawrence de Neufville told Frances Stonor Saunders.[55]

Nightly meetings during the Berlin congress were attended by Lasky, Koestler, Hook, Burnham, and Brown, who discussed the day's doings over a nightcap or two and planned for the morrow. As Hugh Wilford writes, "the notion of a sinister cabal made up of Koestler, Burnham, and other ideologically driven ex-communists soon became fixed in the imagination" of British intellectuals.[56]

Who were these men—arguably the first political intellectuals to receive US government patronage not as employees of the federal government but through backdoor channels as private actors whose literary or polemical skills were thought useful to US policy objectives? Many of the architects of the CIA's front group strategy had themselves been communists or socialists. There was James Burnham, a Trotskyite philosopher associated with the Socialist Workers Party and a prominent figure in both the CIA's OPC and the Congress for Cultural Freedom in its early stages. (Burnham later took a sharp right turn and wound up a columnist for William F. Buckley Jr.'s *National Review*.) An even murkier figure from the world of postwar espionage was Jay Lovestone, who would one day be a chief foreign policy advisor to George Meany's AFL-CIO. Before becoming an anticommunist, Lovestone had been national secretary of the Communist Party USA. His defenders argued that his background made him an acute observer of Communist machinations; others wondered why anyone should listen to a man who had been so disastrously wrong about the Soviet Union.

The CCF inner circle also included Melvin Lasky, a Bronx-born journalist and former Trotskyite who lobbied for and received Marshall Plan funds in order to found *Der Monat*, the German pro-US-foreign policy journal. Lasky, whose penetrating eyes and vaguely sinister beard gave him the aspect of either Lenin or a suave diabolical boulevardier, later edited *Encounter*, the high-brow CIA-funded cultural-political journal around which much of the debate over the propriety of intellectuals accepting government funding was centered. And there was the splenetic Budapest-born, British-residing Arthur Koestler, author of the classic indictment of totalitarianism *Darkness at Noon* (1940), who had been an officer of the Comintern and who once betrayed a lover (who, he later found out, had given him a venereal disease) to the Soviet secret police, leaving her to a grim destiny that can only be guessed.

At the center of this colorful clique stood Sidney Hook, Brooklyn-born Marxist philosopher at New York University, former member of the Communist Party, and fierce anti-Stalinist polemicist. Hook, who had done a stint in Moscow at the Marx-Engels Institute, founded the Committee for Cultural Freedom in 1939 and later headed the American Committee for Cultural Freedom, the CCF's American affiliate. Hook set the template for the CCF-allied American intellectuals. As a young man he had been "[a]ttracted to the muscular, bruising posturing of New Yorkist Communism," as Frances Stonor Saunders writes in her important work on the CCF and its offshoots, *The Cultural Cold War: The CIA and the World of Arts and Letters*.[57]

Hook was not bashful about asking for money. In 1949, he declared, somewhat grandiosely, "Give me a hundred million dollars and a thousand dedicated people, and I will guarantee to generate such a wave of democratic unrest among the masses—yes, even among the soldiers—of Stalin's own empire, that all his problems for a long period of time to come will be internal. I can find the people."[58] It takes considerable brashness to ask for $100 million—back when that was real money, to borrow Senator Everett Dirksen's phrase—and Hook was nothing if not brash.

Participants in the quarrels of the postwar world might be forgiven for their hyperbole. These were days of tension and uncertainty in East-West relations. War had broken out in Korea, and fears ran high that it might explode into yet another world-wide conflict, this time between the communist nations and the democratic nations of the West. The Iron Curtain seemed impenetrable; President Truman was pursuing an activist and interventionist foreign policy over the objections of the dwindling number of Republican isolationists and Western-state antimilitarist Democrats. This aggressively internationalist posture of the US government met with the approval of the intellectuals of the Congress of Cultural Freedom. These men—for almost all were men—would also, perhaps not coincidentally, benefit personally, professionally, and financially from Cold War policies.

There were 118 invitees to the 1950 Berlin conference, representing 21 countries, though only two of those present (an Indian and a Colombian) were from outside Europe. Fully 40 percent were American or German.[59] The overwhelming ideological coloration was social-democratic, and there were far more ex-communists than there were conservatives or libertarians. In fact, there were few if any of the latter; the Congress, like its CIA sponsor, had a distinctly center-left bias.

The Congress was an effort, writes Giles Scott-Smith in his valuable *The Politics of Apolitical Culture* (2002), "to internationalise the American non-communist left" and to organize anti-Soviet intellectuals.[60]

Freedom was the mantra in Berlin. "Friends, freedom has seized the offensive!" Arthur Koestler proclaimed to a large crowd at festival's close.[61] What he meant by that was freedom of conscience, freedom of expression, and the freedom to dissent, though it was an irony that this event was being secretly sponsored by an agency of the US government that had not bothered to request congressional approval for its act. So it was not government per se that Koestler and fellow conferees viewed as the enemy of freedom; rather, it was the governments of the Soviet Bloc. As the US government took on additional police powers over the next two decades and engaged in a disastrous war in Vietnam, the Congress's definition of "freedom" would blur such that many in the West would come to view it not as an organization of freethinkers taking a bold stand for liberty but as a mirror image—more benign, to be sure, but still a mirror image—of the ideologically rigid writers' congresses of the communist world.

In 1950, however, the Congress was largely viewed in the West as a welcome counterpoise to the "peace congresses" of intellectuals and artists that the Soviet Union and its allies had occasionally sponsored. These affairs had been bleak and depressing displays of dogma and cowardice. An example from one such Soviet-friendly peace congress: When asked why he had permitted the Politburo to vet his novel *Young Guard*, Russian Aleksandr Fadeyev, chairman of the Union of Soviet Writers, replied, "The Politburo's criticism helped my work greatly."[62] Then again, *Young Guard* was awarded the Stalin Prize, and since Fadeyev feted Stalin as "the greatest humanist the world has ever known," perhaps Uncle Joe had pruned the novelist's verbosity and polished his sentences to a gemlike precision.[63] Stalin as editor extraordinaire: who knew? In any event, Fadeyev shot himself in 1956, possibly distraught by Khrushchev's denunciation of Stalin earlier that year.

The Berlin Congress, which the inveterate function-attendee Sidney Hook called "the most exciting conference I have ever attended,"[64] issued a Manifesto whose first article read "We hold it to be self-evident that intellectual freedom is one of the inalienable rights of man." This was almost axiomatic; even the grim puppet presidents of the Soviet Bloc might agree with it in principle, if not in practice. The second article was one to which virtually every American would assent: "Such freedom is defined first and foremost by his right to hold and express his own opinions, and particularly opinions which differ from those of his rulers. Deprived of the right to say 'no,' man becomes a slave."[65] This is where the Soviets and their sympathizers would jump off the bandwagon.

There were fourteen articles in all, several of them noncontroversial within the nation that was footing the bill, the United States, though others would certainly draw protests from a not insignificant segment of the citizenry. For instance, article three declared that nations should "submit all questions immediately involving the risk of war to a representative international authority, by whose decisions [they] will abide." This would be difficult for many on the Right to swallow, and the case of the Korean Conflict demonstrated that ceding authority to the United Nations did not automatically mean peace.

The manifesto also contained a curious formulation that might be interpreted by an unsympathetic observer as justification of liberal totalitarianism; that is, the statement in article five that "The principle of toleration does not logically permit the practice of intolerance."[66] This would seem to imply that the liberty of speech and religion, which traditionally have enjoyed the broadest protection in the United States, could be sharply restricted if those liberties are used the "wrong way," say, to promote Marxism. Or to take a more traditionally American example, the liberty to practice one's religion could, by the logic of the CCF manifesto, end at the point where that religious practice displays "intolerance"—for instance, in the belief (shared to an extent by most of the major religions) that nonbelievers are in some way handicapped by their nonbelief. This is especially so if one believes that one should, say, patronize the businesses of one's coreligionists rather than those of nonbelievers. Is a Muslim who refuses to purchase goods from a Christian displaying "intolerance"? It depends on a contested definition of the term. The same is true with respect to speech. If an advocate of traditional morality is harshly critical of, say, the idea of gay marriage, is this "intolerant"? Ought it to be permitted? Anent the First Amendment to the US Constitution, the question seems absurd. Of course it should be permitted. But in recent years, the ever-shrinking zone of protection for speech that might offend someone, somewhere, puts the question in a new light.

That is journeying far from our immediate topic. But the point is that the CCF manifesto was no mere play-acting by posturing intellectuals. It was, rather, a US-government-subsidized proclamation by intellectuals whose bills were being footed by the taxpayers of the United States—people who perhaps had rather different ideas of the limits of "liberty" and "tolerance" than did those who were doing the proclaiming.

It occurred to several of the participants that the lavish hospitality of such a conference was unlikely to have been paid for by private interests—a little-read German magazine?—in a Europe still emerging from underneath the rubble. While many of the CCF's intellectuals would later adopt a tone of wounded innocence as far as the sponsorship of their festivals and conferences went, others figured it out right off the bat. English historian Hugh Trevor-Roper, in an interview with Frances Stonor Saunders, recalled, "When I arrived I found the whole thing was orchestrated on so grandiose a scale. . . . that I realized that. . . . financially it must have been funded by some powerful government organization. So I took it for granted from the beginning that it was organized by the American government in one form or another. That seemed to me obvious from the start."[67]

The Congress was treated respectfully, even worshipfully, by much of the press. Richard Rovere of *The New Yorker* confidently assured readers that it was a "worthy organization, anti-Communist and generally libertarian in outlook, and associated with no government."[68] Whether or not a collection of ex-Trotskyities can be called "libertarian" (or even "anticommunist") is questionable, but Rovere was at antipodes from the truth in his assertion of the Congress's distance from government. (Rovere had second thoughts after the secret subsidy cat was out of the bag. "I have been a contributor to *Encounter*, and my suspicions about its origins and its finances arose well before my last association with it," he confessed in 1967. "Because I cannot recall an occasion when I did nor said anything I did not want to do or say, I have felt no personal guilt. But I am now inclined to think that I have let myself off too lightly."[69])

Quite a different attitude was projected by the Nobel Laureate novelist Sinclair Lewis of Minnesota, who refused the State Department's invitation to tour Czechoslovakia in 1947 on the US government's dime, saying, "Biting journalists should allow no hand to feed them."[70] But Lewis was yesterday's news.

The Congress won the approbation of the likes of Rovere in part because it projected an image that was "urbane, cool, and bureaucratic," in historian Christopher Lasch's phrase. The Congress, Lasch wrote, "asked only that intellectuals avail themselves of the increasing opportunities for travel and enlightenment that the defense of freedom made possible."[71]

Once institutionalized, the CCF was based in Paris and housed in style at 104 Boulevard Haussmann, with Michael Josselson—"pink, well manicured, and. . . . always perfectly groomed"—at its head.[72] The Secretary-General of the Congress was Nicolas Nabokov, Russian-born composer and US citizen, cousin of the author of *Lolita*. (Nabokov and Josselson had worked together on US Army psychological warfare projects in wartime and postwar Germany.) Nabokov explained what was at stake for artists: "Narrow restrictive rules have sought to transform the artist into an instrument of the state, producing works tailored to the utilitarian needs of totalitarian regimes. Free creative imagination of the poets, painters and composers has produced an abundant flow of masterpieces in all the arts."[73] The implication was that the CCF would protect, or perhaps even accelerate, this flow of masterpieces.

At its height, writes Peter Coleman, a prominent member of the CCF's Australian affiliate, the Australian Association for Cultural Freedom, the organization "had offices or representatives in thirty-five countries, employing a total of 280 staff members." Its source of funds was the US Central Intelligence Agency; as Coleman, a defender of the CCF-CIA connection, wrote in 1989, "It is one of the ironies of the story that the CIA gave its support secretly, conspiratorially, and believed it could not—as to this day it does not—claim credit for one of its more imaginative and successful decisions."[74]

Operating through the Chase National Bank—Rockefeller Center branch, appositely—and its Congress for Cultural Freedom front group, the CIA's International Organizations Division shelled out for such events as a month-long 1952 arts festival in Paris, at which the Boston Symphony Orchestra, the New York City Ballet, and various European opera companies performed, and viewers were treated to an "exhibition of 126 modern paintings and sculptures, ranging from Impressionism to works from the 1940s, organised by New York's Museum of Modern Art curator and ACCF member James Johnson Sweeney." (Someone from MOMA always seemed to be around whenever Washington was subsidizing culture.) The cost of the festival was $283,900, while receipts were just $90,000.[75]

A highlight of the Paris festival was the 104-member Boston Symphony Orchestra's performance of Stravinsky's *The Rite of Spring*. Tom Braden was most proud of this, saying in retrospect, "I remember the enormous joy I got when the Boston Symphony Orchestra won more acclaim for the US in Paris than John Foster Dulles or Dwight D. Eisenhower could have with a hundred speeches."[76]

Subsequent CCF conferences were held in Hamburg (1953: "Science and Freedom," which spawned a twice-yearly *Bulletin*), Milan (1955: "The Future of Freedom"), and, less grandly, in Tokyo, Oxford, Vienna, the Greek island of Rhodes, and Switzerland. Other sites where intellectuals, American and non-American, gathered to suss out the questions of the day on the public dime included Bombay, Rome, Mexico City, Venice, and Cairo.

Among the 150 economists and social scientists who participated in the Milan conference was the future Nobel laureate Friedrich Hayek, who was appalled by the suffocating social-democratic consensus. Seymour Martin Lipset, a fellow conferee, summarized Hayek's remarks to the body:

> Professor Hayek, in a closing speech, attacked the delegates for preparing to bury freedom instead of saving it. He alone was disturbed by the general temper. What bothered him was the general agreement among the delegates, regardless of political belief, that the traditional issues separating the left and right had declined to comparative insignificance. In effect all agreed that the increase in state control which had taken place in various countries would not result in a decline in democratic freedom. . . . Hayek, honestly believing that state intervention is bad and inherently totalitarian, found himself in a small minority of those who still took the cleavages in the democratic camp seriously.[77]

The Hayeks of the intellectual world were distant outliers in the affairs of the CCF, its heirs, and its offshoots. They were regarded as radicals, as irresponsibles, as men and women lacking an essential awareness of political realities. The overriding ideological coloration of the subsidized intellectuals was welfare-state democrat; some were more or less socialist in orientation than others, but none was an adherent of laissez-faire economics, none was critical of the New Deal, none was a sharp critic of US military involvement in Europe, Asia, or the Third World, and none was of the sort to question just why taxpayers ought to be underwriting lavish foreign conferences. To even ask such a question was to reveal oneself as a troglodyte.

The CCF, with funds from the CIA, also sponsored traveling exhibitions of Abstract Expressionist work, among them "Masterpieces of the Twentieth Century" (1952), "Modern Art in the United States" (1955), and "The New American Painting" (1958–59), which undertook a yearlong tour of Europe under the direction of Porter McCray.[78] "The New American Painting" included works by Pollock, Rothko, de Kooning,

Motherwell, Arshile Gorky, Barnett Newman. . . . the brightest stars in the AE firmament. The "individualism" of the artists "is uncompromising and as a matter of principle they do nothing deliberately in their work to make 'communication' easy," explained MOMA Director of Museum Collections Alfred H. Barr Jr.[79] Barr, in a *New York Times Magazine* article, lectured that "The modern artists' nonconformity and love of freedom cannot be tolerated within a monolithic tyranny and modern art is useless for the dictator's propaganda."[80] It was, however, useful for the propaganda of the nations of the Free World.

When the Tate Gallery in London pleaded a lack of sufficient funds to mount the exhibit, Julius Fleischmann of America's Fairfield Foundation rode to the rescue. But not, it must be said, with his own money. MOMA was another recipient of Fairfield Foundation grants, though when a museum is buoyed by Rockefeller monies outside grants are not essential to survival.

There were dozens of phony foundations through which CIA monies were laundered, most famously this Fairfield Foundation, which began life as the Heritage Foundation (no relation to the current DC conservative think tank). The American branch of the CCF received regular checks from the Fairfield Foundation, which had been incorporated in 1952 and which supplied about 80 percent of the Congress's funds, relieving Irving Brown of much of his doling the dollars duties.[81] Its president for the next decade was Julius Fleischmann of Cincinnati, son of the former mayor of Cincinnati, heir to the Fleischmann Yeast fortune, and a well-known culture vulture whose causes included the Museum of Modern Art, on whose board he sat and which served as the principal battering ram in the US government's campaign to support modern artists. It helped to have an indisputably rich man like Julius Fleischmann as the public face of the Fairfield Foundation: outsiders would naturally assume that Fairfield's charitable giving was a product of Fleischmann's wealth. The irony was, as Frances Stonor Saunders notes, that Fleischmann, who wore the infra dig nickname of "Junkie," was "a multi-millionaire famed for his stinginess."[82] He was happy, however, to take credit for the CIA's generosity.

The Fairfield Foundation claimed to have been "formed by a group of private American individuals who are interested in preserving the cultural heritage of the free world and encouraging the constant expansion and interchange of knowledge in the fields of the arts, letters, and sciences."[83] Its name was frequently attached to international cultural events, as for instance in its sponsorship of the 1955 Young Painters show, which displayed abstract work by Americans and others in Rome, London, Paris, and Brussels. The cash prizes for best of show came from the US taxpayer by the way of the Fairfield Foundation and, for public consumption, the CCF.

It took a willful blindness for recipients of Fairfield Foundation pass-throughs not to know the source of the lucre. Literary critic Diana Trilling later told Cold Warrior Arnold Beichman that she knew full well that the Fairfield Foundation was a dummy, though she didn't know "whether it was a conduit. . . . for the CIA or the State Department." This did not trouble her, she explained, "because I did not believe that to take the support of my government was a dishonorable act." As Hugh Wilford wrote, while some of "the New York intellectuals seem not to have had many qualms about accepting secret subsidies," they often had decidedly independent ideas about how to spend those subsidies.[84]

The Congress, notes Giles Scott-Smith, "was a very expensive operation." It took flight quickly. By 1954–55, the CIA was passing it between $800,000 and $900,000 annually; in 1956, its income rose to $961,000, and a decade later, on the eve of its exposure as a government front, the Congress for Cultural Freedom was spending approximately $2.07 million.[85]

One large nongovernmental entity did join the US government as a financer of the CCF. The Ford Foundation began funding the Congress for Cultural Freedom in 1957, channeling well over $1 million a year by the early 1960s, and kept at it till the bitter end, even after the revelations that dealt the CCF its death blow. The CCF was hardly unique in pursuing Ford funds. As Dwight Macdonald once cracked, the Ford Foundation was and is "a large body of money completely surrounded by people who want some."[86]

***

Sidney Hook was the first chairman of the American Committee for Cultural Freedom (ACCF), the US branch of the Congress, which was born in late 1950. (Hook had also founded the earlier Committee for Cultural Freedom, an indirect predecessor, in 1939.) The ACCF was one of the pipelines that carried taxpayer monies from the US government to the Congress for Cultural Freedom. Although the CIA was technically forbidden to finance domestic operations, as Hugh Wilford notes, Sidney Hook was a direct beneficiary of such funds, as were various "eastern European émigrés in New York." In fact, "intellectuals' habit of appropriating CCF subsidies for their own private purposes" was "a chronic problem in the United States's cultural Cold War effort."[87] Sidney Hook had his hooks into the CCF.

The ACCF's roster was studded with notables of a generally social-democratic cast, among them novelists Saul Bellow and John Steinbeck; social scientists and historians Daniel Bell, Arthur Schlesinger Jr., and James Burnham; labor figures such as David Dubinsky of the International Ladies' Garment Workers' Union and cloak and dagger CIA operative Irving Brown; and assorted intellectuals and artists (film director Elia Kazan, editor Jason Epstein, cultural essayists Dwight Macdonald and Murray Kempton). Not that all these figures were active members, or supped on the taxpayers' dime.

Irving Kristol, who would edit *Encounter* and become perhaps the preeminent neoconservative of the 1970s–80s, was the ACCF's executive director at a salary of $8,500 in 1954.[88] Kristol was a strong-willed man, not the pliant purveyor of propaganda who might be best suited for such a position.

The ACCF was riven by factionalism and expired of that cause in 1957. This result was not hard to foresee, given that the American Congress's leading lights were largely combative ex-Communists ready to fight—with typewriter keys if not fists—at the drop of a ushanka. The ACCF was big on "freedom" as an abstract cause, but not so big on freedom within its own walls. It made the mistake of elevating the pugnacious novelist James T. Farrell to its chairmanship in 1954. Farrell, a Chicagoan, had been, naturally, a Trotskyite. (That seems to have been almost a prerequisite for involvement in the ACCF and the CCF.) Under the influence, he later said, of "too much beer",[89] in June 1956 Farrell sent a letter to the editor of the *Chicago Tribune* in which he said that US foreign aid was somewhere between wasteful and extortionate, for other nations could "flirt with Communism, insult us, and perhaps get more money out of us."[90] It was time to stop lavishing taxpayer dollars on foreign governments, opined Farrell, who sounded like one of those Middle American isolationists that the socialists and ex-socialists and ex-Trotskyites and ex-communists of the CCF despised: "We honest Americans have taken enough, given enough, and have had enough of the blood of our boys spilled on foreign soil. From here on in, we should have a truly honest partnership in freedom, or else go it alone." He added that Americans "should retire to our own shores"—no more swanky conferences in Paris or Berlin?—"and, if necessary, fight it out to the death with communism."[91]

A good many Americans would agree with Farrell, but his bluntness caused fits of apoplexy at the ACCF. Diana Trilling, an officer of the group (and onetime Trotsky enthusiast), said that any brute who cast Farrell-like doubts about the efficacy of US foreign aid was "not suited" to be chairman of this taxpayer-subsidized club. Farrell resigned. "Cultural Freedom" reigned! As Christopher Lasch observed, "the intellectuals of the ACCF defined cultural freedom as whatever best served the interests of the United States government,"[92] which was, after all, their patron.

***

Some of the more fervent anticommunists—for instance the intractable Burnham and Koestler—were nudged out of the core of the CCF, though their departures were not necessarily involuntary. Koestler was incensed that the Congress "was making overtures" to Jean-Paul Sartre and Simone de Beauvoir, who were outside his conception of noncommunist allies.[93] (In the case of the choleric Koestler, his exceedingly unpleasant personality was a contributing factor to his de facto deposal. His friend Sidney Hook observed, in the paraphrase of Peter Coleman, that "he could not recite the multiplication tables without infuriating somebody."[94]) The Congress, in keeping with the wishes of its CIA handlers, opted for a strategy not of hard-line confrontation but rather a kinder, gentler display of Western artistic and intellectual sophistication. They sought to persuade the noncommunist intellectuals of the European left to side with the US-led West in the Cold War; they feared that the vehemence of the likes of Koestler and Burnham would scare away all but the most ferocious anticommunists.

American conservatives were conspicuous by their absence in the CCF: they were too déclassé, too primitive to mingle with sophisticated Europeans, or so the prejudice went. As Arthur Koestler, a onetime member of the German Communist Party who, like so many of his colleagues in the CCF, spent most of the rest of his life fighting The God That Failed him, said in 1948, "To the Babbitt of the Right I have nothing to say; we have no language in common."[95] The CCF would demonstrate the superiority of the West by sponsoring high-brow journals (*Quadrant*, *Encounter*, *Minerva*, and *Survey*, among others), traveling art shows, conferences of intellectuals, etc. The fact that these entailed, of necessity, subventions and financial sponsorship of intellectuals and artists was a happy facet indeed, at least for those intellectuals and artists who desired government support.

Yet as Giles Scott-Smith frames the question, "How. . . . could the merits of the free society of the West be promoted by those who, outside of the knowledge of the public, were being financed or aided by organs of the state, without their ideas and political positions becoming irreparably tarnished in the process?"[96]

The Congress for Cultural Freedom became, writes Hugh Wilford, "one of the most important artistic patrons in world history" and a godsend to subsidy-seeking intellectuals.[97] From its inception through the revelations that brought it down, the CCF was the front that enabled to CIA to become, in Saunders's phrase, "America's Ministry of Culture."[98] (The American novelists who at one time or another were on the CIA payroll include John Hunt, James Michener, William F. Buckley Jr., Howard Hunt, and Peter Mathiessen.)

"Suddenly there were limousines, parties with lashings of smoked salmon and so on, and people who couldn't normally afford the bus ticket to Newark were now flying first class to India for the summer," amusedly recollected Jason Epstein of the *New York Review of Books*.[99] The CCF had come to town. New York intellectuals were happy, even gluttonous, participants at the feast. Writes Hugh Wilford: "American writers stood to benefit from the clandestine largesse of the CIA in several ways. First, there were travel expenses for attending international meetings of the CCF. . . . [N]ovelists, poets, and critics such as Mary McCarthy, Robert Lowell, and Dwight Macdonald were happy to travel in comfort to glamorous destinations (but often privately scornful of the quality of intellectual discourse at the CCF's meetings). Thanks to rising rents and the decline of old bohemian neighborhoods, the existence of the freelance writer was becoming increasingly precarious. Literary prizes and fellowships donated by such CIA pass-throughs as the Fairfield Foundation made life for the writers a little bit easier. Also welcome were book contracts with one of the publishing houses in which the Agency had an interest, such as Frederick A. Praeger. . . ."[100]

The rent-seekers were using the patronage in part to pay the rent.

Epstein, in a 1967 essay, recalled those swinging days of the early 1950s when the CIA, the State Department, and foundations whose funding source was never quite certain "turned anti-Stalinism into a flourishing sub-profession for a number of former radicals and other left-wing intellectuals."[101] Coincidentally, three decades earlier, some of these same figures had advocated for a greater federal role in the financing of artistic and cultural endeavors through the New Deal's Federal One. But that had a working-class patina to it: wages were modest, the reigning ideologies were Americana and a form of socialist realism, and the projects had a heavy relief component. The CCF, the CIA's modern art ventures, and the world of government-subsidized literary magazines stripped the welfarist brand from government culture programs and made them seem high-toned, cosmopolitan, even James Bondish (though the first Bond novel, *Casino Royale*, was not published until 1953).

They appealed to a certain sort of intellectual, often one who may not have seen combat in the Second World War or Korea or Vietnam but who fancied himself a warrior. As Saunders describes the type, "a lot of them didn't fight, wore glasses and didn't pass the tests, the medicals or whatever. So they had this kind of urge. . . . to get in there and do something."[102] The risks were not physical but intellectual, and it paid much better than being a grunt did. Words do not strike with quite the percussive oomph as do bullets.

The anticommunist industry, observed Jason Epstein sardonically, "was far more luxuriously financed" than the socialist/communist movement of the 1930s had been. It paid for high-brow magazines and their editors and "conferences and seminars on such a scale and in so many countries and with so much air travel to and fro" that even the most credulous recipient of funds had to wonder where it was all coming from—even though "no visible government agency was involved."[103] Epstein was not alone in observing the relative poshness of the world of subsidized intellectuals. Nor was this phenomenon limited to the United States. A correspondent informed the CIA's American labor movement conduit, Irving Brown, that "the expenditure of Congress funds in Britain has not always been marked by that strict economy which would have yielded the greatest advantage in the fight against communism."[104]

Jason Epstein confesses to a bit of jealousy. Though he was involved peripherally in the CCF, he was not on the international lecture circuit, and his journalistic and editorial activities (Random House and the *New York Review of Books*) were not part of the inner circle. Instead, the CIA was financially supporting "an apparatus of intellectuals selected for their correct cold-war positions, as an alternative to what one might call a free intellectual market where ideology was presumed to count for less than individual talent and achievement." He continues, "The fault of the CIA was not that it corrupted the innocent but that it tried, in collusion with a group of insiders, to corner a free market."[105]

Epstein took umbrage at governmental favoritism in the same way that businesspeople resent competitors who receive corporate welfare. It stacks the deck and tilts the playing field; in the case of intellectual life, it gives an imprimatur to the favored few, who may then have a leg up for book contracts, magazine assignments, paid lectures, and the like.

Those intellectuals who were feeding at the CIA trough jealously guarded their positions. Those who crossed them tasted the venom. When in a 1954 issue of *Partisan Review* the socialist Irving Howe criticized intellectuals for collaborating with the state, Hook replied: "The editors of *Partisan Review* have turned out to be disgusting opportunists and morally rotten to the core. Resentful at not being able to gain money from various Foundations, from the Congress or the Committee, so that they could pay themselves fat salaries, they have gotten a Trotskyist by the name of Irving Howe to write a long piece attacking American intellectuals for being conformist."[106]

"Disgusting opportunist"? "Morally rotten"? This is the poisonous language typically bandied about by Stalinists and Trotskyites in their internecine quarrels, which makes Hook's attack on Howe's Trotskyism all the more ironic. The other message is clear: Hook and his confreres have their hooks in the Treasury, and competition for the loot from Howe & Co. is most unwelcome! (Just two years earlier, the mercurial Hook had interceded with the US Department of State on behalf of *Partisan Review* in a tax dispute. Henry Luce of *Time-Life* fame came to the rescue with a $10,000 grant, and in 1953 the American Committee for Cultural Freedom passed along $2,500 of CIA monies to *Partisan Review*.[107]) As the *Partisan Review* imbroglio suggests, the CCF also entangled the US government in the magazine business. Most famous was its sponsorship of *Encounter* magazine, which though based in London featured an American coeditor (Irving Kristol) and a stable of American contributors. *Encounter*, founded in 1953, was in one sense "a very successful venture into the world of literary politics" by the US government, featuring a glittering lineup of such contributors as Albert Camus, Christopher Isherwood, Nathan Glazer, John Kenneth Galbraith, and Bertrand Russell.[108] The poet Robert Lowell said that it was, for a time, "the best literary magazine in English."[109]

Encounter's politics were "Keynesian welfare state capitalism."[110] Its coeditors were Stephen Spender, the British poet of leftist anticommunist sympathies, and the American, Kristol, who had been, of course, a

Trotsykite. It paid well—as much as two hundred pounds per article, a goodly sum in the late 1950s. But then it was well funded: in 1959, *Encounter* received $76,230.30 from its US government sponsor via Fairfield. The French CCF-sponsored magazine *Preuves* received almost as much ($75,765.05). Frances Stonor Saunders, piecing together the fragmentary financial records of the Fairfield Foundation, found that it spent $560,000 on periodicals alone in 1961 and $880,000 in 1962: real money, not the chicken scratch that defensive intellectuals like to claim they received.

Kristol's salary was paid by the Fairfield Foundation, while Spender's paycheques were drawn on the British affiliate of the CCF.[111] *Encounter* enjoyed a real, if limited, editorial freedom. The editors did not wire every proposed article to Langley for agency approval, but in a handful of celebrated instances articles critical of US policy were axed at the direction of the magazine's funders.

Melvin Lasky, equipped with what his former schoolmate Andrew Roth, in an obituary in *The Guardian,* called "his sardonic half-sneer and nasal whine," succeeded Irving Kristol as the American editor in 1958.[112] Dwight Macdonald, whom we will meet at greater length in the next chapter, where he plays the skunk at LBJ's cultural garden party in the White House, was considered for Kristol's successor but was judged either too independent or too eccentric, depending on whom one listens to.

Melvin Lasky traveled well on the taxpayers' dime, including a trip of "several months in 1961 in East and West Africa" that led to the production of a "social democratic, humanist, internationalist" manifesto.[113] The political orientation of *Encounter* under Lasky was welfarist, technocratic, and somewhat abstractly "democratic"—that is, as long as those beneficiaries of democracy voted the right way. Of course it advocated an engaged, internationalist, moderately hawkish foreign policy line, but then that was why it was created in the first place. *Encounter* was not the magazine in which to find articles written from points of view not sanctioned by Cold War liberalism, whether they be neutralist, pacifist, aggressively nationalist, isolationist, or informed by orthodox religious sensibilities, whether Christian, Jewish, Muslim, Hindu, or other. There was a party line, as there often is in ideological journals—but the difference is that *The Nation, National Review, The New Republic,* and the like were not and are not subsidized by the federal government.

Dwight Macdonald penned a corrosive essay titled "America! America!" after which he quickly learned the limits of dissent at *Encounter,* which rejected the piece. For if the piper won't play the proper tune, the payer will just get a new piper. Macdonald said that the response from *Encounter* was "that publication of my article might embarrass the congress in its relations with the American foundations which support it."[114] The Fairfield Foundation, it seems, was a harsh mistress.

The expatriate poet T.S. Eliot rebuffed *Encounter*, for it was "obviously published under American auspices."[115] Eliot was a political conservative and in no way sympathetic to the Soviet Union or even socialism, but he was not willing to be anyone's pawn.

The CCF also served as sugar daddy to such thinking-class publications as *Preuves* (French), *Tempo Presente* (Italy), *Forum* (Austria), *Quest* (India, though it was an English-language publication), *Cuadernos* (Spanish language but published in Paris), *Quadrant* (Australia), and of course Lasky's *Der Monat*. The Congress's brain trust had hopes for *Preuves*, especially, but it never found an audience, peaking in the late 1950s at a circulation of just three thousand. And yet, in 1959 it pulled in $77,283 from the Fairfield Foundation—a hefty American subsidy for a French journal that very few read.[116]

The aforementioned *Partisan Review*, a journal born in 1934 out of the John Reed Club, which also fed the Federal Writers' Project and was associated with the Trotskyite (and anti-Stalinist) far left, was a recipient of CIA funds, though its editors strenuously (and mendaciously) denied the fact. Its contributors included such American notables as Susan Sontag, Leslie Fiedler, and Delmore Schwartz, not to mention George Orwell, though as Sidney Hook noted, the journal was almost wholly uninterested in American cultural life and traditions. "I never sensed," wrote Hook, "that they were as interested in interpreting American culture as they were in playing the role of spokesmen to provincial Americans for modern European culture in its varied manifestations."[117] Its editors were, however, *very* interested in US government funding.

Records show that *Partisan Review* received financing from, at various times, the American Committee for Cultural Freedom, the Congress for Cultural Freedom, and the dummy Fairfield Foundation.[118] Its founder, William Phillips, was an unabashed supplicant before the CIA and its OPC. In the tradition of John Reed Club alumni, he was happy to let the taxpayers underwrite his salary. The Congress proved a lifeline to several high-brow journals. According to Frances Stonor Saunders's investigative work, in the early 1960s the CCF took out 3,000 subscriptions to *Partisan Review* and also bought up a significant portion of the circulations of the *Kenyon Review* (1,500 copies), the *Hudson*

Review (1,500), the *Sewanee Review* (1,000), *Poetry* (750), *Daedalus* (500), and the *Journal of the History of Ideas* (500).[119] For publications with circulations typically in the low thousands, the CCF, with the unwitting assistance of the American taxpayer, kept the presses rolling. (In the case of the *Kenyon Review*, its editor in the early 1960s, Robie Macauley, was a CCF operative. When its circulation skyrocketed to 6,000 copies, Macauley bragged that he had "found ways of making money that Mr. Ransom [the founding editor] had never thought of."[120])

However, *Partisan Review*'s William Phillips would have the gall, in a 1967 symposium, to play the mildly discomforted tut-tutter of those who accepted CIA monies. "I always did think there was something unsavory and conspiratorial about publications, organizations, and individuals rumored to be connected with the CIA," he said in a statement of overwhelming hypocrisy. "The atmosphere they created was a peculiar blend of ulterior aims and immediate self-interest. There was always the smell of the gravy train, and the people supposedly involved—I do not mean the innocents—were usually of a certain type: breezy, rootless, free-wheeling, cynically anti-Communist orgmen."[121] Whether he was an innocent or a breezy "orgman," Phillips protesteth too much. But then as James Agee remarked, "those *Partisan Review* people fear clarity as the devil does holy water."[122]

The Curtain Falls: The CCF Meets the 1960s

The journal *Minerva*, which was founded, with CCF subsidy, in 1962 by sociologist Edward Shils, set forth to study the social and political milieu and consequences of science as it was practiced in the Cold War period. As Shils put it in his first editorial, *Minerva* was to deal with the "governmentalisation of science, and its effect on scholarship and the role of the scientist."[123] He took for granted that the Cold War made governments of East and West intimate partners of the scientific enterprise. This was a new age, and the relationship between state and science was subject to negotiation.

In line with this view, Alvin Weinberg, director of Oak Ridge National Laboratory, described in an influential *Minerva* essay the inevitability of Big Science, with its "czar-like control and. . . . hierarchies," as historian of science Elena Aronova phrased it half a century later in the pages of that same (no longer CCF-subsidized) *Minerva*. There is a sense in which Weinberg's acceptance of a science that is largely the property of mammoth bureaucracies and state-funded enterprises parallels the arguments of the CCF's advocates of a cultural Cold War.

The intervention of a powerful centralized state is a given; the challenge is to see that the necessary propagandistic function of the enterprise does not interfere excessively with freedom of inquiry or exchange.

Yet the philosopher-scientist Michael Polanyi took an opposite tack from Weinberg in *Minerva*. He envisioned a decentralized scholarly community without direction from a single source but instead arranged by "mutual adjustment of independent initiatives." This arrangement was to have the quality of an invisible hand and operate "according to economic principles similar to those by which the production of material goods is regulated."[124] This "Little Science" might be said to have its parallel in the decentralized cultural life which once obtained in America and in some areas still does, and under which, while certain cities become hubs or informal capitals of certain art forms (Boston and later New York City for literature, Los Angeles for motion pictures, Nashville for country music), there is no central authority directing cultural traffic.

Weinberg's model sufficed for the CCF—but Polanyi's was more in keeping with American political and cultural traditions. And as the American establishment came under assault in the 1960s, it was the cult of bigness critiqued by Polanyi that proved the most tempting target for critics.

The New Left historian and social critic Christopher Lasch, dissecting the Congress for Cultural Freedom for *The Nation* as the Vietnam War raged, noted that "the cold-war liberals have not hesitated to criticize American popular culture or popular politics, but the question is whether they have criticized the American government or any other aspect of the officially sanctioned order." The answer, said Lasch, was no. *Encounter* "consistently approved the broad lines and even the details of American policy, until the war in Vietnam shattered the cold-war coalition"—and, not coincidentally, until the source of *Encounter*'s funding was revealed to the world.[125]

There had always been a cloud of suspicion around the CCF and its most prominent regular undertaking, *Encounter*. By the 1960s, those clouds of suspicion had formed into a louring front. In 1964, Rep. Wright Patman, a populist Texas Democrat, revealed that he had learned that the CIA was channeling monies to the J. M. Kaplan Fund of New York, never directly, but through eight CIA-created dummy intermediaries: the Gotham Foundation, the Michigan Fund, the Andrew Hamilton Fund, the Bordon Fund, the Price Fund, the Edsel Fund, the Beacon Fund, and the Kentifield Fund. This caused a mini-tempest: a credible source had let on that government monies were secretly being funneled to foundations, some otherwise legitimate and some simply dummies set up by the CIA, which in turn paid off intellectuals and scholars for work thought helpful to the CIA's mission.

In an editorial in *The Nation* of September 14, 1964, that venerable liberal magazine asked:

> For example, should the CIA be permitted to channel funds to magazines in London—and New York—which pose as "magazines of opinion" and are in competition with independent journals of opinion? Is it proper for CIA-supported magazines to offer large sums in payment of single poems by East European and Russian poets regarded as men of a character who might be encouraged to defect by what, in the context, could be regarded as a bribe? Is it a "legitimate" function of the CIA to finance, indirectly, various congresses, conventions, assemblies and conferences devoted to "cultural freedom" and kindred topics? . . . The secrecy curtain should not be lowered on this subject matter: legitimate questions are involved and they deserve legitimate answers.[126]

The jig was almost up. It ended when in 1965–66 the *New York Times* undertook a major investigative survey, headed by Tom Wicker, of CIA activities and skullduggery around the world. In one of the five articles of the series, the one published on April 27, 1966, the team of correspondents anatomized the ways in which "American newspaper and magazine publishers, authors and universities are often the beneficiaries of direct or indirect CIA subsidies." After detailing the activities of the J. M. Kaplan Fund in funneling CIA monies to researchers, the reporters wrote:

> Through similar channels, the CIA has supported groups of exiles from Cuba and refugees from Communism in Europe, or anti-Communist but liberal organizations of intellectuals such as the Congress for Cultural Freedom, and some of their newspapers and magazines.
>
> *Encounter* magazine, a well-known anti-Communist intellectual monthly with editions in Spanish and German as well as English, was for a long time—though it is not now—one of the indirect beneficiaries of CIA funds. Through arrangements that have never been publicly explained, several American book publishers have also received CIA subsidies.[127]

The *Times* series appeared over the strenuous objections of several mandarins of the American diplomatic and intelligence communities. Secretary of State Dean Rusk pled with *Times* publisher Punch Sulzberger to consider the effect of the revelations on national security. It was giving "comfort to the enemy," he claimed.[128] The legendary James Jesus Angleton, chief of the agency's counterintelligence, tried to use his contacts at the *Times* to hobble, if not undermine, the series. Ambassador to France Charles Bohlen "hit the roof," reported Harrison E. Salisbury in *Without Fear or Favor:* The New York Times *and its Times.*[129]

Establishment liberals mounted a brief defense of the CCF and *Encounter,* though it was often couched in evasive language. John Kenneth Galbraith, George Kennan, Robert Oppenheimer, and Arthur Schlesinger Jr. signed a joint letter to the *New York Times* declaring: "On the basis of our own experience with the congress over the past sixteen years—with its seminars, its artistic festivals, its magazines, its staff—we can say categorically that we have no question regarding the independence of its policy, the integrity of its officials or the value of its contribution. In our experience the congress, under the direction of its Secretary-General, Nicholas Nabokov, has been an entirely free body, responsive only to the wishes of its members and collaborators and the decisions of its Executive Committee."[130]

Note what was *not* said. There was no denial of the facts of the story because there could be no such denial. The intellectuals of the CCF and *Encounter* were accepting (and often soliciting) benefactions from the US government in a manner hidden from public view and not subject to the inspection of the elected representatives of the American people. That was beyond dispute. So the last-ditch defenders of the subsidized intellectuals chose to argue that the source of the subsidies in no way altered or eroded the critical thinking and prose output of those intellectuals.

Current and former *Encounter* editors Irving Kristol, Melvin Lasky, and Stephen Spender wrote the *New York Times* as the cat was crawling out of the bag, claiming that "We know of no 'indirect' benefactions.... We are our own masters and part of nobody's propaganda."[131] Were they fibbing to protect their reputations or the greater cause? Did they believe this? Had they convinced themselves of something they suspected was not true?

When the façade had crumbled, and the fact that *Encounter* was a project of the US government (with additional funding by the British state) was beyond doubt, its stable of editors and writers reacted variously. Frank Kermode, who served as a coeditor with Melvin Lasky, protested, "I was always reassured that there was no truth in the allegations about CIA funds." To which an unrepentant Lasky said, "I probably should have told him all the painful details."[132]

In 1967, *Partisan Review*'s editors and supporters issued a haughty "Statement on the CIA," which read in part: "We would like to make public our opposition to the secret subsidization by the CIA of literary and intellectual publications and organizations, and our conviction that regular subsidization by the CIA can only discredit intellectually and morally such publications and organizations. We lack confidence in the magazines alleged to have been subsidized by the CIA, and we do not think they have responded appropriately to the questions that have been raised." It was so self-importantly obtuse that only an intellectual could have signed it without gagging. When, almost thirty years later, Frances Stonor Saunders showed Tom Braden the statement, he laughed. When he finished laughing he said, "Of course they knew."[133]

The dam had broken, and the condemnation of the bien-pensants of New York intellectual circles washed over the CCF crowd. Norman Mailer, in his inimitable prose, mocked "the enlightened polemics of the cultivated socialism of the Committee for Cultural Freedom which had been brought by the sound-as-brickwork-logic-of-the-next-step in good Socialist *Anti*-Communism to so incisive an infestation by the CIA that it now called up pictures of the cockroaches in a slum sink; not all the wines of the Waldorf could wash out a drop of that!"[134]

For the most part, the begetters of the CCF enterprise regretted not the fact of subsidization but its "political unwisdom," in Sidney Hook's phrase. Hook denied that any action of the Congress was affected in the slightest by its source of patronage, and he scoffed at those pained innocents who professed to be shocked—shocked!—that their hotel rooms and airfare and article fees and editorial payments had come from the big bad wolf instead of the sugar plum fairy. This should have been clear to all since the beginning. Wrote Hook: "In my own mind I had no doubt that the CIA was making some contribution to the congress, but I was never privy to the amount or the mechanism of its operation. Everyone involved in the activities of the Congress had heard rumors of covert CIA support. If anyone had deep moral scruples about it, he should have dropped out. If he did not, he did not want to know."[135]

Just when and how much the satellite figures around the CCF and *Encounter* orbits knew was, then and now, a mystery. In some cases the ignorance may have been, as Hook suggests, by choice. Dwight Macdonald, no timid shrinker from the truth, said, "I was indeed 'involved' in the secret financing of *Encounter* by the CIA during the year I was a special editor, unwittingly and 'unwittily' as they say, and I think I was played for a sucker and I'm still sore about it."[136]

Interviewed years later, former CIA case officer Donald Jameson said, "The main concern for most scholars and writers really is how you get paid for doing what you want to do. I think that, by and large, they would take money from whatever source they could get it. And so it was that the Congress and other similar organizations—both East and West—were looked on as sort of large teats from which anybody could take a swig if they needed it and then go off and do their thing. That is one of the main reasons, really I think, for the success of the Congress: it made it possible to be a sensitive intellectual and eat."[137]

Defenders of the CCF and its works often seemed not to rue its government subsidization so much as they regretted the revelation of such. Peter Coleman, author of *The Liberal Conspiracy: The Congress for Cultural Freedom and the Struggle for the Mind of Postwar Europe* and a former editor of the CCF-supported Australian journal *Quadrant*, opines, with a nod to Michael Jossselson, that the Congress made a significant error in failing to transition from the US government as sugar daddy to one of the major establishment foundations (Rockefeller, Ford, and the like) early enough so as to avoid the messy publicity of the mid-1960s, when the CIA was in bad odor with many Americans.[138] *Encounter* had weaned itself of CIA monies in 1963–64, relying since then on the International Publishing Corp. for its subsistence, but the die had been cast. (Despite this ostensible new independence, Frances Stonor Saunders reports that the CCF remained responsible for editorial salaries and, as a result, retained a say in editorial policies.)[139]

By 1966, the year the lid was blown off, the Congress for Cultural Freedom had a budget of about $2.07 million, the largest portions of which went to its International Secretariat ($200,000) and the Latin American Institute of International Relations ($264,500), the latter indicating the late Kennedy administration's emphasis on Latin American diplomacy through its Alliance for Progress. The most heavily subsidized journals of opinion were *Preuves* ($80,000) and *Der Monat* ($60,000). *Encounter* and its book publishing arm, though ostensibly free of CIA funding by now, did receive $30,000.[140]

In the wake of the *New York Times*'s exposé, CCF leadership scrambled to come up with foundation money to replace the anticipated loss of the no-longer-secret funds from the CIA. The Ford Foundation agreed to a $1.3 million commitment in 1968 (toward a total CCF budget of $1.5 million), with Ford's support gradually declining to $600,000 by 1972.[141]

But the hits to the Congress's reputation just kept on coming. The New Left monthly *Ramparts* published muckraking inquiries into CIA sponsorship of such organizations as the National Students Association. And the knockout punch, perhaps inadvertent, was Thomas Braden's full-throated liberal Cold Warrior defense of the CIA's activities on the cultural front in a blockbuster May 20, 1967, *Saturday Evening Post* article titled "I'm Glad the CIA is 'Immoral.'"

"Back in the early 1950s," explained Braden, "when the cold war was really hot, the idea that Congress would have approved many of our projects was about as likely as the John Birch Society's approving Medicare."[142] Well, perhaps, but does that justify the extralegal nature of the projects: the evasion of congressional scrutiny and the concealment of sponsorship from some of those who were benefitting from the projects?

Braden loved the cloak and dagger aspect of the cultural Cold War. "Money for both the [Boston Symphony Orchestra's] tour and [*Encounter's*] publication came from the CIA, and few outside the CIA knew about it. We had placed one agent in a Europe-based organization of intellectuals called the Congress for Cultural Freedom. Another agent became an editor of *Encounter*. The agents could not only propose anti-Communist programs to the official leaders of the organizations but they could also suggest ways and means to solve the inevitable budgetary problems. Why not see if the needed money could be obtained from 'American foundations'? As the agents knew, the CIA-financed foundations were quite generous when it came to the national interest."

Several informal rules guided the use of front groups, according to Braden: "[T]he first rule of our operational plan [was], 'Limit the money to amounts private organizations can credibly spend.' The other rules were equally obvious: 'Use legitimate, existing organizations; disguise the extent of American interest; protect the integrity of the organization by not requiring it to support every aspect of official American policy.'"[143]

Braden's combative confession set off a firestorm. The independent liberal journalist Murray Kempton, columnist for the *New York Post*, cut Braden's artistic pretensions down to size. "We are fortunate to have Thomas Braden's memoirs of his career as the CIA's paymaster to the anti-Communist Left," he wrote, "because otherwise it would be hard to appreciate the mindless vulgarity of this operation. You pity anyone who had dealings with this sort of man as you ought to pity the Hollywood Communists for the former taxi driver who was their district organizer. Braden's assertion that an editor of *Encounter* was 'an agent of ours' is the language of an *apparatchik*."[144] (That editor was Lasky.)

Braden's revelations disappointed those with whom he had conspired as well as those who had participated, without apologies or regrets, in the activities of the Congress for Cultural Freedom. Allen Dulles believed that Braden had betrayed him and the CIA; he never spoke to Braden again.[145] Michael Josselson resigned as executive director of the CCF in May 1967. He was replaced by a Ford Foundation executive and former *New York Times*-man named Shepard Stone, who had long been rumored to have CIA connections.

The Congress, by then known as the International Association for Cultural Freedom, expired in January 1979, though it had been a virtual shell since the revelations of 1967. It shrunk as its Ford Foundation checks shrunk. In an age of increasing skepticism about US government institutions, there was no CIA there to pick up the tab for lavish conferences, well-paid magazine articles, and ample editorial expense accounts.

Despite the bad press, those who had taken advantage of the CCF munificence for the most part insisted that they had acted in good faith and that their participation had in some perhaps attenuated way furthered the cause of the West in the Cold War. Edward Shils asked himself, "What did it all amount to? How much did it really achieve? Was it merely an opportunity to travel to other countries, to eat good (or even excellent) meals in Geneva or Zurich or Paris or Tokyo?" He concluded that "on a much smaller scale, our efforts were like the efforts of Christians, clergy and laymen, who do not improve human beings—they just keep them from becoming worse than they otherwise would be."[146] This sidesteps the question of funding and frankness—Christians profess their faith openly and act with monies freely given to the church, not taxed from believers and nonbelievers alike—but to the extent the CCF encouraged debate and the exchange of ideas and some fine writing, Shils surely has a point.

Those who wrote and edited on the US government's dime were not mere hirelings or hacks. As Hugh Wilford writes, "the CIA could not always dictate how the money it secretly disbursed was spent, with left-wing literati sometimes purloining it for purposes that had little or nothing to do with the superpower conflict."[147] Seldom were the articles in the government-subsidized journals written by government employees; that would have been too obviously propagandistic, and ineffectual. The CIA was not a "ventriloquist," as Frances Stonor Saunders notes.[148] It did not play Edgar Bergen to an army of cerebral Charlie McCarthys. But neither was the source of funding irrelevant. Writers know that any commission comes with a set of unwritten guidelines and boundaries attached; transgress them and you'll not receive another commission.

When in September 1967 *Commentary* magazine sponsored a symposium on liberal anticommunism, its editors summarized, "As to CIA backing of cultural projects, the consensus appears to be that it was on the whole a disaster, but that the intellectuals who received such subsidies were subject to no actual coercion and were in any case, for better or worse, doing and saying what they would have done and said anyway."[149]

Daniel Bell, for fifteen years a stalwart of the CCF, found *Commentary*'s query whether he had been "a dupe of, or slave to, the darker impulses of American foreign policy" to be "lurid and melodramatic." The conferences in which he had participated "were never propaganda jamborees," protested Bell, but "discussions enlisting some of the best minds of our time in an effort to clarify the intellectual issues of the day." Government funding of such explorations in no way "compromised" him, said Bell.[150]

Taking a more skeptical line in the *Commentary* symposium was Lewis A. Coser, a sociologist at Brandeis, who saw the CCF as part of a "flourishing racket" by which certain intellectuals sought and received "ample funding" from the US government in exchange for toeing the party line. Coser marveled at the "unedifying spectacle of American intellectuals waxing indignant about the kept intellectuals of the Soviet Union while being subsidized by secret or not so secret American government funds."[151] This was, to Coser, a dereliction of duty on the part of the subsidized intellectuals, who had abandoned an ideal stance of critical independence for, in his view, the servile posture of a lapdog.

Irving Howe, editor-in-chief of the socialist journal *Dissent* (of which Coser served as an editor), charged that the recipients of government funds "were no longer autonomous men but had become knowing accomplices of a secret intelligence service. That is not the business of intellectuals; that is not the business of people concerned with a disinterested scrutiny of ideas or a passionate defense of freedom. Even from the viewpoint of people who sincerely believed in an uncritical or almost uncritical support of the West during the cold war, the CIA connection was indefensible."[152]

Coser and Howe were echoed—though not seconded—by the libertarian writer Paul Goodman. Goodman, who praised the "moral advantages" of "a free market and individual enterprise," derided the "socialist nostalgia" of *Dissent.* Yet he also belittled those intellectuals who had taken CIA and State Department money as "paid agents." Goodman cites by name Sidney Hook, also a participant in this contentious symposium.[153] Hook called the charge that he and the other beneficiaries of CIA monies were dupes "absurd" and "vicious." He conceded that accepting government funding without disclosing the source might present a public relations problem, but this was a side issue. "Granted," said Hook, "that it would have been preferable for all [the CCF's] financing to come from private sources. But the pity of it is that the angels of philanthropy have been more willing to subsidize reactionary extremist groups on one side and ritualistic liberal groups on the other than liberal and anti-Communist groups."[154] He never identifies these reactionary extremists who were so lavishly funded by the angels of philanthropy: such outré outfits have never been flush with cash, though perhaps Hook was referring to such moderate Republican-friendly think tanks as the American Enterprise Institute. In any event, if private donations were not forthcoming for the liberal anticommunists, they would happily accept federal tax dollars under the table.

The same point was made by the historian and publicist of Cold War liberalism, Arthur Schlesinger Jr., who justified the clandestine aid in this way: "organizations of the Right in most countries get financial support from the local business communities and oligarchies; organizations of the antidemocratic Left get it from the Russians or the Chinese; but organizations of the democratic Left have no obvious and reliable sources of support. That is the gap the CIA sought in its way to fill. Perhaps the attempt was a mistake, but the problem still exists."[155] Schlesinger's formulation is better applied to Europe than to America, where no real tradition of business sponsorship of "right-wing" politics existed. Yes, the National Association of Manufacturers advocated for economy in government (except when programs might benefit their members), but its primary opponents, the major labor unions, were not without resources. There is also the question of whether the "democratic Left" does not undermine democracy when it receives government funding under the table, without the imprimatur or scrutiny of the elected representatives of the people.

The stigma of being a subsidized intellectual has faded somewhat in the almost half-century since the furor surrounding the revelations by Tom Braden and the *New York Times*. The extraordinary growth of what we might call the university-industrial complex has made federal subsidy a matter of routine for many intellectuals. Are they really all that compromised by the source of funds? Jason Epstein, writing in 1967 about the way that government monies had distorted what he called the free intellectual market, painted the picture in shades of gray: "The depressing fact is that the cadre of intellectuals who had been arbitrarily placed in high journalistic and other cultural positions by means of United States funds, were never, as a result of this sponsorship, to be quite free. What limited them was nothing so simple as coercion, though coercion at some levels may have been involved, but something more like the inevitable relations between employer and employee in which the wishes of the former become implicit in the acts of the latter."[156]

There is also the matter of fairness. Should intellectuals, who by nature are more skilled at the eristic arts than at advocacy, be able to wrangle monies out of the public treasury to subsidize their own interests, e.g., writing and talking? This is a question that is almost never asked anymore, though it was very much in play, at least on the margins, in the debate over the creation of the National Endowments for the Arts and the Humanities, to which we next turn our attention.

Notes

1. Gary O. Larson provides an overview of the post-New Deal, pre-Great Society national arts legislation in *The Reluctant Patron: The United States Government and the Arts, 1943–1965* (Philadelphia, PA: University of Pennsylvania Press, 1983).
2. Frank Thompson, Jr., "Are the Communists Right in Calling Us Cultural Barbarians?" *Music Journal* 13, no. 6 (July/August 1955): 5.
3. Larson, *The Reluctant Patron*, 72.
4. Ibid., 72–73.
5. Charlotte M. Canning, "'In the Interest of the State': A Cold War National Theatre for the United States," *Theatre Journal* 61, no. 3 (October 2009): 414.
6. Ibid., 407–8.
7. Ibid., 417.
8. Laura A. Belmonte, *Selling the American Way: U.S. Propaganda and the Cold War* (Philadelphia, PA: University of Pennsylvania Press, 2008), 19.
9. "Benton & Bowles," *Advertising Age*, September 15, 2003, accessed October 12, 2015, http://adage.com/article/adage-encyclopedia/benton-bowles/98345/.
10. Larson, *The Reluctant Patron*, 27.

11. See "In Memoriam: Everett Franklin Spruce," accessed October 12, 2015, http://www.utexas.edu/faculty/council/2002-2003/memorials/Spruce/spruce.html.
12. Frances Stonor Saunders, "Modern Art Was CIA 'Weapon,'" *The Independent*, October 22, 1995.
13. Lauren Ross, "When art fought the Cold War," *The Art Newspaper*, May 2013, accessed October 12, 2015, http://www.theartnewspaper.com/articles/When-art-fought-the-Cold-War/29407.
14. Larson, *The Reluctant Patron*, 27.
15. John Henry Merryman and Albert E. Elsen, *Law, Ethics and the Visual Arts* (The Hague: Kluwer Law International, 2002), 539.
16. Francis Frascina, ed., *Pollock and After*, 2nd ed. (London: Routlege, 2000/1985), 163.
17. Larson, *The Reluctant Patron*, 27.
18. Hauptman, "The Suppression of Art in the McCarthy Decade," 48.
19. Hugh Wilford, *The Mighty Wurlitzer: How the CIA Played America* (Cambridge, MA: Harvard University Press, 2008), 101.
20. "Abstract Expressionism," accessed October 12, 2015, http://www.metmuseum.org/toah/hd/abex/hd_abex.htm.
21. Frances Stonor Saunders, *The Cultural Cold War: The CIA and the World of Arts and Letters* (New York: New Press, 1999), 253. The book was published in Britain as Frances Stonor Saunders, *Who Paid the Piper? The CIA and the Cultural Cold War* (London: Granta Books, 2000).
22. Tom Braden joked that many of his colleagues in the CIA didn't know "the difference between Socialist Realism and finger painting." This was certainly not true of those making strategic decisions in the cultural Cold War, but the CIA was not singleminded in its promotion of avant-garde art, argues Robert Burstow in "The Limits of Modernist art as a 'Weapon of the Cold War': reassessing the unknown patron of the Monument to the Unknown Political Prisoner," *Oxford Art Journal* (Vol. 20, No. 1, 1997): 68–80. Burstow tells the story of the 1951 competition, organized by London's Institute of Contemporary Arts but underwritten (through fronts) by the CIA, to commission a sculpture memorializing the "Unknown Political Prisoner." The judges selected a design by the modernist British sculptor Reg Butler. The prize's secret sponsors in the U.S. intelligence agency withdrew their sponsorship due to the "ultra modern" (p. 75) style of the winning entry.
23. Mathews, "Art and Politics in Cold War America," 763, 780.
24. Eva Cockcroft, "Abstract Expressionism, Weapon of the Cold War," in *Pollock and After*, ed. Francis Frascina, 1st ed. (London: Routlege, 2000/1985), 126–7.
25. Saunders, *The Cultural Cold War*, 272.
26. John Meroney, "CIA Operative Tom Braden's Plot to Topple the USSR with Modern Art," *Playboy* (November 2013), accessed October 12, 2015, http://playboysfw.kinja.com/cia-operative-tom-braden-s-plot-to-topple-the-ussr-with-1457.
27. Ibid.
28. George Dondero, "Modern Art Shackled to Communism," U.S. House of Representatives, August 16, 1949, in *Art in Theory: 1900–1990*, eds. Charles Harrison and Paul Wood (Cambridge, MA: Blackwell Publishers, 1993), 656–8.

29. Hauptman, "The Suppression of Art in the McCarthy Decade," 48.
30. Dondero, "Modern Art Shackled to Communism," 656–7.
31. Hauptman, "The Suppression of Art in the McCarthy Decade," 48.
32. Mathews, "Art and Politics in Cold War America," 775.
33. Larson, *The Reluctant Patron*, 48.
34. Saunders, *The Cultural Cold War*, 257.
35. Ibid., 259.
36. Thomas W. Braden, "I'm Glad the CIA Is 'Immoral,'" *Saturday Evening Post*, May 20, 1967, 10.
37. David and Cecile Shapiro, "Abstract Expressionism: The Politics of Apolitical Painting," *Prospects* 3 (October 1978): 209–10.
38. Saunders, "Modern Art Was CIA 'Weapon.'"
39. Wilford, *The Mighty Wurlitzer*, 112.
40. Clement Greenberg, *Art and Culture: Critical Essays* (Boston, MA: Beacon Press, 1961), 4.
41. Ibid., 9, 11, 13.
42. Ibid., 5, 21.
43. S.A. Longstaff, "*Partisan Review* and the Second World War," *Salmagundi* 43 (Winter 1979): 109.
44. Shapiro and Shapiro, "Abstract Expressionism: The Politics of Apolitical Painting," 178.
45. Ibid., 180.
46. Ibid., 183, 203–4.
47. Ibid., 206.
48. W. Scott Lucas, "Revealing the Parameters of Opinion: An Interview with Frances Stonor Saunders," in *The Cultural Cold War in Western Europe, 1945–60*, eds. Giles Scott-Smith and Hans Krabbendam (Portland, OR: Frank Cass, 2003), 22.
49. Saunders, *The Cultural Cold War*, 324.
50. Braden, "I'm Glad the CIA Is 'Immoral,'" 12.
51. Saunders, "Modern Art Was CIA 'Weapon.'"
52. Hugh Wilford, *The Mighty Wurlitzer*, 7.
53. Ibid., 71.
54. Ibid., 46.
55. Saunders, *The Cultural Cold War*, 71.
56. Hugh Wilford, "'Unwitting Assets?' British Intellectuals and the Congress for Cultural Freedom," *Twentieth Century British History* 11, no. 1 (2000): 45.
57. Saunders, *The Cultural Cold War*, 53. See also Tony Shaw, "The Politics of Cold War Culture," *Journal of Cold War Studies* 3, no. 3 (Fall 2001): 59–76; James Petras, "The CIA and the Cultural Cold War Revisited," *Monthly Review* 51, no. 6 (November 1999): 47–56; and Kenneth A. Osgood, "Hearts and Minds: The Unconventional Cold War," *Journal of Cold War Studies* 4, no. 2 (Spring 2002): 85–107.
58. "Origins of the Congress for Cultural Freedom, 1949–50," October 12, 2015, https://www.cia.gov/library/center-for-the-study-of-intelligence/csi-publications/csi-studies/studies/95unclass/Warner.html.
59. Giles Scott-Smith, *The Politics of Apolitical Culture: The Congress for Cultural Freedom, the CIA and post-war American Hegemony* (London: Routledge, 2002), 3, 103.

60. Ibid., 102.
61. Peter Coleman, *The Liberal Conspiracy: The Congress for Cultural Freedom and the Struggle for the Mind of Postwar Europe* (New York: Free Press, 1989), 1.
62. Ibid., 5.
63. "Aleksandr Aleksandrovich Fadeyev," *Encyclopaedia Britannica*, accessed October 12, 2015, http://www.britannica.com/EBchecked/topic/200116/Aleksandr-Aleksandrovich-Fadeyev.
64. Sidney Hook, *Out of Step: An Unquiet Life in the 20th Century* (New York: Harper & Row, 1987), 433.
65. Coleman, *The Liberal Conspiracy*, 249.
66. Ibid., 249–50.
67. Saunders, *The Cultural Cold War*, 81–82.
68. Christopher Lasch, *The Agony of the American Left* (New York: Knopf, 1969), 77.
69. "Liberal Anti-Communism Revisited: A Symposium," *Commentary* 44, no. 3 (September 1967): 68.
70. Mark Schorer, *Sinclair Lewis: An American Life* (New York: McGraw-Hill, 1961), 755.
71. Lasch, *The Agony of the American Left*, 78.
72. Edward Shils and Peter Coleman, "Remembering the Congress of [*sic*] Cultural Freedom," *Society* 46, no. 5 (2009): 439.
73. Meroney, "CIA Operative Tom Braden's Plot to Topple the USSR with Modern Art."
74. Coleman, *The Liberal Conspiracy*, 9, 46.
75. Scott-Smith, *The Politics of Apolitical Culture*, 133–4.
76. Braden, "I'm Glad the CIA Is 'Immoral,'" 12.
77. Quoted in Alan O. Ebenstain, *Friedrich Hayek: A Biography* (Chicago: University of Chicago Press, 2003/2001), 180.
78. Saunders, "Modern Art Was CIA 'Weapon.'"
79. "The New American Painting, Large Exhibition, Leaves for Year-Long European Tour Under Auspices of International Council at Museum of Modern Art," press release, MOMA, March 11, 1958, accessed October 12, 2015, http://www.moma.org/momaorg/shared/pdfs/docs/press_archives/2342/releases/MOMA_1958_0025.pdf?2010.
80. Lewis Hyde, "Being Good Ancestors: Reflections on Arts Funding since World War II," *Kenyon Review* 30, no. 1 (Winter 2008): 7.
81. Scott-Smith, *The Politics of Apolitical Culture:*, 124.
82. Saunders, *The Cultural Cold War*, 119.
83. Ibid., 125.
84. Wilford, *The Mighty Wurlitzer*, 87, 97.
85. Scott-Smith, *The Politics of Apolitical Culture*, 123.
86. Dwight Garner, "Dwight Macdonald's War on Mediocrity," *New York Times Book Review*, October 21, 2011. For a look at one Ford-subsidized journal of the cultural Cold War, see Greg Barnhisel, "*Perspectives USA* and the Cultural Cold War: Modernism in Service of the State," *Modernism/modernity* 14, no. 4 (November 2007): 729–54.
87. Wilford, *The Mighty Wurlitzer*, 84–85.
88. Saunders, *The Cultural Cold War*, 157.
89. *Wellsville Daily Report*, August 29, 1956.

90. Lasch, *The Agony of the American Left*, 79.
91. Coleman, *The Liberal Conspiracy*, 169.
92. Lasch, *The Agony of the American Left*, 79, 86.
93. Wilford, "'Unwitting Assets?'," 46.
94. Coleman, *The Liberal Conspiracy*, 34.
95. Ibid., 12.
96. Scott-Smith, *The Politics of Apolitical Culture*, 83–84.
97. Wilford, *The Mighty Wurlitzer*, 101–2.
98. Saunders, *The Cultural Cold War*, 129.
99. Ibid., 220.
100. Wilford, *The Mighty Wurlitzer*, 103.
101. Jason Epstein, "The CIA and the Intellectuals," *New York Review of Books* (April 20, 1967).
102. Lucas, "Revealing the Parameters of Opinion: An Interview with Frances Stonor Saunders," 34.
103. Epstein, "The CIA and the Intellectuals."
104. Wilford, "'Unwitting Assets?'," 56.
105. Epstein, "The CIA and the Intellectuals."
106. Scott-Smith, *The Politics of Apolitical Culture*, 161.
107. Saunders, *The Cultural Cold War*, 163.
108. Scott-Smith, *The Politics of Apolitical Culture*, 127.
109. "Liberal Anti-Communism Revisited: A Symposium," 54.
110. Scott-Smith, *The Politics of Apolitical Culture*, 131.
111. Saunders, *The Cultural Cold War*, 219, 176.
112. Andrew Roth, "Melvin Lasky: Cold Warrior Who Edited the CIA-funded *Encounter* Magazine," *The Guardian*, May 21, 2004.
113. Coleman, *The Liberal Conspiracy*, 184.
114. Lasch, *The Agony of the American Left*, 75.
115. Wilford, *The Mighty Wurlitzer*, 115.
116. Scott-Smith, *The Politics of Apolitical Culture*, 127.
117. Hook, *Out of Step*, 513.
118. Wilford, *The Mighty Wurlitzer*, 104.
119. Saunders, *The Cultural Cold War*, 338.
120. Hyde, "Being Good Ancestors," 9.
121. "Liberal Anti-Communism Revisited: A Symposium," 57.
122. Saunders, *The Cultural Cold War*, 346.
123. Elena Aronova, "The Congress for Cultural Freedom, *Minerva*, and the Quest for Instituting 'Science Studies' in the Age of Cold War," *Minerva* 50 (2012): 316.
124. Ibid., 318.
125. Lasch, *The Agony of the American Left*, 73.
126. "Foundations as 'Fronts,'" *The Nation*, September 14, 1964, accessed October 12, 2015, http://archive.org/stream/nation199julnewy/nation199julnewy_djvu.txt.
127. "Electronic Prying Grows," *New York Times*, April 27, 1966.
128. Harrison E. Salisbury, *Without Fear or Favor:* The New York Times *and Its Times* (New York: Times Books, 1980), 542.
129. Ibid., 535.

130. John Kenneth Galbraith, George Kennan, Robert Oppenheimer, and Arthur Schlesinger Jr., "Record of Congress for Cultural Freedom," *New York Times*, May 9, 1966.
131. Saunders, *The Cultural Cold War*, 378.
132. Roth, "Melvin Lasky."
133. Saunders, *The Cultural Cold War*, 410–1.
134. Norman Mailer, *Armies of the Night* (New York: New American Library, 1968), 85.
135. Hook, *Out of Step*, 455, 451.
136. "Liberal Anti-Communism Revisited: A Symposium," 56.
137. Saunders, *The Cultural Cold War*, 345.
138. Coleman, *The Liberal Conspiracy*, 220.
139. Saunders, *The Cultural Cold War*, 374.
140. Coleman, *The Liberal Conspiracy*, 275–6.
141. Ibid., 225.
142. Braden, "I'm Glad the CIA Is 'Immoral,'" 10.
143. Ibid., 12, 14.
144. "Liberal Anti-Communism Revisited: A Symposium," 53.
145. Reflecting back on the CCF from 1990, Edward Shils, in an essay intended for *Encounter* which met the misfortune of being in the editorial queue when the magazine finally went under, dismissed Braden's *Saturday Evening Post* confession as "evidence of a frivolous character." Shils and Coleman, "Remembering the Congress of [*sic*] Cultural Freedom," 438.
146. Ibid., 441.
147. Wilford, *The Mighty Wurlitzer*, 9–10.
148. Lucas, "Revealing the Parameters of Opinion: An Interview with Frances Stonor Saunders," 25.
149. "Liberal Anti-Communism Revisited: A Symposium," 31.
150. Ibid., 38–39.
151. Ibid., 40.
152. Ibid., 52.
153. Ibid., 41–42.
154. Ibid., 48.
155. Ibid., 70.
156. Epstein, "The CIA and the Intellectuals." Cynthia P. Schneider, an art historian who served as President Clinton's ambassador to The Netherlands, criticized the clandestine nature of the cultural Cold War but called for a new "cultural diplomacy" in a 2002 essay in the *Washington Post*. Cynthia P. Schneider, "There's an Art to Telling the World about America," *Washington Post*, August 25, 2002.

Part Three

Lyndon B. Johnson Does Culture: The National Endowments for the Arts and the Humanities

Federal One hadn't even officially expired before advocates of government arts were drawing up new and better ways to bring artists under federal patronage. The upper-crust artist George Biddle, the Groton-Harvard friend of FDR who in 1933 had lobbied his classmate for aid to muralists, proposed in 1942 a Federal Bureau of Fine Arts.

Biddle's memorandum, which he drew up with the assistance of the National Resources Planning Board—that's the sort of title that strikes fear into the heart of any independent-minded artist; is Georgia O'Keefe a government "resource"?—proposed, in effect, the institutionalization of the New Deal arts projects under one cabinet-level secretary. The aristocratic Biddle took it upon himself to speak for the starving artists of America, saying that they "were the beneficiaries for a period of nine years of the most enlightened and democratic Federal art subsidy that the world has ever seen. At any cost, almost in blind faith, they would like to see such a program perpetuated."[1]

There was a war on in 1942, so the "any cost" rhetoric may have crossed the line into inappropriateness, but Biddle viewed the Federal Bureau of Fine Arts as a national imperative. It would do "the constructive planning which will gear the talent and scope of our 25,000 artists into the needs of 140,000,000 people."[2] This was a language perhaps more suited to certain warring nations across the Atlantic Ocean, but in the twentieth century American politicians became fond of applying the language of mobilization and war to policy initiatives in fields such as education, energy, and poverty relief.

Harper's magazine, after giving Biddle his say, excerpted responses from some of the art and museum world luminaries to whom Biddle had sent his memorandum. They were on the whole favorable, notes *Harper's*, but critics focused on three points: (1) the incompatibility of relief with art; (2) the fear of centralized cultural authority; and (3) the potential for politics to rear its artless head, especially in the selection of the department's secretary.

In the *Harper's* magazine symposium, Henry Allen Moe, Secretary-General of the Guggenheim Foundation, took aim at Biddle:

> I do not myself see that government has any more duty to "artists" than it has to plumbers when "artists" are reckoned in the thousands as was done by WPA and as George Biddle apparently proposes to reckon them. For the plain fact is that there never were five thousand artists (in the sense of original creators) in any one country at any time and there are not anything like that number in the United States now. Apart from a relief program, when the "artist" is entitled to the same help that a plumber needing help is entitled to, but no more. . . . helping artists as artists is justified only when it adds to the creative power and output of the United States. This, WPA never seemed to realize.[3]

Moe leaves himself wiggle room with that penultimate sentence, and so it comes as only a partial surprise that in 1965 he accepted the position of interim chairman of the new National Endowment for the Humanities. His criticisms of federal support of the arts were not from a libertarian or classical liberal direction, and certainly not from a populist angle, but rather from an elitist concern that such aid simply propagated mediocrity.

More forthrightly, the American Artists Professional League (AAPL) opposed a Bureau of the Fine Arts because it feared censorship and political favoritism: "Regardless of who will be President or which party may be in power," stated the AAPL, "such ventures can not escape the political driver in the back seat. . . . After the high and lofty preambles had been stripped from these proposals, there remained nothing but veiled plans for the regimentation of artists and especially all the pseudo artists."[4]

The AAPL declared: "We feel that the essential tendency of this Bill is toward regimentation of the profession under the probable dominance of groups which may be responsive to political control. This we feel would menace if not destroy the creative freedom of our professional artists, endanger their rights of free competition, individual liberty of action and self-initiative, and it would tend inevitably to impair the future achievement of art in America."[5]

The painter John Sloan, a leading light of the Ashcan School of art and former art editor of the socialist journal *The Masses*, made the same point more colorfully: "I am Irish, and so I am naturally 'agin the government.' In government can lurk the foes of all that is best in human life. I want to be able to differ with the government all along the line. I hate nearly everything else it does, its support of privilege, the wars it gets us into. Why shouldn't I hate it in my own line, my own calling. Having the government the advocate of the mediocre in art, the employer of art, would be a good thing. We would know where to locate the enemy."[6]

Though Sloan and the American Artists Professional League occupied different spots on the American political spectrum, they shared the strong suspicion that a central government agency in charge of the arts would inevitably side with a particular school or coterie of artists—and that those artists would be, in large part, conformist mediocrities who would not mind filling out paperwork, obeying guidelines, and permitting bureaucrats to serve as the arbiter of their work.

Biddle's proposal never graduated from the drawing board, but nor did the general idea ever really fade away. In the 1950s, the banner was carried by representatives of a New Jersey congressional district. The first, Rep. Charles Howell (D-NJ), a Trenton insurance broker, bemoaned that "The Federal Government has now been without a comprehensive art program for over 160 years."[7] Eakins, Ives, Twain, Irving, Homer, Hawthorne, Dickinson, Wood, Whistler, Sullivan, Wright. . . . who knows what these men and women might have accomplished if only a Charles Howell had been in previous Congresses to spur on the nation's artists? Indeed, the assumption that support for the arts was conterminous with support for *government* support of the arts was fast embedding itself in the debate.

But Howell was a dilettante when compared with his successor, Rep. Frank Thompson, also a Democrat and among the most determined advocates of a federal arts program the Congress has ever known. Thompson, who can reasonably claim partial paternity for the National Endowment for the Arts, deserves more than a footnote. He left as his legacy numerous paeans to Washington as Muse. "Thompy," as he was known, was dubbed by no less than the *New York Times* as "a liberal's liberal."[8]

Thompy was also a crook. He was nabbed in the FBI's controversial Abscam sting of 1979–80. He had accepted a briefcase packed with $45,000 presented to him by a phony Arab sheik in return for Rep. Thompson's promise to help the sheik obtain a gaming license.[9] Thompson served two years in federal prison. When released in 1985 he became, naturally, a Washington consultant. Which means he was still in the same racket, but this time it was all legal.

In the mid-1950s, Thompson's was the most clamant voice for an extensive federal role in the arts, and the reasons he adduces are not the ones that prop up most court histories of the NEA. He laid them out in a 1955 article that is worth quoting at length. Rep. Thompson got right to the point: "Making Washington the cultural center of the world would be one of the very best and most effective ways to answer the Russian lies and defeat their heavily financed effort to have Communism take over the world." This betrays an ignorance of the organic method by which most art is created, and it conjures images of writers, painters, songwriter, actors, and the like flocking to the nation's capital, where by some congressional snap of the fingers Art will be produced and then weaponized for delivery overseas.

In best "this shall not stand" declamation, Thompson huffed, "I, for one, do not propose to make it easy for the USSR to win the minds, the hearts and the loyalty of men and women throughout the world. I believe the time has come, and indeed is long overdue, for the United States of America to mount an important counteroffensive" against Russian cultural exports. Disarming ourselves in this international contest pitting ballerinas against Western novelists makes it "extremely easy" for the Soviets to convince the gullible masses of the world that "we are gum-chewing, insensitive, materialistic barbarians."

It is beyond rich to read this future denizen of the nation's prison system superciliously condemn gum chewers, but Thompson is on a mission. He calls for "the dynamic and liberal forces to rally around the effort to place our National Capital in the vanguard of our country's cultural and artistic development, in order that the healing influence of the fine arts may become both practical and effective."[10]

Even President Eisenhower, whose idea of cultural adventurism was a night spent in front of the TV with Mamie, concurred, said Thompson, who pointed to the President's call for a Federal Advisory Commission on the Arts within the Department of Health, Education, and Welfare. Eisenhower had given lip service to a federal role in the arts, saying in his 1955 State of the Union that "the

Federal government should do more to give official recognition to the importance of the arts and other cultural activities," but he was too cautious for the likes of Frank Thompson. Thompson was in no mood to listen to worrywarts fret about the threats to freedom of expression inherent in government arts policy. "Nor is it necessary to dig up the old clichés about 'mixing politics in art,'" he said. "Federal recognition is an absolute *must* in this matter, and the bills I have introduced provide the necessary safeguards, since all programs will be in the hands of experts and not politicians."[11]

Here we see, yet again, the boundless faith in experts, who are above petty concerns and are dedicated solely to truth, beauty, and light. Applauding Thompson's efforts was the historian-activist Arthur Schlesinger Jr., soon to be the house intellectual of the Kennedy administration. Unlike Thompson, Schlesinger understood that non-barbarians might object to a federal arts policy, but he viewed such a development as inevitable, given the expanded reach of the central state in modern times. And besides, "Congressmen have learned to defer to experts in other fields, and will learn to defer to experts in this." These experts would include "professional and creative artists" and "responsible executives." Schlesinger conceded that in the production of culture "the role of the state can at best be marginal."[12] Frank Thompson would have considered him a dour pessimist.

Frank Thompson's invocation of the global struggle against the Soviet Union was no anomaly. Historian Donna M. Binkiewicz notes that in the debate over the creation of the NEA in the 1960s, "many of the congressmen advocating the arts programs sandwiched their discussions of the arts between their introduction of other Cold War measures. Nearly half of all arts discussions [in Congress] preceded or followed discussion of such Cold War issues as military strength, funding for the war in Vietnam, or Soviet transgressions."[13] Republicans, especially those who were not ardent Cold Warriors, were skeptical of the Thompson line of argument. "We are dubious, to say the least, of the contention that people abroad are drawn more easily to Communism because we have failed to subsidize, or nationalize, the cultural arts in the United States," said Rep. Albert H. Bosch (R-NY) of Queens.[14]

Senator Herbert Lehman of Bosch's state disagreed. Looking out over the fruited plains in the 1950s, Senator Lehman, a Democrat, saw "an aesthetic Dust Bowl."[15] Presumably the motes in his eye and planks in his ear prevented him from seeing Saul Bellow or Ray Bradbury or Wallace Stegner, or hearing Elvis Presley or Chuck Berry or Meredith

Willson. Culture existed beyond the Hudson River, had Senator Lehman cared to notice.

Members of the country's largest association of orchestras produced a virtual wall of sound against the idea of federal subsidy. As William J. Baumol and William G. Bowen write, "a 1953 survey by the American Symphony Orchestra League (ASOL) showed that 99 percent of the members of orchestra governing boards were strongly opposed to federal aid."[16] The ASOL, as represented by executive secretary Helen M. Thompson, was a vocal critic of bringing its six hundred-plus member orchestras under the federal government's tent. In a 1954 congressional hearing, Helen Thompson asked, "Is it possible that the arts, the thousands of people contributing time and effort to them might become mere pawns in a centrally managed, nationalistic program whose control could be so buried in bureaucracy as to give little hint of its ultimate purpose?"[17] A shrewd question—though federal arts supporters dismissed such concerns as the blathering of right-wingers and paranoids. For surely the motives of the US government were benign, and no attempt would ever be made to manipulate artists for political ends. (The revelations of CIA misconduct and FBI spying on American cultural figures were a decade or more away.)

Typically, in 1950 the director of the University of Oklahoma School of Music, Paul S. Carpenter, remarked of the proposal to create a Department of Fine Arts: "Many of us are disturbed by this proposal. No one can be particularly happy while wearing bureaucratic shackles."[18]

Lending its voice to the chorus was *Musical America*, the venerable classical music publication, which editorialized in 1949 against government subsidy of the arts as a "dangerous expedient." *Musical America*'s concerns were several. Learning from the example of Federal One, with its pitched battles between Communist propagandists and anticommunist fanatics, it worried that the second act would be a heretic-burning episode in which "political witch-hunts" might be directed at orchestras or opera companies which received federal funds. The presence of a stray Communist in the woodwinds section might call down the wrath of demagogues on the entire enterprise.

But there was an economic concern as well. "Subsidy of any kind," lectured the editors, "implies that the people at large do not want music seriously enough to find a way to pay for it themselves." Just so—and in fact the advocates of federal aid to the arts often conceded as much. "But larger musical programs, such as those of symphony orchestras and opera companies, which operate on a wide base and attract audiences of thousands, should pay for themselves," according to *Musical America*, and in so doing "keep music free."[19] (Free, that is, from the interference of political apparatchiks.) A decade later, as the national endowments were taking shape, many within the symphony orchestra community had become enthusiastic about the idea, or at least reconciled to it—but there remained significant opposition to going on the federal dole.

In 1960, Americans supported, to varying degrees, "5,000 theater groups, 20,000 dramatic workshops, 700 opera groups, 200 dance companies, 1,200 symphony orchestras," and a robust book-selling and movie-going culture, all without the benefit of a national arts agency.[20]

In 1963–64, the period just before the emergence of the NEA, seventeen major orchestras received almost a million dollars ($966,000) from subfederal levels of government and another $90,000 from their local boards of education. William J. Baumol and William G. Bowen, authors of the most comprehensive survey of the economics of pre-NEA arts institutions, estimate that this constituted about half of all municipal assistance to performing arts organizations. And they point out that these raw numbers do not include nonmonetary gifts and favors, such as free or discounted fees for auditorium use or lighting.[21]

To the extent the federal government supported the arts, it was through a network of tax exemptions for nonprofit organizations such as museums and "comparatively generous deductions for benefactors" embedded in the tax code.[22] Unlike in France, for example, there was no tradition of royal patronage of the arts, and while the cult of celebrity had grown up around the medium of film, there remained a populist suspicion of intellectuals and high-brows and a disinclination to put them on the public payroll. Good art, it was widely thought, would sell; so would good books. Why subsidize painters or writers whom no one wanted to buy or read?

That question was pushed to the sides as the 1960s dawned. The New Frontier of President John F. Kennedy had a stylistic as well as a political component. Gone was the stodginess of the Eisenhowers, whose idea of high culture, or so the prejudice went, was an evening on the couch watching television. By contrast, the new President and First Lady courted artists and succeeded in coating the White House with a gloss of high culture. Robert Frost—a Grover Cleveland Democrat—had read a poem at the inaugural, cellist Pablo Casals broke a public silence by performing in the White House, composer Igor Stravinsky and French man of letters Andre Malraux were feted at presidential dinners—the contrast with the frumpy Eisenhower administration could not have been more stark. Or at least that was the company line. Kennedy sycophant Arthur Schlesinger Jr. burbled, "In the Executive Mansion, where Fred Waring and his Pennsylvanians once played, we now find Isaac Stern, Pablo Casals, Stravinsky and the Oxford Players. I think we will not leave it to the Soviet Union to discover the Van Cliburns of the future."[23] The oh so erudite Schlesinger gushed that Casals's appearance was "of obvious importance. . . . in transforming the world's impression of the United States as a nation of money-grubbing materialists."[24] After a party Mrs. Kennedy threw for her sister, Princess Lee Radziwill, White House press secretary Pierre Salinger boasted that "There was no twist danced that night." The dance crazes of teenagers and assorted lowest-common-denominator types were not for the beau monde in the White House![25] (Years later, stories of "Princess" Radziwill's affectations made her a figure of sport. For instance, she required her maid to drop a gardenia into the toilet after the Princess had used it.[26])

The novelist Gore Vidal, who shared a stepfather with Jackie Kennedy, said of the President, "He knows the propaganda value of artists and he has. . . . tried to win them over."[27]

Courtiers applauded the *belle époque* of the New Frontier. In his post-assassination hagiography, *A Thousand Days: John F. Kennedy in the White House*, Schlesinger wrote reverently that for John and Jackie, "art had become a normal dimension of existence." He added, "The art to which Kennedy responded most deeply and spontaneously, I think, was literature; but he had a growing interest in architecture, and he had acquired some knowledge of painting—he liked the impressionists, though he was baffled by nonobjective art—and sculpture." JFK's opinion of Abstract Expressionist CIA art was likely the same as that of Dwight Eisenhower, though by the early 1960s AE needed no artificial boost from Washington. "Serious music, it must be said, left him cold," admitted Schlesinger. "But even here he believed it important for the President of the United States to lend his prestige to distinction of creation and performance."[28] This is a curious conception of the presidency: lender of prestige—stamper of approval—to works of art. It simply would not have occurred to presidents of a century earlier—say, the Democrat James Buchanan and the Republican Abraham Lincoln—to endorse novelists, musicians, actors, or playwrights. This is not to say that presidents were indifferent to art or the difficulty artists had in making a living: Franklin Pierce, for one, assisted his friend Nathaniel Hawthorne in obtaining a government sinecure, as did Lincoln for his young admirer William Dean Howells. But the idea that the federal government ought to endorse *The Scarlet Letter* would never have occurred to Pierce. Such an act was so far beyond the bounds of constitutional acceptability as to be unthinkable.

But in 1961, the gloss of high culture was applied to the White House. In the telling of the White House publicists, the debonair young President and his aristocratic wife were elevating the nation's tastes. Beneath the veneer, John F. Kennedy was no more interested in the beaux arts than Ike had been. After sitting through a performance of the Bolshoi Ballet, our Casals-Stern-Stravinsky-loving president muttered, "I don't want my picture taken with all those Russian fairies."[29] When the real JFK runs smack into the myth, the myth always wins. Camelot endures.

In 1961, President Kennedy inserted Secretary of Labor Arthur Goldberg into a labor dispute between the Metropolitan Opera and the American Federation of Musicians. Goldberg's successful mediation of the dispute struck non-New Frontier observers as an overreach of federal power; where in the Constitution was the Secretary of Labor granted such authority? But Secretary Goldberg drew lessons from this episode that pointed toward the need for a more active federal role. "To free our art forms from destructive financial tests is to protect them from the tyranny of the majority," he declared. "If the arts are to flourish, they must be relieved of total dependence upon the market place."[30] The notion that the market, which may thought of as the sum total of the choices of all actors within a given economic sphere, is a *tyranny of the majority* suggests a curious attitude toward the "freedom" that was the usual mantra of government arts advocates.

Once again, those who favored a role for the federal government in the arts had revealed a Manhattan-centered worldview. The *New York Times* editorialized that "everything points to the fact that, if the United States is going to insist that the Metropolitan carry on as a cultural institution that the nation cannot afford to lose, it should provide the opera with a subsidy, with New York State and City sharing the financial responsibility." Just where this nationwide insistence that the Met "carry on" came from was a mystery: certainly the people of Alabama, Montana, Hawaii, and New Mexico demanded no such thing. But the federal government was entering new realms, much to the delight of the New York City cultural industry. As Gary O. Larson notes, Secretary Goldberg's mail ran heavily in favor of his intervention, with support from the likes of John D. Rockefeller III, the Motion Picture Association of America, and the American Federation of Musicians.

The opponents tended to be powerless people from the provinces—the sort who didn't count for much in the new world aborning. For instance, one Mae Gough of Paducah, Kentucky—who used irregular punctuation, Larson observes (John D. Rockefeller III would never misplace a comma)—asked, "Why should Americans who detest Opera and Symphonie be forced to pay taxes to support them. Is America free. If you and the Kennedy bunch like Opera, you support it. You can afford it with all the money in the world behind you."[31] Ms. Gough raises an excellent point, grammatical mistakes aside. Why should she and her neighbors in Paducah be forced to support the Metropolitan Opera, the New York Philharmonic, and other elite cultural organizations that had traditionally been subsidized by the likes of the Rockefellers and other fabulously wealthy families of the New York City metropolitan area?

Momentum for a federal arts agency was growing. Senators Claiborne Pell (D-RI), Jacob Javits (R-NY), Joseph Clark (D-PA), and Hubert Humphrey (D-MN) sponsored legislation to create a National Arts Foundation, which proposed to spawn a new arts bureaucracy and provide grants to approved artists. Senator Javits, impatient with the unlettered bumpkins of the hinterlands, explained, "We are the only major nation on earth whose government still does so little about the nation's cultural treasure in the performing and visual arts, and it is high time we caught up."[32] President Kennedy agreed. He assigned his press secretary Pierre Salinger and highbrow Arthur Schlesinger to formulate some plan for federal encouragement of the arts. The alliterative team of Salinger & Schlesinger recommended August Heckscher as the point man.

August Heckscher was very much in the mold of federal arts advocates. Not only was he a certified blueblood from the environs of New York City (Long Island), he was also a veteran of the US intelligence community, specifically the Office of Strategic Services. Heckscher's grandfather had been a financier and philanthropist. The grandson was educated at St. Paul's School, Yale, and Harvard. He was an editorial writer for the New York *Herald Tribune* and later the Parks Commissioner for New York Mayor John Lindsay, but his most lasting accomplishment was overseeing "The Arts and the National Government," his report for President Kennedy.[33]

Setting the table for an anticipated banquet of arts administrators, in March 1962 President Kennedy appointed August Heckscher as his Special Consultant on the Arts. This was a part-time position envisioned to last for a period of six months, during which time he was to survey the state of the arts in America, with an eye toward gauging the appropriate level of government involvement. Heckscher was not given license to propose any overarching Ministry of Culture-type plan. President Kennedy had told him, "Obviously government can at best play only a marginal role in our cultural affairs," and Arthur Schlesinger says that he, Heckscher, and Salinger concurred.[34] Yet Heckscher was capable of such flights of rhetoric as his announcement that "In place of the older objective of serving the public welfare, there has grown up the new and more delicate objective of serving what I have called the public happiness."[35]

Whose happiness? How is it defined? John F. Kennedy's idea of happiness was, it appears, in a different realm than the average Joe's. The codification of happiness, its legislative enactment and administration, was a challenge beyond what Washington was used to. But this was the age of the New Frontier; anything seemed possible.

The Heckscher Report, as it became known, was submitted to the President on May 28, 1963, and began by citing the increase in leisure and "free time" and "a recognition that life is more than the acquisition of material goods"—the latter would have surprised the Puritans, the Methodists, the Baptists, the Transcendentalists, and millions of other Americans of the past who did not devote their lives to the cartoonish acquisitiveness that modern arts advocates often attribute to our ancestors. With this apparent evolution of American consciousness came a "growing awareness" of the importance of the arts.[36] This was standard boilerplate. The report ventured close to megalomania when Heckscher, using the third person, spoke of his appointment as JFK's Special Consultant on the Art as "mark[ing] the beginning of a new phase in the history of art and government."[37]

Most of the report's recommendations were modest, even insipid. They had to do with such matters as government acquisition of art for public buildings (which should "increase substantially"); art exhibits in US embassies; improving the quality of government posters (who could object?); better public architecture; adjustments to federal tax policy regarding charitable contributions; copyright law; and the recognition of outstanding American artists with medals, awards, and the like. The report contained such sensible suggestions as giving weight to historic preservation in federal policies regarding "construction, highways, and community development."[38] In other words, think, or at least hesitate, before taking the wrecking ball to historic buildings in order to put up a new federal building or highway. (Yet the Heckscher

Report tiptoed around the question of urban renewal, which was then laying waste to huge swaths of American cities using federal dollars. Historic preservation is fine, it seems, but federal bureaucracies are equally deserving of respect.)

Given the world-historical importance of the Special Consultant position, the report urged its continuation as a full-time occupation. The Special Consultant would consult with a proposed new advisory council on the arts, which would "assure the active participation of the artistic community in the Government effort" to nurture the arts in America.

Heckscher ended his report with a bang, not a whimper. The "logical crowning step in a national cultural policy," he declared, would be the establishment of a National Arts Foundation, which would administer grants to arts institutions and to the state arts councils whose birth the foundation would midwife.

Not until the penultimate paragraph does the report deign to reply to those hidebound traditionalists and long-haired radicals who fear government interference in the arts:

> There will always remain those who feel that art and government should exist in different spheres, having nothing to do with each other. But in fact the Government of the United States comes up constantly against choices and decisions where esthetic considerations are involved. In today's world, moreover, artistic talent and creativity are resources vitally important to the Nation, and the well-being of the people is related to progress in the arts as surely as to progress in fields such as recreation and education where government's responsibility is full recognized.

That is not exactly a serious engagement with the arguments of one's opponents, but Heckscher & Co. had the momentum. The tenor of the times was in tune with arts foundation advocates. The report concluded: "Although government's role in the arts must always remain peripheral, with individual creativity and private support being central, that is no reason why the things which the Government can properly do in this field should not be done confidently and expertly."[39]

In his response to Heckscher's resignation as Special Consultant once his task had been completed, the President wrote that "Government can never take over the role of patronage and support filled by private individuals and groups in our society. But government surely has a significant part to play in helping establish the conditions under which art can flourish—in encouraging the arts as it encourages science and learning."[40] He then created, via executive order on June 12, 1963, the President's Advisory Council on the Arts, a body more symbolic than anything else. The Council's creation, according to the President's statement, marked "the first time the arts will have some formal Government body which will be specifically concerned with all aspects of the arts and to which the artist and the arts institutions can present their views and bring their problems."[41]

The painter Larry Rivers was one of many artists immune to the blandishments of the Kennedys and Schlesingers and Hecksсhers. Rivers cracked in 1961, "The government taking a role in art is like a gorilla threading a needle. It is at first cute, then clumsy, and most of all impossible."[42] Nor were those writers who were staking out new frontiers of their own enthusiastic about a federal arts bureaucracy. Lawrence Ferlinghetti, the poet-publisher whose City Lights imprint had issued many of the seminal works of the Beat Generation, including Allen Ginsberg's poem "Howl," which San Francisco authorities had tried to ban in 1957, was a persistent critic of government interference with literature and a mocker of those "cooperating poets and publishers" who sought federal support.[43] But the Beats did not have the ear of President Kennedy.

On October 26, 1963, a month before the murder of John F. Kennedy, the President spoke at Amherst College. "I see little of more importance to the future of our country and our civilization than full recognition of the place of the artist," said Kennedy. "If art is to nourish the roots of our culture, society must set the artist free to follow his vision wherever it takes him.... I look forward to an America which will reward achievement in the arts as we reward achievement in business or statecraft."[44] Achievement in business is generally rewarded within a market economy, of course, though corporate welfare and crony capitalism have a long and dishonorable history in our political economy. Kennedy did not specify whence the rewards to artists would issue, or if they were to be more psychic or remunerative, but he clearly envisaged a more prominent federal role in the arts.

Enter LBJ

Arts advocates wasted no time in capitalizing on President Kennedy's assassination. Arthur Schlesinger Jr., in a memo to President Johnson just days after the murder, wrote that a federal arts policy "can strengthen the connections between the administration and the intellectual and artistic community—something not to be dismissed when victory or defeat next fall will probably depend on who carries New York, Pennsylvania, California, Illinois and Michigan."[45] Mourning, it seems, was not to get in the way of down-and-dirty politics.[46] Schlesinger, anxious to curry favor with the new regime, understood his target well. President Johnson, whom the Kennedy coterie liked to mock as a coarse boor, took up the cause of subsidized culture.

The legislative momentum that would culminate in the creation of the National Endowment for the Arts in 1965 had begun during the Kennedy years. Livingston Biddle, cousin of George Biddle, who had persuaded FDR of the need for federal subsidy of American muralists, was among the forefathers of the endowment. Biddle was descended from Nicholas Biddle, who as president of the Second Bank of the United States was the arch-enemy of President Andrew Jackson. As Michael Macdonald Mooney wrote in his muckraking *The Ministry of Culture: Connections Among Art, Money and Politics*, "The Biddles of Philadelphia had proposed national banks in 1828, national railroads—from which the Main Line took its name—and national commissions of arts."[47] The Biddles were used to ordering about their inferiors, and they were not amused when refractory commoners, whether Andrew Jackson or Republican backbenchers in polyester suits, stood up to them.

The family's blood was the bluest of blues. Livingston had attended St. George's School in Newport, Rhode Island, and then Princeton, where a classmate was Claiborne Pell, the somewhat dotty aristocrat who later served six terms as US senator from Rhode Island. In 1962, Livingston Biddle, then a novelist, went to work for his old friend Senator Pell. The two would become the Lone Ranger and Tonto of the world of government-funded arts. (If the Lone Ranger and Tonto had been ethereal, rather fey upper-class WASPs, that is. Senator Pell was famously odd. His interest in the paranormal, his seeming disconnectedness from everyday life, his resemblance to B-movie horror icon Christopher Lee, and various personal eccentricities led John F. Kennedy to call him—with considerable inaccuracy—the least electable man in America.)[48]

Senator Pell and Livy, as he called his aide, promoted the concept of a National Arts Foundation from the freshman Senator's perch as chairman of the Subcommittee on the Arts of the Committee on Labor and Public Welfare. The senator held five days of hearings on the proposed arts foundation in October–November 1963. Among those testifying was George Biddle, then seventy-eight, who would soon see the realization of his dream of federally subsidized art. Other witnesses included Roger L. Stevens, the Broadway producer who would become LBJ's presidential arts advisor and chairman of the National Endowment for the Arts from 1965–69; John D. Rockefeller III, whose family labored and spent mightily to promote a federal role in supporting the arts and museums; and close to forty advocates of enabling legislation.

There was, however, one discordant note. Wheeler Williams, sculptor and president of the American Artists Professional League, testified on Halloween 1963. His words were more trick than treat for Senator Pell. After befuddling the Senator by mentioning that the two of them were "descended from the same Indian princess"—"I do not think she was a princess," replied Pell, perhaps knowing how little American voters cared for royalty—Williams pronounced himself opposed to the foundation because "the arts should not be supported by the government."

Williams took an especial scunner to modern art, which the federal government had been promoting for over a decade as a weapon in the Cold War. "Just when the bottom is dropping out of the market for the so-called modern art," he told the subcommittee, "confirmed by numerous reports from here and abroad, to have this art rubbish given a shot in the arm would be a blow to all our efforts to keep American art of coherent beauty, integrity, and craftsmanship alive."[49]

In his account of the hearing, Livingston Biddle depicts Williams as a bizarre zealot, fuming about communism and seeing reds under every bed. But there was a little more to him than that. Wheeler Williams, a Chicago native, studied at the Art Institute of Chicago and the Ecole des Beaux-Arts in Paris. He earned an undergraduate degree at Yale and a master's degree in architecture from Harvard. His sculptures and monuments grace American places from the Mission Avenue Bridge in Chicago to the Capitol in Washington, DC, whose Robert A. Taft statue he designed. Wheeler Williams was no philistine—nor was he the only artist who would be critical of the proposed national arts bureaucracy.

Williams was restating the fears of the National Sculpture Society (NSS), which a decade earlier had warned that a national bureau of the arts "would be the end of all freedom of expression and the biased and ruthless shackles of modern art would make conformity to that point of view absolute."[50] Williams was president of the NSS, the most prestigious organization of sculptors in America. (Its founding members included Augustus St. Gaudens and Stanford White.)

Since the 1950s, Williams had been outspoken in his opposition to a federal arts policy. He suspected that the realistic vein in which he worked, and which the NSS represented, would be shortchanged by a modernist-inflected federal bureau of the arts, but more than any perfervid antimodernism, Williams was motivated by an individualist ethos that he saw as grounded in the American Founding. As Williams told a congressional committee in 1957, "The true artist is perforce a rugged individualist and does not want to be kept poodle by the government with dilettante experts as nursemaids."

Adlai S. Hardin, also a president of the National Sculpture Society, told that same committee, "Individual initiative is what our pioneer forefathers had. It is one of the foundation stones on which the whole American philosophy of free enterprise is built. Individual initiative is at the very opposite end of the pole from government encouragement." Such encouragement, said Hardin, carried with it "supervision, direction, conformity, and the danger of subsidizing the support of mediocrity. This is not the American way."[51] Williams and Hardin were speaking the language of a pre-New Deal America. Their words struck a chord with those who harkened back to that earlier period, but to the opinion-molders and au courant journalists, they sounded terribly anachronistic. Their time, it seems, had passed.

When Senator Pell shepherded his legislation to create an arts foundation onto the Senate floor, Senator Strom Thurmond, the old South Carolina warhorse, was there to greet him with a question: "Under what provision of the Constitution does the senator from Rhode Island feel that the national government has jurisdiction to act in legislation of this kind?"[52] Senator Pell pointed to Article 1, Section 8 (which empowers the federal government to "promote the progress of science and useful arts, by securing for limited times to authors and inventors the exclusive right to their respective writings and discoveries") and the ever-useful, if extraordinarily ambiguous, phrase "promote the general welfare," which appears in the preamble to the Constitution.

Senator Thurmond was dubious. "It would require an imagination of truly artistic rather than legalistic talents to justify this measure under the general welfare clause, or under any other section of the Constitution," he said. "This is nothing but an outright subsidy to the arts, despite some attempts to label it as something else." Thurmond went on to examine the consequences of this departure from constitutional orthodoxy: "Although the amount of money involved is by some standards rather low, the principle of the subsidy is the same, and the dangers inherent in the program are many." A federal arts agency, he argued, "will eventually lead to sterility of thought and production.

Centralizing the power of subsidizing. . . . in. . . . a few chosen trustees and officers of the foundation can result in nothing but the stifling of the truly creative mind. . . . Our form of government does not contemplate, nor condone, dabbling in the arts."[53]

Senator Pell replied politely, as was his wont, that the presence of private citizens and artists on the various panels and review groups would keep his National Arts Foundation, as it was to be called, from becoming a repressive ministry of culture. He added that the "cultural renaissance" which the foundation might midwife would enhance "the prestige of our people throughout the world"—a nod to the cultural Cold War.[54] The foundation was approved by voice vote on December 20, 1963. It found tougher sledding in the House, despite its influential champion Rep. Frank Thompson Jr., chairman of the House of Representatives' Special Subcommittee on Labor, whose portfolio included the arts. The House companion bill stripped the proposal of its National Arts Foundation, which was to be a grant-making body, while retaining an advisory National Council on the Arts. It was badly watered down, though even in this form it was ridiculed by a minority report from House Republicans that called this denuded version "a classic example of. . . . the camel's nose under the tent routine." The GOP continued, "We can fully expect, if this bill is sanctioned, that the federal government, in the name of art and culture, will soon be called on to subsidize everything from belly dancing to the ballet, from Handel to the hootenanny, from Brahms to the Beatles, from symphonies to the striptease."

Livingston Biddle called this "absurd," an example of right-wing fearmongering, and yet looking back on half a century of arts subsidies, we can see that in fact NEA monies have gone to rock as well as symphonic and folk-music performers, and to those who dance (or even smear chocolate on themselves) in the nude as well as those who dance classical pieces.[55] The Republicans may have sounded like hyperbolic worry-warts, but what they predicted came to pass.

The measure passed the House in August 1964, but the differences between the House and Senate bills were so great, and the opposition in the House to the more comprehensive measure so spirited (if small in number), that the Senate simply accepted the House bill. Thus was born a National Council on the Arts—a very pale and wan imitation of the robust European cultural agencies which Senator Pell looked to with envy, but it was a start. Roger Stevens, in full Broadway showman mode, envisioned the National Council on the Arts drafting a "Magna Carta of the arts."[56] With an inaugural class of members including actress Elizabeth Ashley, choreographer Agnes deMille, and actor Gregory Peck, we may be grateful, if not surprised, that that never happened.

It was back to the drawing board, though the drawers now had at least an outline to work from. The goal remained the creation of a foundation, an endowment, a grant-making entity whose largesse would permit the arts to flourish in America in ways that they evidently had not during the previous 180 years of the republic.

In the meantime, the Rockefeller family, whose private patronage had been directed toward such elite cultural institutions as the Museum of Modern Art, the Metropolitan Museum of Art, and the Lincoln Center for the Performing Arts, lobbied strenuously for the public to share the burden of patronage. In March 1965, the Rockefeller Brothers Fund, under the direction of Nancy Hanks, the family factotum who would chair the NEA from 1969 to 1977, issued *The Performing Arts: Problems and Prospects.*

This report, which would have an influence all out of proportion to its literary worth—Stanley Kauffmann mocked its "platitude, pedestrian perception" of "a nation teeming with drama devotees, concert-goers, and ballet-lovers"[57]—surveyed the state of the arts in contemporary America and concluded that federal intervention (without censorship or political favoritism, of course) was necessary to a thriving culture. That this aid would be directed, in part, to institutions long dependent on the philanthropy of the Rockefeller family was obvious, though it would have been churlish in the extreme to wonder if this was a way of transferring the burden of such philanthropy from the wealthiest families, who were traditionally the financial bedrock of elite artistic institutions, to the taxpayer. The Museum of Modern Art, the Metropolitan Opera, and other citadels of elite culture had for years been underwritten by munificent arts patrons such as the Rockefellers; perhaps it was time for ordinary citizens to join them. As the critic Richard Kostelanetz wrote of the aftermath of the Rockefeller-sponsored studies, "Public funding of large arts institutions had taken private philanthropy off its increasingly expensive hook."[58]

The family had, from 1958 to 1961, produced a series of six Rockefeller Panel Reports on various aspects of US foreign and domestic policy, including education, the military, and social affairs. These reports, gathered between covers as *Prospect for America,* might be placed within the political tendency then known as Cold War liberalism: they envisioned an active and muscular US government at home and abroad.

Under the auspices of the Rockefeller Brothers Fund, a panel of thirty eminences in the arts was convened in the fall of 1963 to examine "the future development and support of the performing arts in the United States."[59] The panel heard from dozens of witnesses with ties to the arts over a series of five two-day hearings. It also conducted surveys of corporate leaders, invited comments by philanthropists and their beneficiaries, and commissioned shorter papers on the state of dance; Broadway and off-Broadway theater; choral, chamber, and symphonic music; opera; the economic plight of the composer and the playwright; the contributions of labor, the corporate world, and universities to the arts; and the history and prospects of government aid to the performing arts. The lead staffer was Nancy Hanks, who would become perhaps the shrewdest public arts advocate of her time. (Today the NEA and NEH are located within the Nancy Hanks Center, better known as the Old Post Office, in Washington, DC.)

As Stanley Kauffmann observed, the report is pregnant with platitudes, with stirring sentiments about the compatibility of democracy and excellence, and the artist's search for timeless truths. The late President Kennedy's words are invoked on multiple occasions. The necessity of filling leisure time with worthwhile and improving endeavors is emphasized. (That leisure time might be spent profitably, even improvingly, in such activities as fishing with one's son, playing sandlot baseball, snowshoeing, or organizing church bake sales is not acknowledged.) It asserts "the importance of the arts" as though anyone anywhere really disagrees. Of course music and painting and poetry and dance and theater are important to a people. The very statistics the panel cities—the existence, in the United States of 1963–64, of 1,401 symphony orchestras, 754 opera groups, 40,000 theatrical enterprises, and nearly 200 dance companies—suggest a healthy respect for the arts in American life.[60]

Despite an outwardly robust appearance, however, the panel warned the country that the performing arts "are in trouble."[61] You see, the majority of dance, opera, and theater companies, and symphony orchestras, were nonprofessional. For instance, 1,059 of those 1,401 symphony orchestras were community-based and with annual budgets of under $100,000. One might think that this is in the American tradition of voluntarism which was discerned and lauded in the 1830s by the French visitor Alexis de Tocqueville, but one would be mistaken. For it is with the professional that "the highest levels of creative output and quality rests."[62] Moreover, members of professional orchestras were poorly paid, and actors work sporadically, the panel pointed out. Broadway was under siege from the competition of mass media, especially television.

One danger, opined the panel, was "unplanned development."[63] Arts councils must cooperate better. New venues must be constructed. Arts organizations should seek their place in such collective charitable groups as the Community Chest or the United Way. The support of corporate executives must be solicited more skillfully. But these recommendations were ancillary to the centerpiece of *The Performing Arts: Problems and Prospects*: its lengthy chapter on "Government and the Arts."

Concerned and intelligent Americans, the panel advised, were mightily impressed by the practice in some European countries of subsidies to the arts from the central government. (Sweden, France, Italy, and Austria are mentioned; the Soviet Union is not.) In these Edens are "flourishing institutions in which artistic freedom, far from being threatened by the activity of the state, is actually enhanced." (Examples are not provided.) Acknowledging the "strong tradition of voluntary association" that pervades the United States, the panel nevertheless lectured that "we must come to grips with the question of the role of government in our cultural life." Indeed, the question was no longer "whether government should act" but *how* it should act. Just why the former question was now a closed matter was not explained.

While the straitened circumstances and privations suffered by artists and arts institutions had been highlighted earlier, the panel now shifted its focus a bit. "More and more voices," it claimed, "propose that the performing arts turn to government for aid," because "the arts should be made far more widely available to the many than it is possible to make them by private support alone."[64] The penurious oboist or character actor in New York City has given way to the bedraggled child in hardscrabble Arkansas who will only have the opportunity to hear a quality symphony if the government steps in.

The panel issues the expected disclaimer that "no form of government aid to the arts should vitiate private initiative, reduce private responsibility for direction, or hamper complete artistic freedom." Consistent with the country's federalist political arrangement, the panel recommends that city and county governments concern themselves with promoting the arts in schools and "assuring that adequate opportunities are available for. . . . citizens to enjoy the arts," as for instance by building theaters and concert halls. State governments should be responsible for sponsoring "touring activities" and encouraging cooperation between arts groups within the states; one recommended vehicle through which these can be achieved is the state arts agency, a pet project of Governor Nelson Rockefeller in New York. Finally, the federal government "has a vital function in setting a national tone of interest in and concern with the arts," according to the panel.[65]

If this last recommendation seems nebulous, the panel goes on to encourage direct financial support of the arts by Washington, DC. Amusingly, it argues that an arts organization's physical location "has little bearing on the scope of its artistic expression." For instance, though the Lincoln Center for the Performing Arts is in Manhattan, its productions are "of national significance." This seems a preemptive defense against the inevitable complaint, voiced so frequently against Federal One, that a vastly disproportionate amount of federal culture funding will go to New York City. Sure, says the panel, if federal monies were routed to the Lincoln Center "from Washington, its immediate destination would be local, but its ultimate effect would be to advance a national resource."[66] One wonders just how the authors of the report convinced panel members from such far-off burgs as Cleveland, Seattle, Atlanta, St. Louis, and Minneapolis—not a single one of the thirty panelists belonged to a small town or rural area—to sign off on such a claim. It was probably easier to gain the assent of panel members Frank Stanton, the CBS president who was on the board of directors of the Lincoln Center; Charles M. Spofford, chairman of the executive committee of the Lincoln Center; Devereaux C. Josephs, vice chairman of the board of the Lincoln Center; and John D. Rockefeller III, chairman of the board of the Lincoln Center. The idea that the Lincoln Center is somehow central to the flourishing of American arts recalls that old *New Yorker* cartoon in which the known world largely ends at the Hudson River and the rest of the continent is terra incognita.

The arts, concludes the Rockefeller panel, are not a "luxury for the few," though fifty years later, and despite a half century of federal involvement, the audience for, say, opera, is as stratified by class, income, and education as it ever was.[67]

Fortuitously or not, President Johnson proposed a National Foundation on the Arts and the Humanities on March 10, 1965, just two days after the release of the Rockefeller Brothers Fund report. (Two months earlier, in his State of the Union address, Johnson had indicated his support of an arts foundation, sans the humanities. How the humanities hitched a ride on this legislative rocket is a story for later in this section.)

Senator Pell and Rep. Thompson sponsored the administration's plan to create a National Foundation on the Arts and Humanities, though the hopper teemed with kindred proposals by numerous members. Their bill moved through both houses without significant roadblocks. This was the LBJ landslide Congress, and Democrats, who were more inclined to support federal aid to the arts and humanities, were ascendant. The Senate's Labor and Public Welfare Committee reported the bill, which passed the Senate by voice vote on May 10, 1965. Obstacles were more apparent, if easily surmountable, in the House. The House Education and Labor Committee reported its bill on July 14. Seven of the committee's ten Republicans signed a minority report calling the measure "a long step in the wrong direction" and warning of "attempts at political control of culture." The bill, they said, established a "formidable bureaucratic framework" which was "only a portent of the more lavish expenditures of federal funds" in the future. The House Republican Policy Committee added that the arts and humanities were in robust shape just "so long as the deadening hand of the federal bureaucracy is kept from the palette, the chisel and the pen."[68]

The irrepressible skinflint H. R. Gross (R-IA) offered amendments on the House floor that would have added belly dancing, baseball, football, golf, tennis, squash, pinochle, and poker to those activities eligible for NEA subsidy. He also proposed an amendment to define "dance" as "including but not limited to the irregular jactitations and/or rhythmic contractions and coordinated relaxations of the serrate, obliques, and abdominis recti group of muscles—accompanied by rotary undulations, tilts, and turns timed with and attuned to the titillating and blended tones of synchronous woodwinds"—in other words, belly dancing.[69] Gross's mischievous amendments were dismissed by voice vote.

Other critics were just as harsh, if not as waggish. Rep. William S. Broomfield (R-MI) said that there "could be no more painful death to truly creative art in the United States, no surer punishment for the great artists in our country for daring to be different, than passage into law" of the Johnson proposal. Paul Findley (R-IL) pointed out that "the greatest periods in American literature" were those "when not one penny of either state or federal money was spent to support the arts."

Democrats lined up behind the bill, though not unanimously. Oregon's Robert B. Duncan said that it would "force the follower of [*Gunsmoke*'s] Matt Dillon to support the creative efforts in an off-Broadway avant-garde theater he will not only not visit, but does not want to." This was the voice of the old populism speaking, but it was wildly out of fashion during the suave New Frontier. After all, the cachet and glamour was on the side of those who attached themselves to the arts. President Kennedy may have privately sneered at the dancers in the Bolshoi Ballet as "fairies," but pretending to like the ballet was more conducive to status than was referencing Matt Dillon and *Gunsmoke*. Democrats like Robert B. Duncan were in the wrong place at the wrong time.

More representative of his party was Rep. Frank Thompson Jr. (D-NJ), the acknowledged House father of the arts and humanities endowments, who mourned that "we are the last civilized nation on the earth to recognize that the arts and the humanities have a place in our national life."[70] The House agreed. On September 15 it rejected a Republican effort to recommit the bill by a vote of 251–128 and approved the measure.

Amid much fanfare, President Lyndon B. Johnson signed into law the National Foundation on the Arts and Humanities Act on September 29, 1965. Its Declaration of Findings and Purposes announced, as if anyone disagreed, that "The arts and the humanities belong to all the people of the United States." It made a very brief genuflection to the experience of 180 years of non-government-funded art in the United States before disposing of any constitutionalist concerns: "The encouragement and support of national progress and scholarship in the humanities and the arts, while primarily a matter for private and local initiative, are also appropriate matters of concern to the Federal Government."

The language of the New Frontier, with its mixture of Cold War burden-bearing and optimistic American resolve, was central to the enterprise: "The world leadership which has come to the United States cannot rest solely on superior power, wealth, and technology, but must be solidly founded on worldwide respect and admiration for the Nation's high qualities as a leader in the realm of ideas and of the spirit."

The act authorized the appropriation of $5 million for the National Endowment for the Arts (and the same amount for the National Endowment for the Humanities) in fiscal years 1966, 1967, and 1968. Those states and territories with arts agencies were to receive annual matching grants of $50,000, with the implied promise of greater riches down the road. This proved to be an effective incentive.

The "arts" it defined with a broad brush to include, though not be limited to, "music (instrumental and vocal), dance, drama, folk art, creative writing, architecture and allied fields, painting, sculpture, photography, graphic and craft arts, industrial design, costume and fashion design, motion pictures, television, radio, tape and sound recording, and the arts related to the presentation, performance, execution, and exhibition of such major art forms."[71] This list was not quite H. L. Grossian in its scope—poker and baseball were out, though belly-dancing might well be in—but no one could accuse it of narrowly defining its subject.

When signing the bill into law, President Johnson, stepping heavily among the platitudes, opined that "Art is a nation's most precious heritage. For it is in our works of art that we reveal to ourselves, and to others, the inner vision which guides us as a Nation. And where there is no vision, the people perish."[72] It is probably churlish to point out that at that very moment, the President's "vision" was consigning hundreds of thousands, even millions, of people to perish in a war on the other side of the globe. But then the Cold War, of which Vietnam was a sideshow, had been since the late 1940s a bulwark of the pro-federal arts policy argument.

Following closely on the heels of *The Performing Arts: Problems and Prospects*, and the subsequent birth of the NEA, came an influential study by two economists, William J. Baumol and William G. Bowen, entitled *Performing Arts—The Economic Dilemma*, published in 1966. In this thorough economic analysis of the performing arts (with an interesting dollop of history thrown in) Baumol and Bowen assessed "the chronic financial problems of the arts."[73] While the condition of the arts in America in the early 1960s was neither that of a "great cultural renaissance nor. . . . an artistic wilderness," the authors analyzed the "income gap" between income and revenue for the performing arts and concluded that only the popular theater on Broadway even came close to being self-sustaining.[74] If opera, drama, dance, and the less commercial theater were to stay out of the quicksand of red ink, they would need significant boosts in funding, whether from private sources, public sources, or both. Fortunately, "the minority of the public that is interested in the arts is endowed with a disproportionate share of the nation's social, economic and political power." This boded well for government support of the arts, argued the authors. After all, "few legislative programs have been developed and passed in response to a clarion call by an aroused and indignant public." Rather, laws are, for the most part, the product of influential leaders who "take the initiative. . . . to undertake appropriate programs well before their necessity has become patent to everyone."[75] This was music to the ears of those who advocated a more vigorous federal role in the arts.

August Heckscher, who as director of the Twentieth Century Fund oversaw the Baumol-Bowen study, welcomed in the book's foreword what he termed its "disconcerting" message that the performing arts (theater, opera, music, and drama) would be increasingly unable to pay for themselves in the coming years. The solution to this widening chasm between income and revenue, suggested Hecksher, was "a considerably larger contribution by government." It is casting no aspersions on their work to note, as Heckscher proudly did, that professors Baumol and Bowen had been consultants to the Rockefeller Brothers Fund report, and that the Twentieth Century Fund, in preparing the Baumol-Bowen work, had been "given much help" by the Special Studies Project of the Rockefeller Brothers Fund and by its executive secretary, Nancy Hanks.[76]

Any redirection of taxpayer monies toward the performing arts would be, in effect, a regressive tax benefitting the wealthier among our citizens. As Baumol and Bowen found, "despite the allegation of increasing grass roots interest in the arts and the optimist view that audiences include a wide range of social groups. . . . the typical audience at professional performances is drawn from an extremely narrow segment of the population—a group characterized by unusually high levels of education and income." This was true of audiences both within and without New York City. In fact, the authors marveled at the "remarkable consistency of the composition of the audiences from art form to art form, from city to city and from one performance to another."[77]

Not that there's anything wrong with that. The audience for dance or opera is under no more obligation to represent an exact microcosm of America than is the audience for, say, midget car racing, Gospel rap, or televised shows about fishing. But no one advocates federal subsidy of midget car races, Gospel rap, or televised shows about fishing. Their aficionados lack the clout within corridors of power that those who appreciate dance and opera have. That their demographic profile is also poorer and less educated than the profile of those who succeed in having the federal government lend financial support to their chosen entertainments suggests that the rich do indeed get richer, or at least they haven't any compunction about taxing their countrymen to feather their own cultural nests.

As Baumol and Bowen note, even giving tickets away does little to attract "blue-collar workers" to the performing arts examined in their study.[78] People have different tastes, and those tastes are often the result of the milieu in which they have developed. Short of force-feeding them performances of the high arts—perhaps à la *Clockwork Orange*, with eyes taped open to prevent any averting of gaze—there is no obvious way to alter popular tastes. And even if there were, why should this be a function of the federal government? The Baumol-Bowen study made clear that a federal arts agency would, almost inevitably, constitute a federal subsidy to the wealthiest Americans. If this was at odds with the professed philosophy of President Johnson's Great Society, the President seemed not to notice.

LBJ's Garden Party

The NEA and NEH were not the only prong of President Johnson's strategy to court intellectuals—but they were far more successful than his disastrous Garden Party of June 1965. The man who took the blame for this fiasco was Eric F. Goldman, a Princeton University historian who served as a Special Consultant to President Johnson from December 1963 to September 1966. Goldman's task: to serve as LBJ's liaison to the intellectuals, whose more pliable and starstruck personages had been mesmerized into courtiers by John F. Kennedy, but who had nothing but haughty disdain for the uncouth Texan who succeeded the martyred president. Goldman's own mini-tragedy, the White House Festival of the Arts, was an attempt to co-opt artists and intellectuals for LBJ.

As Goldman recounts in *The Tragedy of Lyndon B. Johnson* (1969), the germ of the idea that became the disastrous festival originated with Bess Abell, the White House Social Secretary. With an eye to the Kennedy administration's success in attracting the glitterati of the artistic world, she thought, couldn't President Johnson do something to celebrate, and thereby lure in, those same people? Professor Goldman denies any suggestion that the festival had so crass an intention. Rather, he writes, "I was more interested than ever in having the White House throw its prestige behind the recognition and encouragement of an elite of talent in the United States."[79] Just how the imprimatur of the incult Lyndon Baines Johnson would encourage achievement in the arts and humanities was a question left unexplored.

The seed, once planted, took root and grew into the White House Festival of the Arts, which historians John Rodden and John Rossi call the "sole major example in modern America of a joint cooperative venture in the arts between the federal government and the intellectual elite."[80] In his possibly self-serving account, Goldman stresses his above-the-fray loftiness, while noting the unintellectual Mrs. Abell's concern that "Writers and artists: These people can be troublesome."

He further indicts Mrs. Abell as a turf-guarding airhead who had never heard of some of the most prominent festival invitees and whose primary concern was whether or not a fellow was a "good Democrat."[81] She reportedly objected to playwright Arthur Miller's presence because she believed him to have had past Communist ties. (Mrs. Abell was perhaps not quite so unsophisticated as Goldman makes her out to be. Her father, Earle Clements, was a former governor and US senator from Kentucky. She began as a typist in the speechwriting department of Johnson's vice presidential campaign in 1960 and, through charm and Democratic Party connections, moved into the hapless job of LBJ's social secretary.[82])

The festival was organized hastily. Goldman sent a memo to the President proposing the event on February 25, 1965, and it was carried off less than four months later, on June 14, 1965. The plan called for invitees from the worlds of arts, letters, the arts bureaucracy, and "the heads of representative local symphony associations, art societies, museum boards, etc."[83] The National Council on the Arts was to occupy a central place.

LBJ responded with moderate enthusiasm; he had "no great personal taste for the arts," but he had no objection to attractive photo opportunities.[84] He was less than thrilled to have his turf invaded by the eggheads he disparagingly referred to as "the Harvards." But Lady Bird Johnson, the First Lady, was positively excited.

Seven arts were to be celebrated at the White House fete: painting, sculpture, literature, music, dance, photography, and that most exportable of American art forms, cinema. Though Goldman was careful to say that the White House was not singling out particular artists for official commendation, he did consult "experts and critics" in assembling the works to be exhibited and performed. Goldman expressed astonishment that the establishment experts he consulted exhibited "remarkable agreement" in their tastes and preferences, though another observer might conclude that this is evidence of the pack mentality of much of the critical herd.

From the start, the more individualistic and nonconformist artists promised trouble. The distinguished literary critic Edmund Wilson, who had just two years earlier published a rousing polemic against *The Cold War and the Income Tax*, "declined with a brusqueness that I never experienced before or after in the case of an invitation in the name of the President and First Lady,"[85] noted Goldman, although perhaps he should have read Mr. Wilson's works before inviting him to an event that smacked of state-sponsored art. E.B. White, the essayist, turned Goldman down, too, though he did so gently, protesting that he was no good at public readings.

There were artists who coveted the invitation, however, perhaps as an ego-affirming act. And there was a mad scramble for the limited number of places at the ball among wealthy patrons of the arts, arts administrators, and those who seek the reflected glory of artists. Corporate executives, high-profile philanthropists, and chronic scene-makers lobbied furiously for seats at the king's table.

In the weeks between Goldman's proposal and the festival, the Johnson administration began a major bombing campaign in Vietnam and intervened militarily in the Dominican Republic. The Great Society President was turning his attention from butter to guns.

The poet Robert Lowell, descendant of Boston Brahmins, sent the President an open letter, care of Eric Goldman, that would serve as the first stick of dynamite in the blowing up of LBJ's bridge to the intellectuals. Published in the *New York Times* of June 3, 1965, it read:

> Dear Mr. President:
>
> When I was telephoned last week and asked to read at the White House Festival of the Arts on June fourteenth, I am afraid I accepted somewhat rapidly and greedily. I thought of such an occasion as a purely artistic flourish, even though every serious artist knows that he cannot enjoy public celebration without making subtle public commitments. After a week's wondering, I have decided that I am conscience-bound to refuse your courteous invitation. I do so now in a public letter because my acceptance has been announced in the newspapers, and because of the strangeness of the Administration's recent actions.
>
> Although I am very enthusiastic about most of your domestic legislation and intentions, I nevertheless can only follow our present foreign policy with the greatest dismay and distrust. What we will do and what we ought to do as a sovereign nation facing other sovereign nations seem now to hang in the balance between the better and the worse possibilities. We are in danger of imperceptibly becoming an explosive and suddenly chauvinistic nation, and may even be drifting on our way to the last nuclear ruin. I know it is hard for the responsible man to act; it is also painful for the private and irresolute man to dare criticism. At this anguished, delicate and perhaps determining moment, I feel I am serving you and our country best by not taking part in the White House Festival of the Arts.
>
> Respectfully yours,
> Robert Lowell[86]

Goldman should have known better than to have invited headstrong poets to the festival. Robert Lowell was a Mayflower descendant, a conscientious objector during the Second World War, and an occasional resident of psychiatric hospitals. He was opinionated, principled, and tactless—just the sort of man one should never invite to a solemn affair of state. Better to limit the invitations to artists and intellectuals who are complacent and self-satisfied, or eager to curry favor with the authorities.

As he recounts, on seeing the prepublication letter Goldman telephoned Lowell to ask him to withdraw the letter. It had not yet been made public; perhaps, suggested Goldman, the poet could just quietly back out of the affair, without any public protest. Besides, the President in this instance was acting as the ceremonial embodiment of the American state. A festival celebrating the accomplishment of American artists and intellectuals was, he asserted somewhat implausibly, wholly nonpolitical, and thus an inappropriate venue for political protest.

Lowell was having nothing of it. He objected strongly to the President's interventionist foreign policy, and he believed his presence, and that of the other artists, would imply their approval of policies they found noxious. Then he told Goldman, to the professor's horror, that the letter had already been sent to the *New York Times*. This news sent Goldman running for the smelling salts. LBJ, he knew, would be absolutely furious. Any chance Goldman had of becoming the Arthur Schlesinger of the new administration would go up in smoke. The President would take this as a personal insult, and the fact that it came from one with a New England lineage would intensify the sting. There was an unmistakable dollop of snobbery in the East Coast dismissal of Johnson, and he was keenly aware of the fact.

With a trepidation so acute that one cannot help feeling for him, Eric Goldman forwarded Lowell's letter to the President, along with a proposed conciliatory response. Lyndon B. Johnson was not of conciliatory disposition in this matter, however. He reacted as Goldman feared he would: suffice to say that the conciliatory letter to Lowell was never sent. The *New York Times* ran with the story on Page One. Eric Goldman entered a doghouse he would escape only when he resigned the following year.

Two friends of Lowell, Robert B. Silvers of the *New York Review of Books* and poet Stanley J. Kunitz, solicited signatures for a telegram supporting Lowell's decision. It would be sent to the President, though of course the intended audience was the community (if such a thing can be said to exist) of intellectuals. The telegram declared, "We hope that people in this and other countries will not conclude that a White House arts program testifies to approval of Administration policy by the members of the artistic community." The twenty signers, heavily concentrated in the cliquish world of New York City letters, included authors Hannah Arendt, John Berryman, Jules Feiffer, Lillian Hellman, Alfred Kazin, Dwight Macdonald, Bernard Malamud, Mary McCarthy, Philip Roth, Louis Simpson, William Styron, Peter Taylor, and Robert Penn Warren, and the painters Larry Rivers and Mark Rothko.[87] (Rivers, you will recall, was a sharp critic of publicly subsidized art.)

Goldman noticed, to his dismay, that three of the signers—Macdonald, Rivers, and Rothko—were on the invitation list for the festival. None of them was disinvited, but the President was by now raging at what he imagined to be a phalanx of anti-LBJ artists threatening to skip the festival. Johnson, in the phrase of Eugene McCarthy, the man whose insurgent campaign would drive him from the 1968 race, "personalized" the presidency. He did not see himself foremost as a citizen fulfilling a constitutional duty but rather as an ego-driven man expanding, to the maximum extent possible, the powers of the office into what some called a strong presidency and others an imperial presidency. With reference to that handful of writers and artists who displayed *lese majesty* when invited to the White House, LBJ raged, "Some of them insult me by staying away and some of them insult me by coming." The state, c'est moi. "Don't they know I'm the only President they've got and a war is on?"

The President fumed at the ingratitude on display. As Goldman writes, "For years the intellectuals and artists had been saying that government should encourage and support their work without imposing restrictions on what they did or said. Well, a President had now pushed legislation through Congress to encourage and support them without restrictions, and was about to stage a festival to honor them without policy tests"—and *this* was the thanks he got?!

In all, 102 "writers, artists, and critics" received invitations to the White House Festival of the Arts. Eighteen declined, though only four of them cited Lowellian reasons for their declination. Among those accepting the invitation were writers Saul Bellow and John Hersey.[88] Hersey was yet another headache for the Johnsonites. He was one of five authors asked to read from their works. He announced his plan to read from his nonfiction work *Hiroshima* graphic passages about the mass death and grotesque scenes in the aftermath of the bombing of that Japanese city.

Goldman was summoned to a meeting with Lady Bird Johnson, Bess Abell, and others. Mrs. Johnson spoke bluntly: "The President is being criticized as a bloody warmonger. He can't have writers coming here and denouncing him, in his own house, as a man who wants to use nuclear bombs." Piped in Mrs. Abell, "What right does some writer have to tell the President to come and listen to him so that he can make headlines denouncing the President's foreign policy?" Goldman responded that the President was not even scheduled to be present at the readings, and in any event, he might gain stature in the eyes of the invitees and the wider world if he engaged his critics.

"The President and I do not want this man to come here and read this," declared Mrs. Johnson.[89] Goldman's remonstrances, his protests that disinviting Hersey would make the President look small and the festival look like what its critics said it was—a propaganda party of subservient artists—fell on deaf ears.

As there was no apparent way to tell Hersey not to read from *Hiroshima* without inviting an avalanche of criticism, the author was left free to speak his mind. But he sure as hell would not do it on national television; LBJ made sure of that. The President ordered that "the festival was to be blacked out." Cameras, reporters, and other links to the outside world were banned. He also ordered that several "last-minute invitations" be rescinded after a hasty FBI investigation of the political beliefs of those invitees indicated that they might be anti-LBJ. (As a compromise, the telegrams inviting them went out just before the event, leaving them not enough time to respond or make arrangements for attending.)

When Mrs. Abell and other Johnson loyalists heard the chair of the festival, Mark Van Doren, rehearse his opening remarks the day before the event, they threw yet another fit. Van Doren spoke mostly of Robert Lowell, and while not endorsing his stand, he expressed respect for it. Just as importantly, he "included no word of appreciation for the sponsorship of it by the President and the First Lady."[90] Again, the ingratitude! A no-doubt harried Eric Goldman met with Van Doren and convinced him to thank the First Couple and shorten his remarks about Lowell. All this, remember, in what Americans were being told was a thoroughly nonpolitical affair that was in no way intended to reflect glory on the Johnson administration.

The festival was held on sunny a day that was, for the White House, dour and gloomy. The White House and its grounds were filled with paintings, sculpture, and all manner of artwork from American artists. Lady Bird Johnson greeted the attendees; following her welcome the readers took the podium. John Hersey not only read from *Hiroshima* but also prefaced his reading with a statement that included this passage: "We cannot for a moment forget the truly terminal dangers, in these times, of miscalculation, of arrogance, of accident, of reliance not on moral strength but on mere military power. Wars have a way of getting out of hand."[91] Lady Bird Johnson conspicuously failed to applaud. The President was not yet in attendance.

The afternoon featured a selection of musical pieces by American singers, composers, and orchestras, as well as pieces from American dramas (including Arthur Miller's *Death of a Salesman*, despite Mrs. Abell's concerns).

Much to the vexation of Goldman and the Johnsons, Dwight Macdonald showed up—"wearing a rumpled suit, white shirt *sans* tie, and tennis shoes"—and solicited invitees to sign a petition supporting Robert Lowell and stating that his (and others') attendance should not be interpreted as an expression of support for LBJ's foreign policy.[92] Macdonald, whose journalistic affiliations had ranged from *Fortune* to the anarchist monthly *politics* to *The New Yorker* to *Esquire*, had gone through various ideological phases, notably as a Trotskyite and an anarcho-pacifist, and he was ever the gadfly. He had an independent cast of mind and was perhaps the last person one would invite to a stuffy event aimed at uniting the political and intellectual establishments. Rodden and Rossi write, "as practically all of cultural New York had known for decades, Macdonald was invariably a loose cannon prone to firing off in all directions."[93]

Macdonald's petition read: "We should like to make it clear that in accepting the President's kind invitation to attend the White House Arts Festival, we do not mean either to repudiate the courageous position taken by Robert Lowell, or to endorse the Administration's foreign policy. We quite share Mr. Lowell's dismay at our country's recent actions in Vietnam and the Dominican Republic."[94]

Macdonald buttonholed about fifty people at the festival but succeeded in getting only eight signatures, including his own. The most notable name on the petition was that of Willem de Kooning, the painter whose work had been promoted with such energy by the federal government less than a generation earlier. Macdonald was upbraided by several of the attendees, among them the novelists Ralph Ellison, who decried the petition as "arrogant," and Saul Bellow. He got into a "shouting match" with Charlton Heston; he annoyed the hell out of the organizers; and his day at the White House did not pass unnoticed by the First Family. Lady Bird Johnson, noting the paltry results of Macdonald's impromptu petition drive, joked, "I'll take a 397 to 7 majority any time."[95] The President, for his part, did show up, rather slyly accompanied by Senator William Fulbright (D-AK), a Vietnam skeptic and confirmed intellectual. He shook a few hands, made a few somewhat sour remarks, and left.

The festival had featured superb or at least notable musicians, dramatists, writers, and artists, but as a coup for Lyndon B. Johnson it was an utter failure. Eric Goldman concluded, "I had seen a President acting with arrogant know-nothingism, and influential figures in the cultural world reacting with an equally arrogant know-it-allness."[96] For Goldman, with his aspirations to Schlesingerhood, the event was a resounding failure. He was "irreparably damaged" by the festival, note Rodden and Rossi, and was blamed by Lady Bird for exposing her husband to humiliation.[97] Still, he stuck around for more than a year before resigning. Dreams of political influence die hard, and he who is hopelessly out of favor with the powers-that-be is sometimes the last to know.

This attempt, at least, to co-opt intellectuals by dispensing favors from the federal government had failed. But then the National Endowment for the Arts was just gearing up. . . .

Up and Running

Roger L. Stevens, the first chairman of the arts endowment, shared the Social Register background of the arts advocacy community—he was a product of The Choate School—but he was hardly the sensitive, poetic, soulful stereotype of an artist. When he died in 1998, the *New York Times* eulogized him as a "real estate magnate, legendary Broadway producer and bravura fund-raiser" whose prodigious shaking of the money tree raised the lion's share of the $30.6 million in private financing that went toward the construction of the $77.9 million Kennedy Center.[98] But that wasn't Mr. Stevens's most impressive act of financing; in 1951, he helmed a syndicate of investors that bought the Empire State Building. (The Empire State Building, like the Kennedy Center, was often panned by architecture critics, but then Mr. Stevens was no stranger to bad reviews.)

Roger Stevens, as a Broadway impresario, was an interesting choice as chairman. Broadway and off-Broadway productions are the "main for-profit enclave" in the theater world, as Stefan Toepler and Annette Zimmer note in their survey of the nonprofit arts sector in the United

States and Germany.[99] In the most recent data from the US Bureau of the Census, annual attendance at Broadway shows was 12.2 million, compared to 30 million at nonprofit professional theaters.[100]

The NEA's first grant, in December 1965, in the amount of $100,000, went to the American Ballet Theatre of, naturally, New York City.[101] (The ABT has long been a favorite charity of the Rockefeller family.) As Mark Bauerlein observes in his authorized history of the endowment, the first congressional scrutiny of NEA grants, which was undertaken in 1968, produced no raging controversies but it did reveal certain agency biases.

For one thing, traditional artists complained that the NEA favored the trendy. "Under the protection of the Federal [authority]," worried Michael Werboff, a well-known portraitist whose subjects ranged from Indira Gandhi to Senators Claiborne Pell and Barry Goldwater, "there is nothing to which the traditional artist can appeal for defense of their rights as contemporary American artists. . . . It puts the traditional American artist into the hands of their worst enemy." Rep. John Ashbrook, the conservative Ohio Republican, envisioned an endowment that might "reward the avant-garde artists and discourage the traditional artists."[102] For his part, Werboff's portrait subject, Senator Goldwater, predicted that "the Federal Government eventually will do more harm in this field than good by overregulating it, overcontrolling it."[103] (The Russian-born Werboff took his liberty seriously. In the 1970s, he took a break from painting the rich and famous to do meticulously researched portraits of each of the fifty-six signers of the Declaration of Independence.)[104]

The harshest criticism leveled at the NEA during that 1968 survey was for its partnership with the Rockefeller Foundation and other private organizations in the Theatre Development Fund, which assisted Broadway shows that might not find an audience by, among other things, subsidizing ticket sales. This was about as blatant a giveaway to the theater industry as could be imagined, and the fact that the NEA chieftain was a former Broadway producer did not go unremarked. When the NEA was reauthorized by Congress in 1968, House Republicans voted by a margin of 2–1 to kill the endowment, which still bore the scent of its begetter, Lyndon B. Johnson.

Hanks for the Memories

Roger Stevens was succeeded by Nixon appointee Nancy Hanks, who shared her name with Abraham Lincoln's mother, a distant relation, and had long been a loyal retainer of a rather wealthier Republican: Nelson

Rockefeller. Hanks, a Duke graduate and daughter of a corporate lawyer, arrived in Washington in 1951. As the Truman administration gave way to the Eisenhower administration, she joined Nelson Rockefeller as secretary to the President's Advisory Committee on Government Operations, which Rockefeller chaired. When the future New York Governor and Vice President took the position of undersecretary of the Department of Health, Education, and Welfare in the Eisenhower administration, Nancy Hanks moved with him. She remained within his orbit for most of her professional life.

When Rockefeller, in his role as president of the Rockefeller Brothers Fund, initiated a Special Studies Project in 1956, Nancy Hanks left Washington for New York to serve as the fund's executive secretary. The first major undertaking of the Special Studies Project was a grandiose attempt to define a national policy for the United States during the not-so-quiescent late 1950s. Its focus was on foreign policy and defense; it advocated a significant military buildup. Thus Nancy Hanks, as seems de rigueur for arts administrators, did time in the somewhat murky semiunderworld of Rockefeller-connected Cold War politics.

Emerging from that milieu, she would remain with the Rockefeller Brothers Fund for thirteen years. In her capacity as executive secretary she oversaw the production of the Rockefeller Brothers Fund's enormously influential 1965 report *The Performing Arts: Problems and Prospects.* Hanks was phenomenally well connected in the worlds of art and philanthropy, and in 1968 was elected president of the Associated Councils on the Arts (ACA), an organization consisting of the recently created state and local arts councils. When the new President Nixon was casting about for a successor to Roger Stevens, the Republican—but not very partisan Republican—Hanks was the ideal candidate.

Nancy Hanks, who served as NEA chairwoman from October 1969 until October 1977, was the savviest operator in the agency's history. During her tenure, the NEA's budget increased by 1,200 percent and its staff by 600 percent.[105] The endowment's $7.8 million budget in FY 1969 had ballooned to $124 million by FY 1978—an astonishing expansion, especially given the austerity in vogue in the mid-1970s.

Chairwoman Hanks, under the belief that "there was only so much money in the federal till for culture, and that if the Arts were free of the inhibiting presence of the Humanities then it would inherit the larger share," in the trenchant observation of former NEH chairman Ronald S. Berman, "made repeated attempts to sever [the NEA's] connection with the hapless Humanities Endowment."

From a turf-protecting point of view, Hanks was right, concedes Berman. The NEA "had very quickly become the congressional favorite for a number of reasons. It served large audiences and it did things comprehensible to anyone who watched a performance. It had a fantastically good press. And it was backed by hundreds of institutions well experienced in lobbying for funds."[106] Within a decade, between 1965 and 1974, the NEA's annual appropriation had risen from $8 million to $74 million; Congress was bullish on the arts. But the two endowments remained linked, often at the same appropriation level, and in later years NEA supporters would have reason to be glad that the divorce was never effectuated.

Nancy Hanks was neither an artist nor a writer; her sole venture into the artistic realm was the sewing of "needlepoint typewriter covers." But she was bright, she was charming, and she confessed to a talent for "budgeting."[107] She was also superb at calming little dust-ups before they blew up into full-fledged contretemps.

One of the NEA's earliest controversies involved the endowment-funded *American Literary Anthology* of 1969, edited by George Plimpton, whose journal *The Paris Review* had been founded and kept afloat with CIA and Congress for Cultural Freedom monies.[108] Plimpton's NEA-funded *American Literary Anthology* expended $750 for a one–word poem by Aram Saryon that read, in its entirety: *lighght.* (The author received $500 and the *Chicago Review*, the publication in which the poem first appeared, was awarded $250.) Presented properly, the poem is in the center of the page, surrounded only by white space. It means. . . . well, according to Saroyan, it had to do with the way that his generation, the generation that grew up bathed in the cold light of television, had been "exposed to a number of variations on the phenomenon of light."[109] Rep. William Scherle, an Iowa Republican with limited taste for avant-garde poetry, objected that the NEA was spending $107 per letter for Saroyan's effort. When a Scherle aide phoned George Plimpton to ask what the poem meant, Plimpton haughtily replied, "You are from the Midwest. You are culturally deprived, so you would not understand it anyway."[110] That did not exactly appease Scherle, and it was a rather impudent response for a man who was a regular dipper at the government trough. Even supporters of the endowment were puzzled. Michael Whitney Straight, a Hanks adjutant, says that in the days that followed the *lighght* public relations tempest, thirty-five members of Congress, many of them friends of the NEA, called to ask what on earth was going on. Straight asked the endowment's acting director of literature to explain the poem to him. The best she could come up with was, "light was flickering. . . . and so was the poem."[111]

At a House subcommittee hearing at which this cacographic poesy was brought up, Rep. Clarence Long, a Maryland Democrat, cracked, "I don't pretend to know too much about poetry or poems—but this is the first one I've been able to memorize."[112] The controversy soon faded—one word, and a nonobscene one at that, and $750 were not the stuff of grand philosophical tilts—though Saroyan's misspelled poem has been adduced now and then over the years whenever someone wishes to criticize the judgment of the endowers. George Plimpton, with a wee bit of exaggeration, later opined that "*lighght*" might be "one of the most important poems of the 20th century" because "those seven letters may have contributed more than any other single factor to the dismantling of the National Endowment for the Arts."[113]

The National Endowment for the Arts was not dismantled in 1969 or in 1981, despite Plimpton's hyperbole, nor was it dismantled in 1995, when Newt Gingrich was cast in the role of Rep. Scherle. But the NEA's sometimes hysterical defenders never seem to run short of right-wing bogeymen with which to scare the "arts community."

The relentless disparagement of popular taste rankled some. Writing in 1963, Nobel Prize-winning economist George Stigler had insisted: "Our society's tastes are judged by those of the vast majority of the population, and this majority today is generous, uncomplacent, and hardworking, with unprecedentedly large numbers engaged in further self-education, or in eager patronage of the arts. Our market-supported legitimate theater, which is surely the best in the world, is a suggestive measure of popular tastes."[114]

The haughtiness embodied in the frequent dismissals of materialism and commercialism by arts advocates struck a nerve with the critic Stanley Kauffmann. Writing in *Commentary*, Kauffmann protested that "many of the best people in the arts—especially the performing arts—are also capitalist entrepreneurs or are connected with them."[115] He instanced Roger Stevens, the showman and theatrical producer who headed the National Council on the Arts and later the National Endowment for the Arts. Was not Stevens's career, which included such productions as *Cat on a Hot Tin Roof*, *A Man for All Seasons*, and *Bus Stop*, a rebuke to those who claimed that the profit motive resulted in endless dross? Sure, Stevens might not have understood the meaning of *lighght,* and neither did most Americans, but they flocked to Tennessee Williams's plays, and those were hardly Punch and Judy shows.

More substantial than the *lighght* debate was the NEA's awarding of a $5,000 Literature Fellowship in 1973 to novelist Erica Jong for her notorious erotic novel *Fear of Flying.* In her acknowledgments to the sexually explicit novel, Jong expressed her "thanks to the National Endowment for the Arts for a grant which helped."[116] Jong's thank-you would hardly have been noticed had not *Fear of Flying* sold twenty million copies worldwide. That the NEA was underwriting sexually charged books was a red flag to some conservatives, though the more pertinent (yet seldom voiced) concern ought to have been the propriety of the taxpayers supporting a published poet, daughter of a wealthy family, who was no one's idea of a starving artist.

Fear of Flying became a smash best-seller, though its critical notices were decidedly mixed. The novelist and travel writer Paul Theroux, writing in *The New Statesman,* took notice of Jong's source of subvention: "This crappy novel, misusing vulgarity to the point where it becomes purely foolish, picturing woman as a hapless organ animated by the simplest ridicule, and devaluing imagination in every line.... represents everything that is to be loathed in American fiction today. It does not have the excuse of humour, nor is its pretence to topicality anything but tedious. That it was written with a grant. . . . from the National Endowment for the Arts should surprise no one already familiar with the ways American money is used, though is ample justification for any of us to refuse paying his taxes this year."[117]

Casting light, if not lighght, on these early NEA contretemps were similar disputes taking place across the sea. The post-CIA and barely breathing *Encounter* magazine, of all curious venues, was the site of one such row, when the English poet and former Oxford professor Roy Fuller explained his reasons for resigning from the Arts Council of Great Britain in the middle of a three-year term. Fuller, no populist, found many of the objects of the council's benefactions ridiculously frivolous. As he lists them you can almost hear his faint snorts of derision: the Amazing Professor Crump, John Bull Puncture Repair Kit, Forkbeard Fantasy, Phantom Captain, and the ineffable Harry's Big Balloonz, whose reputation was unfortunately deflated by Fuller's pinpricks. Such "community arts" projects seemed unworthy of support to Fuller, who noted that they consumed a greater part of arts funding in the land of Shakespeare than did literature. Public monies were expended on the "show-biz, the amateur, and the ludicrous," argued Fuller, who meant to cast no aspersions on Harry's Big Balloonz, not having seen the artists in question ply their trade, but he noted that standards of quality were irrelevant to most community art, which existed, it seemed, to provide employment, however transient, to the unemployable.

"The bestowal of money for the arts inevitably attracts the idle, the dotty, the minimally talented, the self-promoters," wrote Fuller. "In my opinion too much public money gets into the hands of such people."[118] Even in the literature program Fuller found what he dubbed "Arts Council pensioners": writers without audiences, industrious work ethics, or in some cases talent who received their dole every year without having to produce a book, a story, or even a seven-letter poem. Fuller indicted what he called the "Give 'im the money, Barney" mentality of too many Arts Council members, who had come to look on these allotments as entitlements to be distributed to any writer or self-styled writer who bothered to ask for them.[119] (As the American critic Jonathan Yardley, a sharp detractor of subsidies to individual artists, puts it, "there is little reason to believe that income unearned by work does the artist any real good beyond keeping him afloat. Receiving a free lunch inspires not a desire to work but an expectation that another lunch sooner or later will be served.")[120]

Roy Fuller ended his abbreviated stint on the Arts Council by lending a sympathetic if not entirely supportive ear to such critics of government aid to artists as the poet Philip Larkin and Ian Robinson, the British literary critic, who had written, "if literature is to survive, if works of literature are to be freely created, published, and judged. . . . [t]he best thing the Arts Council can do for it is to leave it alone."[121] Roy Shaw, Secretary-General of the Arts Council, responded with the ruefulness of the arts bureaucrat in the pages of *Encounter*. Shaw complains that Fuller's essay was "intemperate" and relays that some of Fuller's colleagues were appalled by the poet's habit of referring to various petitioners for literature grants as "layabouts." But Shaw's real grievance is that Fuller has not been properly deferential to "experts." Fuller is "an excellent poet," concedes Shaw, "but he is not an authority on contemporary painting and neither am I; the paintings are bought on the advice of people who are."[122]

The alternative, it seems, is rule by philistines. As the evidently nonpopulist Shaw explains, "Members of the Arts Council and its paid staff must continue to make value judgments, otherwise we might as well replace the Director of Art (for example) by a bus driver."[123]

The bus driver, though wholly unqualified to judge art, is perfectly capable of paying the taxes to support that art.

This is the same cult of the credentialed that the more bureaucratic defenders of government arts tend to fall back on. Questions of quality and standards are punted to the experts, who are said to be capable of offering preternaturally objective assessments of works in their specialized fields.

(Fuller was no anomaly. British poets and novelists of Tory or libertarian disposition harrumphed with style over the infelicities of the British arts bureaucracy. Kingsley Amis, in a speech to the Centre for Policy Studies, marveled at such Labour Party pronouncement as "Politics are inextricably sewn into the fabric of the arts," a ham-fisted phrase that would seem inapplicable to, say a string quartet; and literature is "an underfinanced artistic area," to which Amis replies: "Would you let someone who talked about 'underfinanced artistic areas' recommend you a book?"[124] Amis also seconded Roy Fuller's pan of "layabouts," observing that because "we all spend other people's money more freely than our own," the "State-supported artist is likely to be wasteful.")[125]

For the most part, the National Endowment for the Arts avoided controversy in its first quarter century of life. Not that everyone was reconciled to its existence. Many artists remained critical of state-sponsored culture, and from time to time a member of Congress rose in opposition to an authorization or appropriation. In 1973, Senator William Proxmire (D-WI), scourge of government waste, proposed a 40 percent cut in the three-year authorization bill offered by Senator Pell (who was trying to pad the combined budgets of the two national endowments from $80 million in FY 1973 to $400 million in FY 1976). Proxmire argued that an expanded endowment would "promote stale, sterile, establishment art. There is no way to promote excellence in the arts by shoveling out the money," said Promxire. "There is no way to prevent official censorship if government pays the freight."[126] But Nancy Hanks's sedulous attention to congressional relations paid off. Fiscal conservatives such as Senators Barry Goldwater (R-AZ) and John Tower (R-TX) extolled the mighty infusions of NEA cash into their states, and Proxmire could attract only thirty votes in his effort to downsize the endowments.

While Richard Nixon viewed artists warily, as part of the noisy minority in opposition to his silent majority, he was not averse to flattery, and he understood that it is better to be viewed by the nation's opinion makers as cultured than a boor. His counselor Leonard Garment, lawyer and jazz saxophonist, was a powerful in-house voice for arts spending—in fact, next to Nancy Hanks, Garment was the greatest ally the culture industry had within the Nixon administration. In late 1969, Hanks and Garment, an effective tandem, encouraged the President to propose a near-doubling of the budget of both the arts and humanities endowments, citing as among the reasons for this boost that it would "be a high impact move among opinion leaders."[127] The President concurred, and the Congress easily approved a doubling of the endowments' combined appropriations to $40 million. In the House, only seventy-eight nay votes were cast. The NEA, though its budget be modest, was becoming an untouchable.

In a 1989 lecture, Leonard Garment explained Nixon's support of the endowment: "Richard Nixon knew the extent to which the Vietnam War had turned America into two mutually hostile camps. The president wanted for his own an issue that would not divide his audience into sympathetic hawks and hostile doves. It was more an effort to soften and survive than divide and conquer, but this was the reason my arguments found favor."[128] So the NEA, which a few short years earlier had been hailed as the potential catalyst in an American cultural renaissance, was being used as a political object by a political man. This was the least surprising development since the rising of the sun that morning in the east.

His pro-NEA posture won Nixon consistently good press. The *Washington Post,* his bête noire, went so far as to opine in 1972 that he could "go down in history as the nation's most enlightened presidential patron of governmental architecture and design as well as a great patron of the arts."[129] Nixon was, in fact, the president under whom the NEA knew its greatest growth. Once he, Hanks, and Garment got rolling, appropriations for the endowment increased fivefold between 1971 and 1975, from $15 million in to $75 million.

Nixon was, to judge by the agencies his administration begat and fattened, the most liberal domestic president since FDR. And a relatively robust National Endowment for the Arts is among his legacies. (After the 1972 election, Nixon told aide H.R. Haldeman, "The arts are not our people. We should dump the whole culture business."[130] But Watergate intervened, and whether this was a serious remark or just one of Nixon's piqued asides we do not know.)

Throughout the 1970s, dissident voices raised the question of the geographic imbalance of NEA activities. Rep. Albert Quie (R-MN) remarked at a congressional hearing in 1973, with reference to the distribution of agency grants, "it seems like they are congregated along the East Coast from Washington up to Boston. I know there are a lot of people up there, but there are a lot of people in California, too, and quite a number of people in between."[131] The in-betweens had been relatively quiet during the Nancy Hanks era, so much so that frank voices were lauding the endowment for favoring New York City over the rest of the country. The neoconservative writer Hilton Kramer told readers of the *New York Times* in 1976,

> To put the matter bluntly, the arts thrive in situations of urban concentration and cosmopolitan vitality. It is in the cities that standards are set and ideas are generated, in the cities that talent is nurtured and recognized, in the cities—and in this country, one city in particular—where the arts really grow, where they receive significant intellectual nourishment and criticism and new creative energy. Without Paris and New York, there would be no Calder to admire in Grand Rapids; without New York there would be no Martha Graham legend for the White House to celebrate. The arts need the cities, and the cities need the arts—that is a fundamental fact of our cultural life, and it ought to be the cornerstone of any national arts policy.[132]

The idea that New York City of the mid-1970s was the fountainhead of American cultural life is highly debatable, yet in any event Kramer despaired. President Ford, he thought, was a Michigan dolt, and Jimmy Carter had spoken of decentralizing arts policy, when what was needed, according to Kramer, was its further centralization. Those of the Kramer school looked with mounting disfavor on the NEA sending monies to increasingly vocal state arts agencies. The first state to conceive an arts agency of its own was Utah, which in 1899 enacted the "Art Law," the legislative progeny of State Rep. Alice Merrill Horne, daughter of Utah pioneers and an artist who had studied at the Art Institute of Chicago and other schools. The law was intended to "advance the interest of fine arts, to develop the influence of art in education, to sponsor an annual art exhibition, establish a state art collection and present public lectures on art."[133] The Utah Art Institute created by Rep. Horne's bill predated the second state agency—that of New York—by three score years.

A 1959 Library of Congress survey found that thirty-four states "gave no support"—let alone a dedicated agency—to the arts.[134] The paucity of state support of the arts seems to have accurately reflected public opinion. A 1963 Opinion Research Corporation survey found "that only 5% of Americans believed the federal government should sponsor the arts and a similar proportion suggested state or local governments should do so, while 'the other 90 percent preferred private leadership or, more often, saw no need for concerted action at all.'"[135]

Nevertheless, the Empire State pushed ahead. The New York State Council on the Arts (NYSCA) was another Rockefeller arts organization, though in this case the funding was explicitly public. Created in 1960 at the behest of Governor Nelson Rockefeller, who once said "it takes courage to vote for culture when you're in public life"[136]—perhaps not so much if you're voting to support with tax dollars your favorite personal causes—NYSCA quickly became the most prominent state arts council. In FY 1966, the year before the NEA began sending out block grants to state agencies, NYSCA's state appropriation of $766,000 was greater than the combined total of the appropriations ($505,000) to the other twenty-one then-existing state agencies.[137]

Flush with cash, contemptuous of the bonds of fiscal discipline, Governor Rockefeller successfully pushed the New York legislature to increase NYSCA's budget tenfold, from $2 million in 1970 to $20 million in 1971. Richard Kostelanetz speculates that Rockefeller was "socializing the costs" of the enormous New York City cultural institutions his family had supported, such as MOMA and the Lincoln Center. NYSCA was a means by which "the tax-paying middle class would implicitly collaborate with a wealthier class in paying for the museums and symphony orchestras."[138] Despite the lead role played by private donors and foundations, "most advocates of [a federal] arts policy regarded philanthropy as an inadequate substitute for public policy," as Daniel M. Fox noted in his study of the politics of art museums.[139] Some of the great philanthropists agreed.

Befitting a Rockefeller-begotten program, NYSCA concentrated its efforts in New York City, particularly Manhattan, so much so that in 1974 the state legislature had to slap a "geographic-distribution requirement" on NYSCA in order to ensure that some pittance made its way into the rural counties in the hinterland upstate.[140]

The Art of Backscratching

After Nancy Hanks reluctantly took leave of the chairmanship—Senator Pell told her that he did not believe in third terms, at least for this kind of president—Pell's right-hand man, Livingston Biddle, took the helm, nominated by Jimmy Carter.

(During a brief interregnum between Hanks's departure and Biddle's ascension, Hanks's deputy, Michael Straight, former editor of *The New Republic*, served as acting chairman. The New York City-born and Cambridge-educated Straight was an upper-class toff. He had also been a communist spy in the 1930s and 40s while studying at Cambridge and later working at a fairly low level in the Roosevelt administration. Straight's revelations of his early espionage led to the outing of Anthony Blunt as a spy.[141] Extreme wealth and communist sympathies: two traits that showed up with a certain frequency in the government arts advocates of the 1930s–60s.)

Livingston Biddle had a valuable ally in Joan Mondale, wife of the Vice President, whose ardor for arts spending was such that she won the sobriquet "Joan of Art." But the endowment was entering a difficult period. There was a widespread perception that the NEA and the NEH had grown fat, happy, and self-satisfied by the late 1970s. They had become, for some, a means of dispensing favors to clubbable writers and intellectuals. Back-scratching and tit-for-tat grant-giving among a small circle of friends were rife. Even the *Washington Post*, hardly a crusty foe of cronyism, editorialized of the NEA in 1979, "The charge that a 'closed circle' of acquaintanceship runs the Endowment through overlapping appointments to panels and committees is a serious one, and one both the Arts and Humanities [endowments] have been guilty of for a long time. Besides the obvious wrong of creating situations where friends make grants to friends, or friends of friends, there is also the patently unhealthy set-up in which stale ideas recycle like so much dead air."[142] To expect a government grant-making apparatus to ventilate fresh new ideas is, admittedly, asking a lot.

The raw details of this cronyism in the Carter-era NEA were laid bare by Hilary Masters, whose father, poet Edgar Lee Masters, was the Illinois attorney who had gained lasting fame with *Spoon River Anthology*. Hilary Masters took on the endowment as a favors-for-friends machine in an eye-opening essay in the Summer 1981 *Georgia Review*. Masters focused on the NEA's 1979–80 literature awards. These fellowships came with a not inconsiderable sum of $10,000 each as well as "an imprimatur that certifies on curricula vitae, book flaps, and letters home that the recipients are (to use the NEA's own language) 'published writers of exceptional talent'—America's Best, officially recognized by a bureau of culture created by the United States Congress and funded by the U.S. taxpayer."[143]

As usual with a centralized bureau of culture, the preponderance of money flowed to the wealthiest cities. Masters notes that in 1979–80, "[m]ost of the grants went to New York and California," while "few found their way to Middle America or the South." In other words, the regions that bred such writers as Faulkner and Hemingway, Fitzgerald and Harper Lee, Dreiser and Zora Neale Hurston, were afterthoughts. Missouri, birthplace of Mark Twain and those archetypal American characters Huck Finn and Tom Sawyer, was shut out altogether. Not a single one of the 274 fellowships—which attracted 3,750 applicants—went to a writer from the Show-Me State.[144]

Yet seven fellowships went to writers associated with a small, by then defunct, California publisher, Big Sky Press. This was the best showing of any publisher: Random House, Doubleday, Henry Holt—none could best Big Sky Press in the grant-winning department. Moreover, another obscure outfit, This Press, which had the same mailing address as Big Sky Press, had four of its authors win grants. Which means that writers associated with these two almost wholly unknown publishers sharing one address took home more than $100,000 in fellowships in a single year.

This might seem a heartwarming tale of an underdog getting recognized for its quality and not its flash or glitz, but as Hilary Masters demonstrates, the real reason behind this cluster of awards was old-fashioned cronyism and log-rolling. These writers and the editors of the two presses had personal ties to the NEA Literature Panel that amounted to a "transcontinental daisy chain," in Masters's phrase. To make matters worse, several of the small presses whose writers received an inordinately high number of fellowships refused to consider unsolicited manuscripts and largely published the work of their editors and an inner circle, which "put the Federal Government in the position of actively supporting if not encouraging the equivalent of a sizable vanity press—and one with an elitist attitude at that."[145]

Subsequent reforms in the grant-making process were designed to reduce such backscratching, though any time government funds are being expended a degree of favor-trading is inevitable. The NEA still subsidizes small presses and journals, as well as public readings, residencies, translations of foreign works into English, and, most controversially, writers. Despite the glaring defects in NEA Literature grantsmanship that Hilary Masters exposed, when Congress abolished individual grants in all artistic disciplines in the wake of the 1990s controversies, it preserved the Literature Fellowships. As the NEA

Literature Director at the time, Gigi Bradford, said, "People all across America came together to prioritize the fellowships."[146] (The use of the hideous bureaucratic word "prioritize" by the NEA Literature Director ought to have—though it did not—given pause to the program's partisans.)

Contra Gigi Bradford, not all people—certainly not all writers—came together to prioritize these fellowships. In 1992, the godfather of the Beat poetry movement, Lawrence Ferlinghetti, registered his "object[ion] to a welfare system that would turn wild artists into tame lapdogs."[147] Lapdogs, however, eat regularly, even if it is from twenty-five-pound bags of Uncle Roy's dog food. Wild dogs, like wild artists, have to scrounge and forage.

The NEA Literature Fellowships are in the form of grants to individual creative writers. At their inception in 1967, the awards were worth $5,000; they have been bumped up periodically to their current value in the sum of $25,000. Fellowships are gifted on poets and prose writers in alternating years.

The roster of NEA Literature Fellows contains numerous prominent American writers. In that first year of 1967, awardees included Isaac Bashevis Singer, William Gaddis, and Richard Yates. A distinguished list, to be sure: Singer would win the Nobel Prize in Literature in 1978, and Yates was already the author of his classic novel *Revolutionary Road* (1961). Subsequent NEA creative writing fellowships went to such writers as Andre Dubus, Annie Dillard, and T. C. Boyle.

The NEA Literature program has also supported lesser-known writers at lower levels of financial aid over the years, though various of its programs (notably the Discovery Awards for obscure young writers) have vanished. The NEA, like all bureaucracies governmental and academic, pledges undying fealty to "diversity," though it measures diversity in race and gender terms and does not even pretend that artisans whose bent may be aesthetically traditionalist or politically conservative are represented among NEA recipients in anything close to their representation in the general population. Some diversities are more equal than others.

Not all NEA grantees have a sense of entitlement. The reluctance to be identified as a charity case—the same sense of pride that kept many writers from enlisting in Federal One—is still apparent in some artists. For instance, novelist Kaye Gibbons of North Carolina explained in 2006, "Before I received an NEA Literature Fellowship in 1989, I did not have the money for the February rent. But that grant enabled me to pay the rent, feed my children, and work in peace. However, I never saw the grant as something to which I was entitled. I felt I could contribute something of value to the American letters and therefore to my country. Because of the book I wrote with the grant and because of subsequent books, I have paid over $750,000 in federal income tax. The government has been more than repaid for its investment in my work, and for that, we should both be grateful."[148] Similarly, the late Oscar Hijuelos, the Cuban-American novelist, NEA fellow, and winner of the Pulitzer Prize, proudly declared that "I was able to repay the government's largesse back many times over, by way of taxes."[149]

Hijuelos and Gibbons are obviously not spoiled trust fund performance artists demanding the financial backing of unenlightened taxpayers while mocking those taxpayers' lives and religious beliefs. They are serious writers who are, or were in the case of the late Hijuelos, mindful of the obligations implied by government sponsorship.

The Reagan Age Cometh

If the revelations of NEA machinations in the Carter years proved an easily overcome nuisance, the arrival of the purported budget-slasher from the West, Ronald Reagan, sent government arts advocates into a chorus of caterwauling. The Reagan administration proposed a reduction of about 50 percent in the NEA's budget authority through 1986. Given that its FY 1981 budget was $158 million, and the outgoing Carter administration had proposed an increase to $175 million for FY 1982, the prospect of a sub-$100 million budget aroused horror in the world of arts administrators. Such a meager allotment for the arts was hardly worthy of a great nation; with the cowboy Reagan in the White House, philistines were in the saddle!

The Office of Management and Budget, directed by the parsimonious ex-Michigan congressman David Stockman, produced a working paper on the NEA that indicted the endowment for "promoting the notion that the federal government should be the financial patron of first resort for. . . . artistic and literary pursuits." The OMB paper speculated that slicing the NEA's budget would stimulate "private individual and corporate philanthropic support of the arts," which had been disincentivized by the endowment's existence.[150] And though not articulated by the bean-counters, another motivation of the more ardent Reaganauts was the desire to "defund the left": that is, to reduce or eliminate those government agencies, among them the Legal Services Corporation, the Corporation for Public Broadcasting, and the two

National Endowments, whose ideological coloration was decidedly left of center and whose budgets were dedicated, in part, to promoting what conservative critics believed to be a liberal or left-wing agenda. Some conservatives held the endowments to be little more than liberal slush funds whose monies were allocated to promote an aggressively statist liberal agenda.[151]

For the first time since its birth, the NEA was threatened by the budget cutter's knife. Heretofore it had avoided close scrutiny, largely by virtue of that combination of concentrated benefits and diffused costs that makes it so difficult for taxpayers to mount effective challenges to corporate welfare. Outgoing NEA chair Livingston Biddle ascribed the Reaganauts' penny-pinching with respect to the endowment to "ignorance," that all-purpose epithet applied to those with whom an establishment figure disagrees. Biddle and his allies felt "deep indignation."[152]

NEA defenders took to the ramparts and sprayed their fire without fine discrimination. In the March 22, 1981, *Washington Post*, novelist Toni Morrison, a member of the National Council on the Arts, protested the "brutal," "foolish and uninformed" Stockman-proposed cut, which was really a "deft strangulation" based on "shabby scholarship, inaccurate data and an astonishing ignorance of the workings of the NEA itself." Morrison skips from this denunciation of shabbiness to make such unsupported claims as that almost half of all artists are unemployed and that every dollar spent by the NEA is multiplied eighteen times by matching "corporate and private money." She also claims that NEA grants to museums and institutions produce "billions of dollars in income" for the affected cities, though again she does not favor readers with a source for this assertion. Take her word for it—she's a novelist.

Morrison invokes Hitler, naturally, since anyone desirous of cutting the budget must be tarred as a genocidal dictator. (Never mind the fact that Hitler believed in government-funded art that glorified the state and the "master race.") And she concludes in rousing fashion with a rhetorical swirl that suggests that she has never examined the demographic breakdown of which social, economic, and ethnic groups profit most from the NEA: To advocate a reduction in government aid to the arts, says Morrison, "is saying to poor people in Tucson, the Bronx and Oakland: You must not only live in substandard housing, with poor health care, inadequate protection and subsistence diets, you must also relinquish your cultural life-line—the reason, sometimes, you get up in the mornings; the respite you look forward to of an afternoon; the relish of working at your own art."[153]

If this was the NEA's self-image, it bore little resemblance to the agency as it actually was.

Who *Really* Benefits from the NEA?

Toni Morrison was flat-out wrong in her ideation of the folks for whom the National Endowment for the Arts is a "cultural life-line." One consistent finding across the years is that the "arts audience" is "much wealthier than the general population."[154] This has remained constant despite the professed efforts of the National Endowment for the Arts to make the arts accessible to all. In their significant study, *Performing Arts—The Economic Dilemma* (1966), William J. Baumol and William G. Bowen found that the audience for dance, theater, opera, and music was overwhelmingly drawn from the highest levels of income, education, and occupation.

Visitors to art museums are disproportionately drawn from the top economic and education levels. The "arts institution audience," determined Alan L. Feld, Michael O'Hare, and J. Mark Davidson Schuster in *Patrons Despite Themselves: Taxpayers and Arts Policy* (1983), "is extremely well educated."[155] College graduates and those with post-graduate educations are far more likely to visit an art museum than are those who did not attend college.[156]

As a side issue, a populist might ask why federal subsidies should direct art into the cloisters known as museums. If the ostensible purpose of such subsidies is to disseminate art as widely as possible, why funnel it to museums, whose patrons are drawn largely from the top strata of the economic, social, and educational world? Rather, as mentioned earlier, the painter Thomas Hart Benton preferred to have his work shown less fashionable venues. After all, he asserted, "People go to saloons, but never to museums."[157]

A letter writer to the *New York Times* in 1961 made a similarly anti-elitist point: "The small percentage of people who enjoy opera does not qualify it for public financial support. If opera cannot pay for itself, the fault is with opera. . . . It has never been a principle of our society that the people as a whole should be forced to pay for the entertainment of a few—and it must not be so now."[158]

The special case of opera was also treated by the social critic Ernest van den Haag. Opera, wrote van den Haag in 1979 in *Policy Review*, was and is "an exotic import of and for the rich." Though van den Haag professed to be an opera-lover, he wondered "why those who want opera are entitled to compel others to pay for it—even though these others, in the main, prefer unsubsidized movies or Broadway shows. A subsidy to opera supports or expands our national consciousness as much as a subsidy to the manufacture or the wearing of tails and top hats would." He continues, "Tin pan alley, jazz, rock, or baseball are more important in the celebration of American values, not only in the working classes and among adolescents, but also in the upper classes and even among educated groups."[159] They receive no subsidy, he observes—so why should public monies flow to opera, which is of infinitely less salience to all demographic groups except, perhaps, a narrow slice of the Old Money rich?

Van den Haag was wrong to say that jazz, which has been favored on occasion by the NEA, is unsubsidized, and as for baseball, the profusion of taxpayer-built stadia stand as a gold-plated rebuttal. But his assertions about the class bias of the NEA's support of opera—as well as classical music and museums—are irrefutable.

According to the most recent US Bureau of the Census statistics, while 22.8 percent of those eighteen years of age and older who made at least $150,000 had gone to a classical music concert at least once in the previous year, only 4 percent of those making less than $10,000 had done so. The corresponding figures at higher income levels are 3.9 percent for those making $10,000–$19,999; 4.4 percent for $20,000–$29,999; 6.8 percent for $30,000–$39,999; 8.7 percent for $40,000–$49,999; 9.5 percent for $50,000–$74,999; 11.7 percent for $75,000–$99,999; and 14.8 percent for $100,000–$149,999.[160] A similar relationship exists for other manifestations of high culture. While 9.4 percent of those making less than $10,000 and 10.3 percent of those making $10,000–$19,999 had visited an art gallery or museum in the prior year, 34.4 percent of those making $100,000–$149,000 and 51.9 percent of those with incomes above $150,000 had done so. (Those with middle-range incomes—middle-class taxpayers—were in the 25–30 percent range.)[161]

Those who patronize NEA-supported high culture are also those who favor its public subsidy. In a paper published in *Public Choice*, Arthur C. Brooks confirmed that "the benefits of public arts funding accrue primarily to those in the highest income class."[162] Relying on data from the 1998 General Social Survey of the National Opinion Research Center, Brooks tested variables for their association with strong support or opposition to arts subsidies. He found that holding all else constant, "those in the highest income classes are more likely to support public arts funding." Since these people are also the likeliest to make private donations to the arts (and, as we have seen elsewhere, attend artistic events), Brooks notes that his findings add "legitimacy to the position that government arts funding, as currently administered, is primarily a public subsidy to the rich."[163]

Variables significantly associated with opposition to government funding of the arts include maleness and a self-applied "conservative" ideology; those significantly associated with support *for* such funding included high income, private donations to the arts, and residence in the Midwest. Which means that if the country were populated primarily by wealthy liberal women from the Midwest who donate to the arts, the NEA budget would rival that of the Pentagon.[164]

And Now, Back to the Reagan Threat

The early months of the Reagan administration evoked widespread panic in subsidized intellectuals. An axe-wielding David Stockman haunted their dreams. For instance, although Reagan had actually recommended a 6 percent *increase* in the budget for the National Institutes of Health, from $3.6 billion to $3.8 billion, the *New York Times* reported a "deep undercurrent of unease" in its twelve thousand-person staff.[165] One assumes that the undercurrent had disappeared by the last budget of the Reagan era, that of FY 1989, when NIH's appropriation topped $7.1 billion.

Or consider the National Science Foundation. When an administration ally, Rep. Larry Winn (R-KS), offered an amendment in the House to reduce the NSF's FY 1982 $1.1 billion appropriation by $70 million, or about 6 percent, social and physical scientists launched what the newsletter of the American Sociological Association called an "unprecedented" lobbying blitz. True, the Reagan administration had actually recommended *increases* in the NSF's basic research budget, but it called for reducing monies allotted for "social, behavioral, and economic research." The Winn amendment, which incorporated the Reagan recommendations, was defeated on July 21, 1981, by a vote of 264–152, with 69 Republicans deserting the administration. One such Republican, Rep. Margaret Heckler (MA), attributed the defections to "letters and calls they received from the scientific community in their districts."[166] In other words, old-fashioned lobbying by recipients of federal funds for more federal funds.

This "sophisticated lobbying effort" by psychologists, economists, sociologists, and others, "has begun to change the way Washington views them," according to the *New York Times*.[167] They were no longer wool-gathering eggheads, suggested the *Times*, but a potent and battle-hardened lobby. One reason for the panic, suggested Nobel Laureate economist Lawrence Klein of the University of Pennsylvania, was that "support of social research" had "shifted from private foundations to the NSF," as Constance Holden explained in *Science*, and therefore "social scientists have no other source to turn to" for support.[168] The central government, which had become their rock and their stay, had left them no alternative, at least none that they could perceive, to importuning Washington.

Like the National Institutes of Health and the National Science Foundation, the National Endowment for the Arts survived the supposed onslaught. In this fight the NEA, and the NEH, were assisted by that reliable ally of the status quo: the task force. A Presidential Task Force on the Arts and Humanities was born amidst the hubbub of Reagan's first months in office. The fear among endowment supporters was that the purpose of the task force was to supply intellectual cover for the abolition of the endowments, though its three co-chairs—actor Charlton Heston, art collector Daniel J. Terra, and University of Chicago President Hanna Gray—seemed exceedingly unlikely to preside over any group that would make such a recommendation. And in fact in October 1981 the task force, which Reagan had charged with proposing "methods to increase private support for the arts and humanities,"[169] disgorged its report, which concluded, "Basically, the Endowments are sound and should remain as originally conceived."[170] The task force included Daniel Boorstin, the eminent historian who was serving as Librarian of Congress at the time. "The countries that have cultural policies are, of course, totalitarian countries," remarked Boorstin in a 1981 roundtable, though his own position as a federally funded intellectual suggested that he was hardly a firebrand on the matter.[171]

The Reagan NEA chairman, Frank Hodsoll, had little familiarity with the endowment before his nomination and certainly bore it no enmity. To the contrary, this former aide to that consummate political insider James Baker became an intra-administration defender of the agency, as appointees often do. As Milton C. Cummings Jr. and Richard S. Katz note, "Apparently it is the case for arts agencies, as it is known to be more generally, that once a politician assumes control of a government department, he often develops an incentive to support its programs and position within the total governmental structure, no matter what he may have thought of the department before."[172]

The influence of the David Stockman budget-cutting wing of the Reagan administration soon diminished. The crisis passed. Although the administration again proposed cuts in the NEA's FY 1983 budget, its lobbying effort was feeble and the funds were restored. By the time Reagan left office, the NEA's budget stood at $169 million—not as much as Claiborne Pell or Joan of Art might have wished, but far from the abolition which had been forecast in early 1981 by alarmed public arts supporters. In only one of Reagan's eight years in office did NEA funding decline. The revolution wasn't.

After 1981, the NEA largely steered clear of controversy during the Reagan years. One exception came in 1984, when the Metropolitan Opera, recipient of $850,000 in endowment funds for that year, staged Verdi's *Rigoletto* with its Renaissance-era setting updated to 1950s Little Italy, with Mafia hitmen and stereotyped Italians romping around the stage. Italian-American organizations such as the Sons of Italy and the Coalition of Italo-American Organizations protested what they regarded as an ethnic defamation. Rep. Mario Biaggi (D-NY) demanded that NEA Chairman Hodsoll use the agency's leverage to convince the Met to cancel the production.[173]

The show was not cancelled. The Met did throw a bone to Rep. Biaggi and Senator Alfonse D'Amato (R-NY) when it pulled the libretto of this updated *Rigoletto* from its bookstore. Anthony A. Bliss, general manager of the Met, denied that this in any way constituted "censorship," which was, he righteously declared, "a thing I could not entertain." Rep. Biaggi sought, unsuccessfully, to prohibit the NEA from funding "ethnic or racially offensive material" in the future.[174]

One agency innovation under Reagan was the awarding by the NEA of a National Medal of Arts, which the endowment calls "the highest award given to artists and arts patrons by the United States government." It is awarded by the President of the United States to individuals or groups who "are deserving of special recognition by reason of their outstanding contributions to the excellence, growth, support and availability of the arts in the United States."[175]

The medal was authorized by legislation enacted in the symbolic year of 1984. The National Medal of Arts is the kind of government imprimatur on artists that the early opponents of federally subsidized art had warned against. It smacked of official art, of writers and poets and painters and actors and dancers and musicians being honored not for the purity and independence of their vision, or for their prodigious talents, but rather for their usefulness to the authorities. Yet in

1984, few saw it that way. The first crop of honorees in 1985 included distinguished personages such as Ralph Ellison and Martha Graham, and over the next three decades the National Medal of Arts has been bestowed on dozens of prominent American artists. There has been an unquestionable political tint to the honorees—under Republican presidents, awardees are likelier to be right-leaning figures such as Frank Capra, Saul Bellow, and Ray Bradbury, while under Democrats, medal winners have included such left-leaning partisans as Edward Albee, Harry Belafonte, and Tony Kushner.

Very few observers found anything troubling about the existence of a National Medal of Arts in the United States. For Americans in 1984, it did not conjure a *1984*-ish Orwellian nightmare of government-approved art. Instead, the specter of *1984* would be raised five years later, and not by libertarian skeptics of the NEA but by subsidized artists themselves.

The Culture Wars

The NEA's culture wars, as they came to be known, began with two endowment grants in the visual arts. The first, issued in September 1987—the Reagan years—was a matching grant in the amount of $75,000 to the Awards in the Visual Arts program of the Southeastern Center for Contemporary Art (SECCA) in Winston-Salem, North Carolina. Among the ten artists chosen for this traveling program, which included stops in Los Angeles, Pittsburgh, and Richmond, was Andres Serrano, one of whose selected works bore the undainty title *Piss Christ.* This specimen was a plastic crucifix soaking in Mr. Serrano's urine. (George H.W. Bush's NEA chairman John Frohnmayer observed, cluelessly, that if not for the urine "the work probably would have been revered by believers, since it had a translucent and mystical feel."[176] Yes, and by the way, Mrs. Lincoln, other than that unfortunate interruption, how did you like the play?)

Many Christians viewed this as tax-supported blasphemy. Why, they asked, should their tax dollars go toward mocking images of the central symbol of their faith? Serrano's defenders suggested that *Piss Christ* was a statement about the devaluing of the Christian message, though this seemed a tad disingenuous. Whatever the artist's intent, *Piss Christ* would have elicited nary a condemnation had its creator not been the recipient, at second hand, of NEA monies.

In fact, its 1988–89 journey was largely without controversy; *Piss Christ* only became a cause célèbre after the SECCA exhibit had run its course. The real trigger for the controversy was a March 19, 1989, letter to the editor of the Richmond *Times-Dispatch* by Philip L. Smith objecting to the inclusion of Serrano's work in a recently concluded show at the Virginia Museum of Fine Arts. Wrote Smith: "The Virginia Museum should not be in the business of promoting and subsidizing hatred and intolerance. Would they pay the KKK to do a work defaming blacks? Would they display a Jewish symbol under urine? Has Christianity become fair game in our society for any kind of blasphemy and slander?"[177] A representative of the American Family Association, a group generally identified with the Religious Right, saw the Smith letter. The AFA swung into action, asking its members if they believed that their tax dollars should fund this kind of art.

The expenditure of tax monies on *Piss Christ* provoked a firestorm of criticism. Twenty-four US senators, ranging from conservative stalwart Jesse Helms (R-NC) to such liberals as Bob Kerrey (D-NE), Harry Reid (D-NV), and Tom Harkin (D-IA), issued a letter in May 1989 condemning *Piss Christ* as "trash."[178] At about the same time, the NEA gifted the Institute of Contemporary Art of the University of Pennsylvania with $30,000 to stage *The Perfect Moment*, a traveling exhibition of the photographs of Robert Mapplethorpe. The images on display featured, among other things, bondage, sadomasochism, urine-drinking, and a bullwhip sticking out of Mr. Mapplethorpe's anus. The show was scheduled to visit the private Corcoran Gallery of Art in Washington, DC, in the summer of 1989, but the Corcoran administrators cancelled the exhibit, whether out of prurience or good taste, depending on one's point of view.

Washingtonians were not deprived of Mapplethorpe's visions; the show went up at DC's Washington Project for the Arts. The Corcoran suffered for its stand, as at least one major bequest to the museum was cancelled, and several artists pulled their works from the gallery. In fact, the commotion surrounding *The Perfect Moment* was a boon to art dealers specializing in Mapplethorpe works, as the prices of his works skyrocketed. There is no such thing as bad publicity for an artist, especially if sex is in the mix.

Seemingly overnight, the polemical hysteria on both sides of the issue reached fever pitch. Gary Indiana, a playwright who was part of the art-world demimonde, raged against the "provincial spite" motivating the "morality brigade." He termed a speech by Senator Alfonse D'Amato (R-NY) a "Hitlerite tirade" and almost ran out of epithets to describe Senator Jesse Helms (R-NC), leader of the Senate's social conservative bloc. At least Indiana did describe the Mapplethorpe photos whose government sponsorship these assorted bigots and yahoos objected to: "a self-portrait in which the photographer offers his bum to the camera, having inserted into said bum the handle of a bullwhip; and a portrait of two men in leather, one pissing in the other's mouth."[179] Many of those who castigated what they regarded as the censorious anti-Mapplethorpe crowd primly refused to say just what was in those photographs.

The anti-NEA furor set off by the Serrano and Mapplethorpe exhibits was, in the mass media, ascribed to the machinations of the Reverend Donald E. Wildmon, a Methodist minister and antipornography activist who ran the aforementioned American Family Association. Wildmon, based in Tupelo, Mississippi, was adept at generating press coverage as well as letters to members of Congress from outraged citizens. As a Southern minister, he was also an easy target for caricature; subsidized artists and their defenders found it easy to feel superior to this man (and his admirers), whom they regarded as a redneck fundamentalist hick.

This was no ginned-up issue, no instance of the fake grass-roots movements later mocked as "astroturf." Many Americans were genuinely upset that federal monies were going to sponsor art they found offensive. *Congressional Quarterly* noted in 1990 that "Congressional staffers say constituent mail is running 100–1 in favor of restrictions on obscene art."[180]

Yet it was also misleading to blame Washington for the exhibits. As Ryan M. MacPherson, senior editor of *The Family in America*, a scholarly journal associated with traditional conservatism, writes, "Already in 1989 it was a stretch for social conservatives to blame the NEA for funding Serrano and Mapplethorpe, since the funding decisions were made by local agencies that received block grants from the Endowment."[181] So even proposals to decentralize arts funding by transferring much or all of the NEA's budget to state and local agencies would not satisfy the objections of groups like the American Family Association.

For the first time, really, in its history, the NEA feared for its corporate life. Talk of abolition was in the air. In July 1989, an amendment was offered on the House floor by Rep. Dana Rohrabacher (R-CA) to zero out funding for the endowment. Rohrabacher, whose background was in the libertarian movement, said that "Artists can do whatever they want on their own time and with their own dime."[182] Though his amendment lost overwhelmingly, the House did vote by a margin of 361–65 to reduce the NEA appropriation by $45,000, or the approximate amount the agency had contributed toward the Serrano and Mapplethorpe exhibits. Notice had been served.

The House debate ought to have been a lesson to artists in just who calls the piper's tune. Rep. Pat Williams (D-MT), chairman of the House subcommittee with jurisdiction over the NEA, told artists that the endowment must not be "a funnel for sanitized, government-approved art." But to arts advocates like William Nolan of the Florida Arts Council, who said at the time that an NEA grant is "like giving an artist the Good Housekeeping Seal of Approval," that would seem to be the point: the endowment *is* the arbiter of government-approved art. Rep. Rohrabacher echoed that point when he said, "The National Endowment for the Arts should be able to say to a group, 'You're going to get cut off if you don't use better judgment with this money.'"[183]

In other words, play our tune—do not play forbidden tunes—or we turn the spigot off. Any artist who doesn't find that disconcerting—and who isn't moved to at least wonder whether or not accepting government monies for art is compromising her artistic integrity—is either dense or willfully obtuse.

On July 27, 1989, the Senate approved by voice vote an amendment to an appropriations bill by Senator Jesse Helms (R-NC) that would bar the expenditure of funds by the NEA or NEH to "promote, disseminate or produce obscene or indecent materials, including but not limited to depictions of sadomasochism, homoeroticism, the exploitation of children, or individuals engaged in sex acts; or material which denigrates the objects or beliefs of the adherents of a particular religion or nonreligion."[184]

Senator Helms was to liberals what Senator Ted Kennedy was to conservatives: a bogeyman who was supremely useful as a fund-raising tool in the burgeoning industry of direct mail. But Helms, no less than Kennedy, was a serious legislator, no matter how strongly one might disagree with him, and he deserves to be heard in non-caricatured form. He explained his antiobscenity amendment in a 1990 article in the *Nova Law Review*. Helms traced his anti-NEA awakening to *Piss Christ*, which he regarded as an intentional insult to Christians. He quoted at length from a letter he had received from a federal judge:

> when a federally-funded artist creates an anti-Christian piece of so-called art, it is a violation of an important part of the First Amendment, which guarantees the right of all religious faiths to be free from

> governmentally-sanctioned criticism. When the National Endowment for the Arts contributes money to an artist for him to use to dip a crucifix in his own urine for public display, it is no different [in terms of church and state entanglement] from a municipality's spending taxpayers' money for putting a crucifix on the top of city hall.[185]

The "so-called art" phraseology is reminiscent of Rep. Dondero, but unlike Dondero, scourge of the subsidized modernists, Helms, in this instance, chooses to characterize his amendment in libertarian rather than moralistic terms. He denies that his intent is censorship. Censorship, he says, is not the same as sponsorship. He seeks only to forbid federal funds from flowing to the likes of Andres Serrano. His amendment, he says, "in no way 'censors' artists; it does not prevent artists from producing, creating, or displaying blasphemous or obscene 'art' at their own expense in the private sector." Artists remain free "to shock and offend the public," insists Helms, "but at their own expense, not the taxpayers'. . . . People who want to scrawl dirty words on the men's-room wall should furnish their own walls and their own crayons."[186] He adds that "refusing to subsidize something does not 'ban' it."[187]

The Helms amendment was dropped in conference, replaced by language less constrictive but still condemnatory of grants to "obscene" works lacking "serious literary, artistic, political, or scientific value." An antiobscenity pledge was thereupon included in NEA contracts at the behest of the George H. W. Bush-appointed NEA chair, Oregon attorney John Frohnmayer, who assumed his position in October 1989. Frohnmayer proved to be a hapless bumbler whose political skills were unequal to what was admittedly a daunting task: dispensing federal funds to arts and arts institutions whose works will inevitably prove offensive, in some cases, to the citizens who fund them.

Frohnmayer claimed that he inserted the antiobscenity wording into NEA grants in order to provoke a lawsuit, which he believed would overturn the obscenity ban. But he was too clever by half: the subsidized art world raged at what its spokespeople claimed hyperbolically was a virtual American Inquisition, akin to an epidemic of book-burning and artist-incinerating that lit the night from Manhattan to Los Angeles. New York cultural fixtures such as producer Joseph Papp and conductor-composer Leonard Bernstein publicly protested the alleged censorship, Papp by turning down NEA grants and Bernstein by refusing a National Medal of Arts. Frohnmayer later protested that he wished he could have told the world, "Hey, folks, I'm trying to force a lawsuit here so that your language can be declared unconstitutional," but dissimulation is tough for amateurs to pull off.[188]

The case of Joseph Papp is illuminating. In response to the anti-obscenity language in NEA grants, Papp thundered to Frohnmayer, "As head of a major theatrical institution, I have always cherished my freedom, defending it whenever it was challenged. My privileged right to make my own judgment in choosing this over that and that over this regardless of great varieties of societal pressure, have been matters of principle, taste and artistic standards. To be asked, after meeting the tests of 35 years, to yield to circumscription and legislative prohibitions in the most vulnerable and inexplicable area of the arts, its content, is unthinkable, if not downright subversive."[189] A bit prolix, but stirring. Though this raises the question: Why was Joseph Papp, who had become rich through his production (and stake in) such blockbusters as *A Chorus Line*, receiving federal assistance?

In his memoir, *Leaving Town Alive: Confessions of an Art Warrior*, Frohnmayer complains that to the Right he was "the government's official smut purveyor" while to the world of government-nurtured artists he was a "coward" who was fair game for all sort of "ad hominem attacks."[190] On the whole, though, he blames the "distorted, homophobic, and anti-intellectual" forces of the Right for his problems.[191] Typical of his missteps, Frohnmayer cancelled a $10,000 NEA grant to Artists Space, a New York City art gallery, for "Witness: Against Our Vanishing," a show about AIDS. The cancellation elicited the predicted squeals of protest, and after viewing the show, Frohnmayer flip-flopped, restoring the money. But as an observer sympathetic to the endowment writes, this show was not merely about the scourge of AIDS, as circumspect descriptions in the press usually had it. Rather, it featured graphic depictions of sexual acts and a catalogue that was, to put it mildly, "highly polemical,"[192] as for instance in the statement by artist David Wojnarowicz that he would like to "douse Helms with a bucket of gasoline and set his putrid ass on fire or throw Rep. William Dannemeyer off the Empire State Building."[193]

Putting aside the question of whether such juvenilia qualifies under even the most generous definition as "art," for an artist to expect federal subsidy for this work suggests an entitlement mentality that would put such consummate corporate welfare recipients as Boeing and Archer Daniels Midland to shame. Wojnarowicz was welcome to his fantasies, but to expect your Aunt Minnie's tax dollars to fund them was a bit much.

The weakened Helms amendment language expired with the NEA's then-current authorization on September 30, 1990. The reauthorization act substituted for the Helms strictures a direction that when judging applications for funding, the NEA and its panels should take "into consideration general standards of decency and respect for the diverse beliefs and values of the American public."[194] This "decency clause" was almost immediately tested in court.

Performance artists, especially, had come to believe that a federal check was their birthright. When in June 1990 Frohnmayer, responding to reservations expressed by the National Council on the Arts about recommendations of its Theater panel, refused to award grants to performance artists Karen Finley, Holly Hughes, Tim Miller, and John Fleck, the artists promptly dubbed themselves the NEA Four and sued the endowment. The case wended its way to the US Supreme Court, which upheld the legitimacy of the vaguely defined "decency" standards in *National Endowment for the Arts v. Finley*. Each of the NEA Four included sexually explicit material in his or her show. Finley became the best known of the quartet when the syndicated columnists Evans and Novak revealed to the wider world that Ms. Finley sometimes smeared chocolate over her nude body to protest the mistreatment of women. The chocolate was supposed to represent feces, though Ms. Finley's choice to use a symbol rather than the real thing may or may not be instructive.

You have to expend some pity on poor Frohnmayer. He asked the NEA panel that had approved the grant to Fleck, "What am I going to say when one of our critics says that we funded a guy who whizzes on the stage?"[195] He might have reassured them that at least Fleck wasn't urinating into a bottle containing a crucifix.

That writers and artists grown used to the dole were affronted when their grants came under attack in the 1990s only showed how little they knew of the history of public art, says the Dutch culture critic Kees Vuyk. He points to the unusual conjunction in the early Cold War era between the anything-goes aesthetic in avant-garde art, for instance among the Abstract Expressionists, and the political climate, which emphasized the freedom of the West in contrast to the conformity and repression of the East. The artists of this era, writes Vuyk, "developed the idea that governments supported the arts for no other reason than the arts themselves," when in fact, the arts were being "used as weapons in an ideological war."[196] It is no coincidence, says Vuyk, that the NEA came under attack simultaneously with the fall of the Berlin Wall and the demise of Soviet communism. The arts were no longer a useful component of US strategy; they had become expendable, and the artists with them.

One performance artist who was not lucky (or self-dramatizing) enough to be included in the NEA Four but whose work drew the disapproval of Republican politicians was Annie Sprinkle, nee Ellen Steinberg, who had acted in hardcore pornographic films before discovering art school. Her show, *Annie Sprinkle: Post-Porn Modernist*, an explicit account of Ms. Sprinkle's career as porn star cum feminist, was staged in 1990 at The Kitchen, a New York City performance venue. This did not go unnoticed by anti-NEA campaigners. In February 1990, Rep. Dana Rohrabacher circulated a "Dear Colleague" letter alleging that "Ms. Sprinkle is manipulating herself with toys and selling opportunities for the audience to participate in her sex act with tax dollars generously provided by the New York State Council on the Arts which receives half a million dollars in unrestricted funds annually from the National Endowment for the Arts."[197]

For its part, NYSCA denied that Sprinkle was pleasuring herself with its money, though the performer opened a show by announcing, "Usually I get paid a lot of money for this, but tonight it's government funded!"[198] Ms. Sprinkle had a gift for attracting publicity, but this was (perhaps undeserved) bad news for the NEA. When it rains, it pours.

John Frohnmayer stepped down in February 1992, without protest from President Bush, who was being bludgeoned with the NEA issue by maverick candidate Patrick J. Buchanan in the Republican primary campaign. Maybe "stepped down" isn't quite the right phrase: Frohnmayer says they "canned my ass."[199] And yet for all the tempest and roil and bluster, the NEA's budget remained more or less unassailable: in FY 1992, it stood at $176 million. An amendment to the appropriations bill by Rep. Phil Crane (R-IL) to abolish the endowment won only sixty-five votes. A proposal by Republican congressmen Thomas Coleman (MO) and Steve Gunderson (WI) to boost the share of the NEA's budget that goes to state arts councils from 20 percent to 60 percent—a decentralizing measure that was applauded by some state councils—frightened NEA defenders but never posed a serious threat to the agency. The storm had been weathered, rather easily.

The Gingrich Panic

Actress Jane Alexander, a liberal political activist, was President Clinton's choice for chairwoman of the endowment. She was not above histrionics or rhetorical stretches; at a 1994 arts conclave,

Alexander described the mission of government-funded art thusly: "We then begin, person by person, child by child, to build a new America."[200] A more immodest mission would be hard to imagine.

As an actress, Alexander had a stately, calming presence, which she would need when in January 1995 the House of Representatives welcomed a Republican majority for the first time since the Congress that was elected in 1952. The new Speaker of the House, Newt Gingrich of Georgia, fancied himself an intellectual, but he was, or seemed to be, a skeptic of federal subsidies to intellectuals. The NEA became one of the targets of his new majority.

Bills to eliminate the endowment showed up in the hopper. Conservative and libertarian writers made the case against a federal arts policy. Groups with ties to the religious right found that the likes of Serrano and Mapplethorpe still made good fundraising copy. But in the halls of Congress, where the NEA's fate would be decided, the agency was never really in danger of abolition. In 1995, the House kicked the can down the road, voting $99.9 million for both the NEA and NEH in FY 1996 with a threat to zero out funding in two years for the NEA and three years for the NEH, but the Senate would entertain no such abolitionist notions. A conference committee settled on an FY 1996 appropriation of $110 million for the NEH and $99.5 million for the NEA. This was a sharp dip from the Nixon-era levels—and the roles had been reversed, as the NEH had become more popular, or less objectionable, than its big brother—but the endowments survived. In the event, any measure to kill either or both endowments would have met a sure and sustainable veto by President Clinton—despite the fact that Leon Panetta, Clinton's budget director, had recommended defunding the NEA.[201]

In July 1997, the House actually voted 217–216 to shutter the NEA, but the endowment had significant Republican support in the Senate, which ensured it a $98 million appropriation in FY 1998. For the remainder of President Clinton's term, House Republicans would offer motions to abolish the endowment, but the Senate would ensure its survival at levels verging on $100 million. The storm had passed.[202]

Nevertheless, the NEA's hour of darkness produced, in its condemnation and in its defense, some of the most overheated rhetoric this side of a direct-mail barrage. No claim was too hyperbolic to make when the agency's existence was at stake. For as Barbra Streisand described the political landscape in a 1995 speech at Harvard, "The far right is waging a war for the soul of America by making art a partisan issue. And by trying to cut these arts programs, which bring culture, education, and joy into the lives of ordinary Americans, they are hurting the very people they claim to represent."[203] That Hollywood and Harvard might be the allies of "ordinary Americans" in any fight would come as news to many ordinary Americans, but Streisand's formulation was positively milquetoast compared to some outraged arts advocates.

Defenders saw themselves as heroic paladins of the arts standing up to the mob of yahoos with torches who were trying to burn down every museum and library in America. To them, American cultural and intellectual life began, it seems, in 1965; before that annus mirabilis all was darkness and dolor. If this seems an exaggeration, consider the cover story of the August 7, 1995, issue of *Time*, which then was nearing the end of its long run but remained the news magazine of choice for the middle class. "Pulling the Fuse on Culture" was written—one is tempted to say *expectorated*—by Robert Hughes, its eminent Australian art critic.

Hughes was exorcised that "The Republican leadership in Congress means to sever all links between American government and American culture." (One can almost hear the roar of approval—"It's about time!"—from the long line of anarchistic and rebellious American artists.) "These boys and girls aren't even cultural Neanderthals," fumed Hughes, whose diatribe went on to excoriate, predictably, the "blitzkrieg" by the "insatiable Fundamentalist Christian right wing," which was motivated by "meanness" and "smug Philistinism." The NEA (and its eclipsed junior partner, the NEH, which was doing its best to keep a low profile and avoid the brickbats), represent "[i]ntelligent appreciation of the arts and humanities"; its opponents are either "shortsighted materialists or mere yahoos," whose political spokesmen are "bigots and populist lowbrows." These "zealots," with their "ranting queer hatred," are about to subject the country to a "[p]artial lobotom[y]."

Whew!

To give Hughes credit, he did observe of Andres "*Piss Christ*" Serrano: "Artists who call themselves sociopolitical subversives, and then ask for state handouts, are either fools or hypocrites." And in an echo of the internal debates over Federal One, Hughes came down emphatically on the side of "the dreaded Q word: quality," opining that the agency "should be more elitist."[204] These are arguable propositions that would have the effect of making the NEA an even more regressive redistributor of tax monies from the middle class to the affluent, but they are not banal bromides or hackneyed art-ese.

So over-the-top was Hughes's screed that it provoked a reasoned response from, of all people, House Speaker Newt Gingrich. Eschewing the red-meat approach, Gingrich quoted art historian Alice Goldfarb Marquis, author of the valuable *Art Lessons: Learning from the Rise and Fall of Public Arts Funding* (1995), that "Art is not a product like soybeans, but rather the outcome of imaginative endeavor by talented people, of whom there is always a limited supply. When grants prop up artists unable to attract audiences, individuals with limited abilities persist, crowding out superior talents." Gingrich then asked, "Should the American people be forced to underwrite cultural dependents who add to our decay and undermine our values rather than enhance our lives?"

He soft-pedaled the smut stuff, though he did object to "putting the government's imprimatur on *Piss Christ*," which gave "a signal that it is acceptable to mock and blaspheme faith in the Creator." Rejecting the philistine label—and whatever one thinks of the colorful Mr. Gingrich, he is and was no philistine—the Speaker put forth, in brief, an alternative vision that he claimed would "improve the arts and the country by returning power and authority to the private sector." This included changes to the tax code to encourage gifts to private foundations, a somewhat hazy plan to privatize the NEA and NEH by transferring them to "the arts community" (one imagines a game of hot potato, as the supposed beneficiaries frantically pass the "gift" back and forth), and, less radically, a requirement that artists whose NEA-supported work proves valuable in the commercial market must give the endowment a percentage of their royalties.[205] Substance aside, Gingrich won the round by not losing his head.

What was remarkable was the paucity of artists on the anti-NEA side in this debate. As Michael Kammen noted in 1996 in the *Journal of American History*, "We tend to forget that in 1964–1965, when the NEA was being hesitantly created, some of the most prestigious artists, art critics, and arts institutions felt suspicious of politicians and believed that they had more to lose than to gain from any involvement in the political process. Three decades later that pattern of mistrust has been turned inside out."[206]

There were throwbacks: for instance novelist John Updike, who in a speech intended for the American Academy and Institute of Arts and Letters in May 1989—it was undelivered due to a fire scare, though the *Wall Street Journal* later published it—lectured supplicants, "The ancient law that he who pays the piper calls the tune has not been repealed even in this permissive democracy, and the cultural entrepreneurs so eager to welcome NEH and NEA money into the arts may now be aware that they have invited a dog—wooly and winsome but not without teeth and an ugly bark—into their manger."[207]

But arts advocates had won the public relations battle. The middlebrow and elite press depicted NEA foes as knuckle-dragging anti-intellectuals who hated art and artists.

Jane Alexander left the chairmanship after a single four-year term, and President Clinton nominated Bill Ivey, a folklorist, academic, and director of Nashville's Country Music Foundation, to replace her. It was, culturally, a masterstroke. The populist Ivey's interests included folk music, bluegrass, and local cultures. His was not the résumé of a Karen Finley groupie, or someone who would be intimidated by the hectoring of grant-seeking performance artists.

The FY 2001 NEA appropriation increased slightly, from $97.4 million in FY 2000 to $105 million, and under President George W. Bush the endowment fully regained its political footing. Bush's first appointed NEA chairman, composer and dean of Rice University's Shepherd School of Music, Michael Hammond, died just a week into his term. An acting chair, Eileen Mason, bridged the thirteen-month gap until Bush's next nominee, the respected poet Dana Gioia, assumed the position.

Gioia was widely praised for his skill in directing endowment funds toward artistically worthy projects, such as the Shakespeare in American Communities program, under which touring theatrical companies brought the Bard to schools and (largely) smaller cities and towns as well as military bases; and the Jazz Masters Initiative, which sent American jazz virtuosos fanning out across the country in an attempt to inject new vitality into an American art form that seemed to be dying from a lack of an audience.

As the NEA's reputation improved, so did its funding. Under Gioia's one-and-a-half term chairmanship (he resigned early to resume his poetry: he was foremost an artist, not a bureaucrat), the NEA budget grew from $115.7 million in FY 2003 to $155 million in FY 2009.

As if conjuring up the ghost of Roger Stevens, President Obama nominated Broadway impresario Rocco Landesman to be his first chair of the NEA. Landesman, who seemed to revel in the role of brash New Yorker (even though he was born in St. Louis, son of a cabaret owner), had produced such Broadway blockbusters as "The Producers" and "Angels in America." He made an immediate misstep when, picking a Middle American city out of the air, he said, "I don't know if there's a theater in Peoria," and he doubted that even if such a thing existed it would be worthy of NEA support.[208] After his impolitic remark, Landesman went on what was widely joked to be a crow-eating tour. He toured Peoria's artistic sites, pronounced them fabulous, and even took in a production of *Rent* at East Peoria High School.

Lee Rosenbaum of the *Wall Street Journal*, in a sympathetic profile of Landesman, wrote, "Lost in the Peoria euphoria is the important point Mr. Landesman was trying to make—that the chief criterion for grants should be artistic excellence, not geographic distribution."[209] Once again, New York's culturati was insisting that the city's offerings were superior to those of the hinterlands—and when the hinterlands merely offers pale imitations of New York City productions, à la *Rent*, they may have a point.

Landesman was succeeded by a much lower-profile arts bureaucrat, Jane Chu, a skilled fund-raiser who had been president and chief executive of the Kauffman Center for the Performing Arts in Kansas City, Missouri.[210] She was unlikely to insult Peoria, and her talents at shaking the money tree were much desired, as the NEA's budget ($146 million in FY 2015) was lower than it was when George W. Bush left office.

An Irrelevancy

If the imputed immorality of selected NEA grant-getters no longer fueled opposition to the agency, a new criticism of the endowment appeared on the distant horizon as the twenty-first century dawned: It was no longer necessary. It had been passed by. It was yesterday's news.

The NEA reforms of the Clinton and G. W. Bush administrations had muted much of the opposition. Among the alterations to the endowment in the wake of the 1990s controversies was the elimination of grants to individual artists (literature excepted) and a change in the composition of the National Council on the Arts, which was reduced from twenty-six members to (currently) eighteen private members plus six members of Congress in an ex officio capacity. This latter reform may be seen as a way of putting the endowment further under the congressional thumb or as a means of injecting some political reality into decisions about whether to fund institutions that will use those funds to exhibit works offensive to the taxpayers to whom, at least in theory, the members of Congress must answer.

The great decentralization threat of the mid-1990s, when moderate Republicans looked with favor on bypassing the NEA and sending federal funds directly to state arts agencies, has also passed. At present,

40 percent of the NEA's program funds are sent to state arts agencies, an amount too high, in the view of the endowment's true believers, but just high enough to satisfy potentially troublesome hinterlands Republicans.

The endowment's current programs include Theater, Media Arts, Museums and Visual Arts, Dance, Literature, and Music and Opera—no pinochle, squash, or belly dancing, pace H. R. Gross. The antielitist argument with respect to opera has faded, and the formerly suspicious local orchestras have fallen into line. The Music and Opera programs support orchestras, opera companies, choruses, jazz and chamber music, and various festivals. The American Symphony Orchestra League, quondam doubter of the efficacy of a federal ministry of culture, changed its tune (and its name to the League of American Orchestras); its website now offers visitors and its approximately eight hundred member orchestras "opportunities for orchestra advocates to urge Congress to restore NEA funding."[211] In FY 2014, the NEA sent $2,891,500 to 116 orchestras through its Grants for Arts projects.[212]

The NEA never did become a Ministry of Culture or a Federal Bureau of the Arts. The wildest warnings of its opponents did not pan out. Unlike the WPA's Federal One, the NEA has not been a patron of a distinctive school of art. The New Deal project had favored, though not exclusively, of course, murals and Americanist realism (or what the English art historian Jonathan Harris calls "democratic realism") in art[213]; social democratic didacticism in its plays, particularly of the "Living Newspaper" variety; and a flat and factual (though sometimes enlivened by colorful details and asides) style in its guidebooks. But as Mark Bauerlein, editor of an NEA-published 2008 history of the endowment, notes, "Neither the Arts Endowment nor the artists or arts administrators who advised the agency over the past four decades have sought to align the NEA with a sociopolitical agenda."[214] (The early 1990s partisans and antipartisans of Karen Finley, Holly Hughes, and Annie Sprinkle would disagree.)

But the endowment now runs workshops for critics and journalists in dance, theater, opera, and classical music, and while the potential for political propagandizing through classical opera may be limited, the thought of government sponsoring the education of art critics would be deeply troubling to those skeptics of government-funded art who suspected that one goal of Federal One and the NEA and NEH was to encourage or discourage certain artistic schools or traditions, be they avant-garde, traditional, or modern.

Yet concerns that the NEA might become an instrument of propaganda seem to have receded as its profile has lessened. A new generation of critics is asking not what *harm* it does but what *good* it does. The American model of arts funding, argues economist Tyler Cowen, "encourages artistic creativity, keeps the politicization of art to a minimum, and brings economics and aesthetics into a symbiotic relationship."[215] That model is marked by decentralized funding, minimal direction by the central government, indirect subsidies (often via the federal tax code), and significant contributions from philanthropy.

In recent years scholarly attention has turned from the potential of direct subsidy—which seems limited, as the NEA's budget has achieved an unimpressive stasis—to the very real and vast network of indirect subsidies that have played a largely unacknowledged part in supporting American arts.

In *Patrons Despite Themselves: Taxpayers and Arts Policy*, a study sponsored by the Twentieth Century Fund, authors Alan L. Feld, Michael O'Hare, and J. Mark Davidson Schuster examine the role that indirect subsidies to the arts have played. They liken this support to "an underground river through the tax system" that "provides the arts with about two-thirds of all the government support they receive."[216]

This indirect government aid takes various forms. The most obvious is tax deductions for charitable contributions by individuals or corporations, which may be in the form of money or artwork. Federal deductions for charitable donations to nonprofit charitable organizations, including museums and those related to the arts, have been a feature of the federal tax code since 1917, when a 15 percent deduction for such contributions was established. The deduction for charitable contributions encourages support for the arts while permitting the donor to target her eleemosynary to favored organizations or activities rather than some monolithic agency labeled "Art." As Joel Feinberg writes, such tax measures "allow taxpayers to some degree to choose the direct beneficiaries of their own tax payments, and escape to some degree the requirement that they support causes from which they do not themselves benefit and of which they may even disapprove."[217]

Tax policy has broad implications for arts funding. Reductions in income tax rates may spur greater contributions to the arts, since taxpayers have more disposable income, or they may reduce incentives for giving by lessening the value of such contributions. The same is true of changes in estate or capital gains taxes. Deductions for donated artwork (by collectors) and expenses (by artists) can indirectly assist (or penalize) artists and those who collect their work. Tax exemptions for nonprofits, including cultural institutions such as art museums, are another indirect subsidy.

One notable advantage of indirect subsidies, at least in the view of those who share John Sloan's fear of a Ministry of Culture directing artistic affairs, is that, as economist Tyler Cowen notes, "Tax subsidies allow the government to support the arts while avoiding judgments about artistic merit."[218]

Feld, O'Hare, and Schuster recommend that if governments are to subsidize the arts, they do so publicly, via direct subsidy, rather than through the tax code. This would certainly be more transparent, though it is hard to imagine museums and other cultural institutions preferring to lobby elected bodies for more money rather than rely on the tax-advantaged charitable giving of the current system.

Arthur C. Brooks, formerly a professor at Syracuse University's Maxwell School of Citizenship and Public Affairs, now president of the American Enterprise Institute, has estimated that for every dollar of direct federal aid to the arts, Americans contribute $14 in tax-deductible contributions. As previously noted, Brooks finds that the likeliest supporters of government aid to the arts and culture are not identical to those who actually donate to the arts and cultural groups. The former—supporters of government—are disproportionately "nonwhite, educated, self-described liberals," while the latter—those who actually donate, and thus are in practice supporters of indirect aid—are likeliest to be "upper-income, educated white women."[219]

Given the far greater resources available from indirect rather than direct aid, Brooks counsels arts groups to target potential private donors rather than government officials. Relying on philanthropy—indirect giving—"appears to be more of a winning fund-raising strategy than shaking the tree of direct aid," he concludes.[220]

NEA defenders love the word *leverage*, for they emphasize that the endowment, though its annual appropriation is modest, permits grantees to leverage NEA monies into additional grants and greater sums. The endowment limits its role to that of co-financer; the grantee must raise the remainder of the sum necessary to execute the project from foundations, corporations, or private support. Yet as Romina Boccia, a fellow at the Hoover Institution, points out, "Even Kickstarter raises more money for the arts than is available from NEA's budget. Federal funding for the arts is neither necessary nor within the proper scope of the federal government. . . . The NEA should be eliminated."[221]

Indeed, Kickstarter, the website through which writers, filmmakers, artists, game designers, and other creative people solicit donors, has been the medium through which $2 billion has been raised for over 78,000 projects since 2009. Over that same period, the cumulative budgets for the NEA—and this includes administrative and other costs that wind up nowhere near an actual living breathing artist or intellectual—have been $906 million. As is the case with those who receive benefactions from the NEA, those who raise money via Kickstarter are under no financial obligation to those who invest, though they often promise them film or book credits, first editions, tickets, and the like. As Kickstarter explains on its website, "Creative works were funded this way for centuries. Mozart, Beethoven, Whitman, Twain, and other artists funded works in similar ways—not just with help from large patrons, but by soliciting money from smaller patrons, often called subscribers. In return for their support, these subscribers might have received an early copy or special edition of the work. Kickstarter is an extension of this model, turbocharged by the web."

Kickstarter projects are not vetted by the credentialed experts who were so prized by those who conceived the NEA. There are regulations pertaining to the website and its users, but there are no real gatekeepers or quality-control experts. Donors—*voluntary* donors—pledge their funds to projects that sound worthy or interesting or offbeat or that just tickle their fancy. If the project fails to meet its funding goal, no money changes hands. But in almost half—44 percent—of the cases, pledges meet or top the goal, and the green light flashes.[222] Kickstarter is in the best tradition of voluntaristic American endeavor. And it is a harbinger of web-enabled fundraising for artistic ventures.

Other Internet sites supporting various aspects of the arts are emerging. For example, whereas music projects are the largest category on Kickstarter, "artists have been flocking to the crowdfunding sites. Indiego . . . hosted more than 9,000 theater and music campaigns" in 2014. That number has ballooned more than 110 percent since 2011."[223]

At all events, the National Endowment for the Arts is in no danger of disappearing.[224] That brief period during which fundamental questions were being raised, and criticisms both trenchant and overblown were being leveled at the NEA, is long over. If the NEA ever dies, it seems likely that the cause of death will be irrelevance instead of irreverence.[225]

The Great Afterthought: The National Endowment for the Humanities

The "Open for Business" sign in the great game of subsidizing the research of intellectuals was hung out in 1950, with the creation of the National Science Foundation. (For an extended treatment of the NSF's birth in the context of federal subsidization of science, see my book *The Doomsday Lobby: Hype and Panic from Sputniks, Martians, and Marauding Meteors.*)[226] Basic research was now a subject of government benefaction, though NSF advocates were always careful, especially in those early years, to tie in their work with national defense.

The congressional hearings preceding the birth of the National Science Foundation featured just a single harsh critic of the various proposals. He was Frank Jewett, a University of Chicago Ph.D. who had taught physics at the Massachusetts Institute of Technology before embarking on a storied career as a research scientist, head of Bell Telephone Laboratories, and president of the National Academy of Sciences from 1939 to 1947.

Jewett warned the heedless members of Congress against placing science under the federal heel, which he said would be a "radical departure from the normal American way, which during the past 150 years has taken American science and technology to the highest pinnacle man has ever achieved." That pinnacle was scaled by men whose genius and inventiveness were nurtured by liberty, not government grants or state coercion, Jewett emphasized. He reminded the solons that "Every direct or indirect subvention by Government is not only coupled inevitably with bureaucratic types of control, but likewise with political control and with the urge to create pressure groups seeking to advance special interests."[227]

His testimony was fruitless. The 1940s and 50s were the era of Big Science, which received an even more potent boost when the Russians launched the 184-pound artificial satellite dubbed *Sputnik* on October 4, 1957. Suddenly, the American political establishment panicked that the sky was falling. Although the unflappable President Eisenhower dismissed *Sputnik* as a "one small ball in the air," politicians raced each other to introduce and then take credit for legislation that spawned, among other entities, the National Defense Education Act, the National Aeronautics and Space Administration, and the Office of Science and Technology.[228]

No one flipped the panic switch with quite the alacrity of Senate Majority Leader Lyndon B. Johnson, who told the Senate Armed

Services Subcommittee on Preparedness Investigation in November 1957, a month after *Sputnik I* orbited the Earth, "We meet today in an atmosphere of another Pearl Harbor."[229]

Scholars in the arts and letters cast a jealous eye on their brethren in the hard sciences. If physicists could be awarded federal grants, why not philologists? As Stephen R. Graubard, Brown University historian and editor of *Daedalus: The Journal of the American Academy of Arts and Sciences*, wrote in his assessment of the National Endowment for the Humanities in its twentieth year, the "most significant fact, certainly, about the Endowment's founding is that it modelled itself very deliberately on the National Science Foundation."[230] And yet, as Graubard notes, peer review is not as useful in the humanities as in the sciences, and there was no analogue in the humanities to Vannevar Bush's *Science—The Endless Frontier* (1945), to make the case for a major federal investment in the field. The humanities, unlike Big Science, had not appreciably helped the Allies win the Second World War, and the Soviet Union was fighting the Cold War with Sputnik, not Pasternak and Solzhenitsyn.

Yet the dim outlines of a government program were visible. Ronald Berman, who would chair the National Endowment for the Humanities, observed that the establishment of the NSF "indicated to part of the academic profession that it could rely on the federal government for subsidies." The sciences had gotten a foot inside the door of the US Treasury. The humanities demanded their share. And so "historians, philosophers and literary critics campaigned for federal patronage."[231]

On January 21, 1962, at the annual meeting of the American Council of Learned Societies (ACLS), which was founded in 1919 and described itself as "a private, nonprofit federation of national scholarly organizations concerned with the humanities and the humanistic aspects of the social sciences,"[232] the ACLS adopted a resolution that read, in part: "That this council very strongly urges that the Federal Government, in the national interest and for the strengthening of our scholarly and intellectual resources on the broadest possible front, extend its support of higher education and research to include all the humanities and the social sciences on the same basis as mathematics, the natural sciences, and technology."[233]

In early 1963 a National Commission on the Humanities was born, its parentage a tripartite affair of the American Council of Learned Societies, the Council of Graduate Schools in the United States, and the United Chapters of Phi Beta Kappa. The commission's job was "to consider the state of the humanities in America and to report its findings and recommendations to the sponsoring organizations."[234] Everyone knew that the commission was intended to do for the humanities what Vannevar Bush's report on *Science—The Endless Frontier* had done for the hard sciences: lay the foundation for a foundation. Before Congress could act, however, there was the formality of an official report.

The commission's chairman was Brown University President Barnaby C. Keeney, who had long and intricate ties with the Central Intelligence Agency. Its twenty members included luminaries from academic administration (Presidents Kingman Brewster of Yale, Theodore M. Hesburgh of Notre Dame, and Clark Kerr of the University of California Berkeley, and Chancellor Herman B. Wells of Indiana University); business (Thomas J. Watson Jr., chairman of IBM; Devereaux C. Josephs, former chairman of New York Life Insurance); and academe (professors of history, philosophy, French, classics, and English from such schools as Brown, Duke, Princeton, and the University of Michigan). The result was, as poet and Director of the Folger Shakespeare Library O. B. Hardison Jr. wrote, "a statement by the academic establishment for the academic establishment."[235]

The commission issued its report on April 30, 1964. Its members unanimously urged that the three sponsoring societies "take appropriate steps to promote the establishment of a National Humanities Foundation, particularly the enactment of legislation authorizing the appointment of the board of the National Humanities Foundation and the director and staff, and the appropriation of funds for organization and planning."[236] Bingo! The National Commission on the Humanities had done exactly what it was supposed to do: transfer the prestige and cachet associated with its individual members and their institutions to the idea of a government bureaucracy that would subsidize those doing work in the humanities.

The commission's report begins by affirming the importance of the humanities as "the study of that which is most human." After some gauzy rhetoric about the humanities being about all of us, it gets down to cases. The humanities include the study of "history, literature, the arts, religion, and philosophy."[237]

These disciplines have gotten on tolerably well without state subvention, and the commission does not bother to dispute that fact. So the c-word must be introduced. "The state of the humanities today creates a crisis for national leadership." A crisis? What crisis? Well, there looms a "danger that wavering purpose and lack of well-conceived effort may leave us second-best in a world correspondingly impoverished by our incomplete success." This sentence is hard to unpack, but key words therein—"danger," "wavering purpose," "second-best"—are classic locutions of Cold War-era fundraising.[238] There's a Cold War going on, a nuclear arms race, a contest for world supremacy—and finishing "second-best" is tantamount to being finished, period. There is no second-best in competition in which there can be only one winner. There is the winner and there is the loser. And God help the USA if it finishes second in *this* competition.

The commission goes on in the same vein, emphasizing that "World leadership of the kind which has come upon the United States cannot rest solely upon superior force, vast wealth, or preponderant technology." Government commitment to the humanities is thus an essential piece of US world leadership. Yet Americans are falling down on the job. "American practitioners of the humanities—the professionals, so to speak—are now prevented in certain specific ways from realizing their full capacities and from attracting enough first-rate individuals into their ranks."

And how are these "professionals" prevented from carrying out their profession? Lack of money. Like the jealous sibling complaining that Mom and Dad like Big Sister better, the commissioners fret that Big Brother in Washington is favoring Science. They explain:

> The laudable practice of the federal government of making large sums of money available for scientific research has brought great benefits, but it has also brought about an imbalance within academic institutions by the very fact of abundance in one field of study and dearth in another. Much of the federal money for science requires a proportionate commitment of general university funds to sustain the higher level of activity in the scientific departments. Students, moreover, are no different from other people in that they can quickly observe where money is being made available and draw the logical conclusion as to which activities their society considers important. The nation's need for balanced education demands that this imbalance be remedied.[239]

One solution would be to end government subsidization of science—which in practice tended to be Big Science with military applications. This view would achieve a brief vogue several years later, when for a short time public scrutiny focused on the military-industrial-science-university complex, but as of 1964, it was inconceivable to the substantial men (and one woman) who made up the Commission on the Humanities that government funding of scholarship might have insidious or nefarious consequences.

The commission asks the question that was on the lips of mossback conservatives and far-out libertarians: "Is it then in the interest of the United States and its federal government to give greater support to the humanities?" Not to spoil the suspense, but the answer was a resounding *Yes*! The national government, they point out, has "greatly extended" its reach into many aspects of American social and economic life. "Health was once considered a private problem; it is now a national one. The newer forms of transportation are heavily subsidized and, to some extent, controlled by the federal government. In World War II the federal government undertook an active role in technology and since then. . . . it has greatly extended its activities in the fields of science. Education was once entirely the concern of private foundations or local government, but it has long since ceased to be so."[240]

One would think that the cautionary example of science might slow down the headlong rush of our commission into the advocacy of a national cultural policy. No less than President Dwight Eisenhower had quite recently and ominously warned, in his Farewell Address of January 17, 1961:

> Today, the solitary inventor, tinkering in his shop, has been overshadowed by task forces of scientists in laboratories and testing fields. In the same fashion, the free university, historically the fountainhead of free ideas and scientific discovery, has experienced a revolution in the conduct of research. Partly because of the huge costs involved, a government contract becomes virtually a substitute for intellectual curiosity. For every old blackboard there are now hundreds of electric computers.
>
> The prospect of domination of the nation's scholars by federal employment, project allocations, and the power of money is ever present—and is gravely to be regarded.
>
> Yet, in holding scientific research and discovery in respect, as we should, we must be alert to the equal and opposite danger that public policy could itself become the captive of the scientific-technological elite.[241]

The prospect of a humanities-government complex seemed remote. The commission and its sponsors had seen the main chance, and they intended to seize it. "Traditionally our government has entered areas where there were overt difficulties or where an opportunity had opened for exceptional achievement," stated the National Commission on the Humanities, with a childlike faith in the sincerity of politicians' pronouncements. (Were they entirely unacquainted with, say, the history of US railroad policy?) "The humanities fit both categories, for the potential achievements are enormous while the troubles stemming from inadequate support are comparably great."

This is asserted rather than demonstrated or proven. Was there really a humanities crisis in the United States in the early 1960s? Impressive, even stunning or monumental works of the visual, musical, and literary arts were distinguishing American culture; so, too, were scholarly achievements in fields as disparate as Biblical studies, American literature, and biography. No one outside, perhaps, a *Pravda* editorialist really believed the United States to be a vast wasteland whose population was doltish, materialistic, and wholly uninterested in the finer things or the most profound questions.

But you wouldn't know that from reading the apologists for state subsidy. "The stakes are so high and the issues of such magnitude that the humanities must have substantial help both from the federal government and from other sources," the report states. Then it comes to the crux of the matter—indeed, to the commission's very reason for being: "It is for these reasons that the Commission recommends the establishment of a National Humanities Foundation to parallel the National Science Foundation, which is so successfully carrying out the public responsibilities entrusted to it."

The NSF was the obvious model for the proposed NHF. The commissioners went so far as to attest that the NSF was basically apolitical: "It is encouraging to note that the federal government in its massive program of subsidy for the sciences and technology has not imposed control and, indeed has not even shown an inclination to control the thoughts and activities of scientists."[242]

Sure it hasn't. As Joseph P. Martino discovered in his study *Science Funding: Politics and Porkbarrel* (1992), "the dominant influence of the NSF in certain disciplines means that a handful of individual project officers in the NSF can shape the content of entire disciplines."[243]

The commission does acknowledge a potential downside of a government humanities agency: "A government which gives no support at all to humane values [a nice substitution for "humanities scholars"] is careless of its own destiny, but that government which gives too much support—and seeks to acquire influence—may be more dangerous still." After all, while it is imperative that we "increase the. . . . flow of funds" to intellectuals working in the humanities, "we must safeguard the independence, the originality, and the freedom of expression of all who are concerned with liberal learning."[244]

And how to do that? By creating a new federal agency, of course! This agency, the National Humanities Foundation, would consist of a Director and a twenty-four-member Board, all of whom would be appointed by the President with the advice and consent of the Senate. The proposed board would be composed of persons "selected for their general cultivation and competence in the humanities." The foundation would be charged with ensuring "that suitable means are provided for educating and developing scholars, artists, and teachers at every stage of their growth." The "means of publishing or otherwise disseminating the results of their endeavors, both within the academic community and to the public at large, must be available." Which means subsidies for book publishers and scholarly journals. Specifically, "the Foundation should concentrate its subsidies for publication in university presses or in experimental and scholarly works which under present circumstances cannot be financed." And lest anyone worry that more direct assistance is being forgotten, "Grants to properly qualified and endorsed individuals are a fruitful and efficient way to accomplish these ends." Finally, humanities scholars would get what was coming to them: cash from the taxpayer from the federal government.[245]

Other deserving recipients of funds from the proposed National Humanities Foundation included public and school libraries (especially "major research libraries"), institutions that train teachers, cultural buildings, and "any corporate or private body involved in the humanities or the arts for the promoting of research, teaching, performance, and publication."[246] Academic conferences, both domestic and international, were to fall within the bailiwick of the foundation as well.

And what about any lurking pitfalls involved in the national government's sponsorship of humanities research? "If the director and members of the board are men of acknowledged competence and courage, as are the director and members of the National Science Board, there should be no problem of improper control."[247] With the government involved, what could possibly go wrong?

For their part, the three institutional sponsors of the commission summed up its findings thus: "The *Report* stresses two fundamental points: (1) that expansion and improvement of activities in the humanities are in the national interest and consequently deserve financial support by the federal government; and (2) that federal funds for this purpose should be administered by a new independent agency to be known as the National Humanities Foundation." The kicker came in the next sentence: "On the first of these points the sponsors believe there is no room for debate."[248]

Well that settles that! Never mind that for nigh unto 180 years of the republic the idea that the national government ought to financially support scholarship in the humanities had been anything *but* a settled question. Indeed, the preponderance of sentiment had been on the negative side of the question. But that was before humanities professors and the institutions for which they worked had become supplicants and lobbyists. The authors of the report understood that one way to forestall opposition was to declare the question closed. Declare that all people with triple-digit IQs were in agreement on the question. Dissentients were either mentally feeble, eccentric, or reactionaries.

The sponsors did allow that debate was permissible over whether governmental support of the humanities should be administered through a new humanities foundation or an existing agency. They endorsed the commission's recommendation of a new independent agency in part because it would "correct the view of those who see America as a nation interested only in the material aspects of life and Americans as a people skilled only in gadgeteering."[249] As we have seen in other cases, the advocates of state subsidy like to fall back on the alleged disrespect Europeans have for Americans, a disrespect that can best be dissipated by generous infusions of taxpayer monies to intellectuals.

Twenty-four learned societies contributed to a supplement of the *Report of the Commission on Humanities*. Most are worthy and earnest and dull, though some repay reading half a century later. Striking a note that comes close to parody, the American Society for Aesthetics takes aim at the philistine taxpayers whose monies they crave but whose characters they condemn. Huff the aestheticians:

> The New Leisure finds the "quiet American" spending more and more of his time and money on the arts. Yet, troubled by his Puritan and practicalist upbringing, he is at a loss to know what role the arts may rightfully play in the social order, beyond that of private amusements. The "unquiet American," on the other hand, sees the contemporary artist as some kind of public menace to be met with contempt and anger. Surely the blatancy and malaproprism of some Americans' talk about art are symptoms of an unexamined life more discordant than they will admit. The "unquiet American" may "know what he likes," but he is really not very happy with it.[250]

Finding a more straightforward expression of contempt for one's fellow Americans would be difficult, but the aestheticians—who are neither "quiet" nor "unquiet" Americans but, instead, belong to some presumably superior category—are perfectly happy to take the tax dollars of these dullards and simpletons.

Getting down to cases, the American Society for Aesthetics lists as the number one need of aestheticians "Support for Individual Research." Specifically, aestheticians "need time; relief from teaching loads; travel (both domestic and foreign); funds for books, music, photos, microfilms and other instruments of scholarship, and secretarial assistance." The aestheticians also insist on the "need to meet with our fellow inquirers, both for stimulation and for joint research." Moreover, the lack of a commercial market for books by members of the society, as well as "difficulty in obtaining support for illustrated books," demonstrates the crying need for government subsidy of the publishing industry, or at least that niche of it devoted to aesthetics.[251]

If the price of receiving such aid was traffic or intercourse with the boob-like quiet and unquiet Americans whose taxes filled the Treasury's larder, well, the aestheticians would probably endure that, though not with a smile. The sacrifices intellectuals have to make to live the life of the mind boggle the imagination!

Few organizations were quite as obvious as the American Society for Aesthetics in their disdain for the nonintellectuals from whom they were demanding support, but many were just as insistent that the "need for a national foundation for the humanities" was "self-evident," as the statement of the American Studies Association put it.[252]

The American Historical Association, while endorsing a national foundation, added that in the case of the humanities, it was "most dangerous to entrust to the benevolence or direction of any single authority, whether of church or of party or of state." Therefore any support for the humanities from the federal government must be "limited and indirect," "matched by support from many other sources," and controlled "by a mixed body or by several bodies of policy-makers."[253] Raising the specter of Orwell's *1984*, the AHA warned of "history politically controlled."[254] It was a concern seldom raised by other dunners for dollars.

Even the Metaphysical Society of America weighed in on the subject, suggesting that among the benefits of a national humanities foundation would be the emplacement of grant-makers who are "humanists who realize that quantitative results are not the purpose of research in the humanities," and that "the lack of specificity which would invalidate a proposal for a scientific research contract might be exactly appropriate in application for a grant in the humanities."[255] Again, this was a way of bypassing those practical-minded philistines (or Puritans, or Babbitts, or whatever the term of disapprobation happened to be) and ensuring that monies flowed to intellectuals without visible strings attached.

The American Political Science Association (APSA) betrayed no such worries about the prospect of governmental misbehavior, except to concede that the board of directors of the NHF should be drawn "from outside the ranks of government personnel." It endorsed a national humanities foundation as something that "would greatly encourage the cultivation of that kind of intellectual activity in which we can take legitimate pride." The APSA saw nothing but blue skies as far as the federal government's activity could stretch: "It has become apparent that governments can do much to stimulate scientific and technological advancement, and under the motivation of national defense and the threat of communism throughout the world the United States government has already appropriately encouraged the training of future scientists and engineers and encouraged scientists to probe the frontiers of outer space. In its legitimate concern for such advancement of knowledge and technology it should not neglect the cultivation of those ingredients of the good life that identify the kind of civilization we all want to defend."[256]

The political scientists knew which bells to ring. They spoke the language of Cold War liberalism, which granted to the national government powers and capabilities far outstripping those previously entertained by the US government and the public. In this formulation, the defense industry and Big Science were unalloyed national benefits, as were the social-welfare infrastructure and the burgeoning bureaucracy on the Potomac. To this bureaucracy the APSA wished to add a national humanities foundation. It would aid the political science community by funding fellowships, supporting dissertations, underwriting travel, sponsoring seminars and conferences, designing courses on "communism and Marxism" for secondary schools, and, of course, financing research by political scientists. Its eyes fixed on the prize, the APSA noted that the "need to understand Marxist-Leninist thought" is "obvious."[257] Should government fund scholars who are studying that very government? The question never arises in the APSA's contribution to the *Report of the Commission on the Humanities.*

Other scholarly organizations endorsing the creation of a national humanities foundation included the American Anthropological

Association, the Archaeological Institute of America, the Society of Biblical Literature, the Association of American Geographers (though its preference was for the NSF to incorporate the humanities), the History of Science Society, the Modern Language Association, the American Musicological Society, and the Renaissance Society of America, which could not help pointing out the injustice of "the grant to a science college of $30,000 plus costly equipment" from the National Science Foundation, while Renaissance scholars scrounge for a spare thousand here or there from foundations.[258]

Interestingly, the Society of Architectural Historians, while endorsing federal support of "the physical appearance of the cities," admitted that their ranks were far from unanimous on the desirability of more extensive federal support of their work. "[A] number of those consulted," said the society's statement, "have strongly expressed the view that the expense of research and publication concerned with knowledge for its own sake are more related to the aims of the foundations—particularly at a time when government debts are mounting."[259] This display of unselfish fiscal responsibility was not widely imitated.

Another note of skepticism was sounded by the American Sociological Association, perhaps because the chairman of its committee to consider the NHF, Robert Nisbet, was an admirer of voluntary and mediating institutions rather than large coercive states. Concluded the ASA report: "Finally, should we think in terms of a large, NSF-type of foundation for the humanities? Yes, if this is the only means of channeling federal funds for research in the humanities. But, given the familiar problems of organizational ethos and management, it may be doubted whether sociologists and political scientists would encounter any greater hostility for their humanistic projects than they do in existing organizations."[260]

Advocates for a national humanities foundation understood that their discipline lacked the cachet and glamour of the arts and the military patina and astronautical sexiness of the sciences. Standing alone, they were quite likely to be the odd man out. So they sought linkage with the more popular and established campaign to create an agency or department of culture. As historian John Higham wrote in his account of the genesis of the NEH, "the humanities would have a better chance of gaining federal aid if their drive were tied to the more broadly based and fully developed campaign for governmental support of the arts."[261]

The arts world, or that segment thereof that solicited federal support, was at first nonplussed by these johnny-come-latelies. Who were they to horn in on the carefully laid plans of the arts advocates? (The difference between the two broad fields, according to some administrators, was "If they do it, it's art. If they talk about it, it's humanities."[262]) And Americans have always preferred doers to talkers. In line with this aphorism, NEH recipients are barred from using their funding to "create original works of art."[263] Yet in retrospect, Senator Claiborne Pell, the Rhode Island Brahmin who was among the founding fathers of the endowments, claimed that the humanities had the broader base of support. "The arts, except in Boston, New York, Chicago, and Los Angeles," said Pell, "didn't have much strength across the country. Humanities had it right across the country. . . . so we combined, we. . . . rode 'piggy-back' on the humanities." Pell's surprising assessment was seconded by Robert Lumiansky, then acting president of the American Council of Learned Societies, who said in 1985 that "[t]he arts bills could never be pushed through Congress because of the lasting memories among some members of Congress of the supposed communist leanings of persons in the theatre during the Depression."[264] The arts endowment needed the staid but decidedly non-Red humanities aboard to make it to enactment.

President Lyndon B. Johnson, not hitherto acknowledged as a man with an especial interest in the humanities, gave his imprimatur to the nationalization of humanities scholarship in a speech at Brown University on September 28, 1964. His host was Brown President Barnaby Keeney, who soon chaired the very endowment whose creation President Johnson was endorsing. Johnson was aware, as subsequent studies found, that he enjoyed the overwhelming support of academics in the humanities, and as a canny politician he believed in rewarding his supporters.[265]

President Johnson told the audience at Brown that "the sum of human knowledge" was increasing, and it was the responsibility of the universities, in conjunction with the federal government, to keep up with it, lest. . . . well, lest we fail to compute the sum, or comprehend the sum, or reduce the sum, or something. The metaphor was not clear. But what was clear was that in the President's view, it was time for the "partnership of the Government, your Government—not an enemy way-off-yonder, but something that belongs to you. . . . and the universities" to ascend to a new level. He continued: "And there just simply must be no neglect of humanities. The values of our free and compassionate society are as vital to our national success as the skills of our technical and scientific age. And I look with the greatest of favor upon the proposal by your own able President Keeney's

Commission for a National Foundation for the Humanities." As with the National Science Foundation, the National Defense Education Act, and other putatively pro-education measures of the Cold War era, the proposed humanities foundation was being sold as "vital to our national success." The study of Shakespeare, Melville, Austen, Fitzgerald & Co. was not to be defended as scholarship for its own sake, for the simple sake of furthering knowledge and coming to a deeper understanding of our cultural heritage. No, it was bound up in "national success," whose measurements were a mystery but which seemed to have something to do with international prestige, the arms race, and boosting the GNP.[266]

Johnson linked his vision with that of the martyred President who preceded him, and in this matter, as in others, the momentum for the achievement of the Kennedy-Johnson agenda seemed irresistible. The LBJ landslide Congress that assumed office in January 1965 was awash in a blizzard of bills proposing the creation of foundations or endowments for the arts and humanities, as was described earlier in this section.

When possible, national defense and the threat of nuclear war were conscripted by the champions of a humanities foundation. Glenn T. Seaborg, chairman of the Atomic Energy Commission, was a member of the Commission on the Humanities. He told a Senate committee: "We cannot afford to drift physically, morally, or esthetically in a world in which the current moves so rapidly perhaps toward an abyss. Science and technology are providing us with the means to travel swiftly. But what course do we take? This is the question that no computer can answer."[267]

In the eyes of its most fervent supporters, the humanities foundation promised a new renaissance. The usually phlegmatic Republican congressman Frank Horton, a pork-barrel-dipping timeserver representing a Rochester district, gushed that "this measure proposes nothing less than the restoration of man."[268]

Who knew?

The NEH would never generate anywhere near the level of controversy as did its fraternal twin, the NEA, but then its constituency was less varied, more stodgy, more tweedy and respectable. As skeptic Stanley Kauffmann wrote in *Commentary*, "Scholarship has at least as many dullards and almost as many fakers as the arts, but qualifications are more reliably demonstrable."[269] Annie Sprinkle was never going to receive, even indirectly, NEH funds, nor would they be expended on a misspelled word masquerading as poetry.

On September 29, 1965, the President signed into law the National Foundation on the Arts and the Humanities Act, which authorized the "establishment of the National Foundation on the Arts and the Humanities to promote progress and scholarship in the humanities and the arts in the United States." The purpose of this foundation was "to develop and promote a broadly conceived national policy of support for the humanities and the arts in the United States." The Foundation consisted of a National Endowment for the Arts, a National Endowment for the Humanities, and a Federal Council on the Arts and Humanities.

The act defined the humanities as the study of "language, both modern and classic; linguistics; literature; history; jurisprudence; philosophy; archeology; the history, criticism, theory, and practice of the arts; and those aspects of the social sciences which have humanistic content and employ humanistic methods." The chief administrator of the NEH was to be a chairman, appointed by the President with the advice and consent of the Senate. He or she would serve a four-year term and be eligible for reappointment. With the advice of the aforementioned Federal Council on the Arts and Humanities as well as the newly created National Council on the Humanities, which was a set of twenty-six "distinguished" private citizens, the chairman was charged with six primary tasks. To wit, to

1. develop and encourage the pursuit of a national policy for the promotion of progress and scholarship in the humanities;
2. initiate and support research and programs to strengthen the research potential of the United States in the humanities by making arrangements (including grants, loans, and other forms of assistance) with individuals or groups to support such activities;
3. award fellowships and grants to institutions or individuals for training and workshops in the humanities (fellowships awarded to individuals under this authority may be for the purpose of study or research at appropriate nonprofit institutions selected by the recipient of such aid, for stated periods of time);
4. foster the interchange of information in the humanities;
5. foster, through grants or other arrangements with groups, public understanding and appreciation of the humanities; and
6. support the publication of scholarly works in the humanities.[270]

The enabling act authorized the appropriation of $10 million per year for the fiscal years 1966, 1967, and 1968 for the two endowments, to be divided evenly. Appropriations for 1966 were set at $2.5 million for each endowment, with additional monies available for matching-funds programs.

The first chairman was a stopgap: Henry Allen Moe, who had been president of the American Philosophical Society and the John Simon Guggenheim Foundation, served until the President's first choice, Barnaby Keeney of Brown—who had been, as it were, present at the creation—was able to assume the helm in July 1966. Keeney was like many of the Cold War-era advocates of subsidies for intellectuals in that he, too, had been deeply involved with the Central Intelligence Agency. He had done intelligence work during the Second World War and later spent two decades working closely with the CIA—including the entirety of the period while he was president of Brown (1955–66), as detailed by Danielle Cerny in the "Electric Keeney Acid Test" (*Brown Daily Herald*).[271]

From the start, the NEH seemed designed to channel tax monies from states with few academic institutions to states—usually more affluent states—that were teeming with universities. This grated on politicians from the former states, since "It did Nevada, with one university, no noticeable good to insure a constant flow of academic rewards to Massachusetts."[272] The oldest dilemma in politics surfaced: once the pork is on the table, how do you divvy it up?

The American Council of Learned Societies, having begotten, indirectly, the NEH, maintained a fiercely paternal attitude toward the agency. ACLS executive associate Thomas J. Condon complained in a 1969 symposium that the "starved condition" of the NEH (1969 appropriation: $5.6 million) meant that scholars were essentially "cottage-industry workers in a space-age economy." He insisted that "the days of laissez-faire scholarship must surely be limited," though he despaired that "we do not yet have an adequate model for the organization and support of scholarship in the future."[273] That it must be government-generated, however, was beyond dispute.

President Nixon's attempt to appoint a former Eisenhower-Nixon aide, Stephen Hess, to succeed Barnaby Keeney in 1970 elicited a fusillade of criticism from the ACLS. His lack of a Ph.D. and his previous service on two White House staffs were seen as disabling flaws. The head of NEH was supposed to be "above politics," asserted Hess's opponents, though in what way Keeney, who was not exactly a retiring hermetic scholar, was "above politics" is not clear.[274] To say that a political appointee who had millions of tax dollars to dole out could ever be "above politics" is the mark of an ingénue or a hypocrite, but that was the illusion under which public discourse was conducted.

The clientage of the NEH enforced academic standards on its chair in a way that NEA clients did not. There was to be no Nancy Hanks of the humanities endowment. And Stephen Hess never found a constituency. Dismissed by the ACLS as a lightweight, he was also criticized as a liberal by the conservative publication *Human Events*. The administration pulled back, and Hess went on to become a fellow at the Brookings Institution and a Washington fixture in the centrist establishment.

Ronald S. Berman, the Nixon appointee who served as chairman of the NEH from December 1971 until January 1977, when the Carter administration replaced him with Joseph D. Duffey, was a respected Shakespearean academic who was also a political conservative, a combination not pleasing to liberal Senators Pell and Javits, the senatorial gatekeepers of all things cultural. But they relented, and he was confirmed. (Curiously, the relevant Senate committee was that of Labor and Public Welfare, which one does not readily associate with inquiries into the humanities.) Berman, who has left us a valuable account of his stewardship of NEH, had a pugnacity about him and a preference for large grants to established institutions and scholars. His disdain for the fledgling state humanities councils, as well as his overt elitism, brought him into a conflict with Senator Pell that ended with Pell holding up his renomination and sending him back to academe.

Berman was characterized by Kevin V. Mulcahy, a scholar of national cultural policy, as a "bureaucratic 'zealot' concerned with the correctness of a narrow policy viewpoint," though Mulcahy also allowed that Berman was "a forthright, outspoken, and often combative defender of what he saw as the classical values of the liberal arts."[275]

As Berman recounts in his memoir of life at the NEH, *Culture & Politics*, his confirmation hearing featured hostile questioning from Senator Jacob Javits, the New York Republican who been a long-term advocate of greatly increased subsidies for the arts and humanities. But only, it seems, if those scholars and artists had political viewpoints that were somewhat congruent with those of Senator Javits. For Javits grilled Berman over the criticisms he had made of the New Left in his book *America in the Sixties* (1968), and he even asked whether or not Norman Mailer, the iconoclastic novelist-essayist-pugilist, and not a favorite of Berman's, would be "eligible for a grant from NEH." "I replied that he would probably not need one," recalls Berman.[276] There is no record of Javits asking a liberal NEH appointee if, under his chairmanship, William F. Buckley Jr. would be eligible for an NEH grant.

Berman was ever at odds with Senator Pell, whose fiefdom included the NEH. The two developed a dislike for each other that no amount of applied diplomacy could lessen. The irony was that Berman, who had been a Professor of Literature at the University of California at San Diego, was tagged with the sin of "elitism"—and yet his chief foe, Senator Pell, had the reputation of a doddering aristocrat who was preposterously out of touch with the common man and woman.[277] Although Berman was an advocate of "large and useful projects," and drew criticism for emphasizing big splashy King Tut-like programs intended to raise the endowment's profile, his sin in Pell's eyes, it seems, was in also emphasizing academic fellowships and research as opposed to broadening the public understanding of the humanities. For instance, Pell, taking the populist approach, called for reserving 5 percent of the NEH research budget for people lacking college degrees, using the examples of "grocers" and "lumberjacks."[278] Senator Pell also wanted a set percentage of NEH monies to go directly to the states, and the prospect of such outliers as Utah and Wyoming gaining while New York lost enraged Senator Javits and other representatives of purportedly culture-heavy states.

Chairman Berman was instrumental in expanding the NEH into the field of television, as it helped to underwrite such public television series as the 1976 PBS mini-series *The Adams Chronicles, War and Peace* (a BBC production), and *The Scarlet Letter*, which were conceived or produced at various stages of Berman's tenure. (It might be pointed out that commercial moviemakers have at various times filmed both *War and Peace* and *The Scarlet Letter* without a dime from Washington.) The quality of such productions aside, the fact that scripts were vetted at some point during the funding process by NEH officials carries the faint air of Official Art.[279] Certainly heterodox accounts of American history were not going to find favor.

The agency, which since its founding had been the dowdy overlooked sibling of the flashier NEA, made its first real public relations splash as 1976 drew near. The goal? "Kidnaping the Bicentennial."[280] The fear among many was that 1976 would be a travesty. Instead of intelligently commemorating the two hundredth anniversary of the Declaration of Independence and the Revolution, the federal government's Bicentennial Commission was expected to engage in various gaudy and garish activities and mindless ceremonies, punctuated by boring "eat your broccoli" lectures to which no one would pay any attention whatsoever. The NEH, which had already sponsored work on the papers of various Founders, funded an array of projects, ranging from *The Adams Chronicles* on television to museum exhibits to a 52-volume series of histories of the states, Puerto Rico, and the District of Columbia called *The States and the Nation*. And while the Egyptian king predated the American Republic by three millennia or so, the NEH-supported exhibition "The Treasures of Tutankhamun" toured Washington, DC, New York, Chicago, New Orleans, Los Angeles, and Seattle to overflow crowds in 1976.

Hitching a ride on the Bicentennial, NEH funding zoomed upward, from $8.85 million in FY 1970 to $40.66 million in FY 1973 to $79.14 million in FY 1975 to $99.3 million in FY 1977.[281] Whether Thomas Jefferson would have applauded this use of federal monies is perhaps an open question. But the Bicentennial was very good to the NEH.

This populist outreach—if a PBS series can be called populist—met with protest by those who preferred the NEH to focus on professional scholarship. Robert Lumiansky, the ACLS president and a medieval scholar, lamented that the "money it costs to put on the *Adams Chronicles* or whatever, could.... have been better used in support of research libraries, either in acquisition, preservation, or whatever.... That's one hell of a lot of money that goes into those TV things."[282]

As Ronald Berman later rued, Congress had a more expansive vision of the humanities, one that extended far beyond an academic cloister. Indeed, NEH grants were seen as ways to "enhance rural life; make teenagers less destructive; illuminate the golden years of senior citizens; awaken ethnic pride; and raise the national consciousness."

It's not clear just how a $10,000 grant to a Melville scholar can do any of these things. And so the earliest conception of the NEH, that on display in the *Report of the Commission on the Humanities*—as a granter of monies to professors and students working in literature, history, philosophy, and kindred fields; to libraries; to scholarly journals and university presses—evolved. By 1968, the National Council on the Humanities envisioned the NEH's mission as comprehending such issues as "urbanization, minority problems, war, peace, and foreign policy; problems of governmental decision, civil liberties, and the wider applications of humanistic knowledge and insights to the general public interest." As Ronald Berman observed, "There is not much in this resolution about scholarship or education; but there is a great deal about the issues concerning Lyndon Johnson's Great Society."[283]

Berman, in the manner of Leonard Garment with the NEA, sold the idea of boosting the endowment's appropriation by pointing out "the isolation of Republicanism from the intellectual mainstream." Would it not profit the GOP, and President Nixon himself, if intellectuals were to view the party as an ally—a granter of funds to intellectuals, that is—rather than an adversary? It would be too crude to say that the NEH was envisioned, for a moment at least, as a way of buying off the clerisy, but certainly there was an attempt to rent them. And it worked, briefly: by 1973, "the academic world, traditionally hostile to the Nixon administration, was now very much behind that part of his policy dealing with their own interests."[284] Not that it did him much good when Watergate came down.

One of the endowment's major grants in the Nixon era was that of $2 million to the New York Public Library (which was matched and exceeded by nonfederal grants). This was very much in the federal cultural policy tradition of the FWP, MOMA, and the Rockefeller Brothers Fund.

As Berman notes in his illuminating memoir, the expansion of the NEH under his leadership vexed many on the Right, for "In the case of culture. . . . those who benefit from the patronage of government tend to be liberal technocrats." Why, wondered conservatives, was a Republican administration boosting appropriations for an agency that suckled academic liberals? The NEH represented "socialism for the rich and free enterprise for the poor," as the free-marketeer Rep. Phil Crane (R-IL) put it during one congressional debate.[285]

Though less vocal than the NEA's constituency, the American Council of Learned Societies and its members became effective lobbyists for the NEH's fellowship and research programs, which put money into the accounts of those for whom they spoke. They did have one complaint: As Ronald Berman writes of those on the NEH dole, "Our grantees were grateful for our services, but most of them would have preferred a steady flow of federal subsidy. They did not like to make repeated applications, and it was their dream to become line-items on the Federal Budget: mandated recipients of funds given by entitlement."[286]

The NEH has largely avoided NEA-style controversies. Its glamour projects have never included crucifixes immersed in urine or bullwhips crammed up the nether regions of naked men. Rather, they are such widely admired efforts as cosponsorship of the Library of America series, which republishes classic works of American literature; PBS shows such as Ken Burns's immensely popular series on the Civil

War; and the publication of the papers of Washington, Jefferson, John Marshall, and other luminaries of the early republic. Libertarians may object to such projects, pointing out that private sources can and have funded similar efforts, but there is no real populist juice behind such criticisms.

The great gadfly Senator William Proxmire (D-WI) occasionally went after the NEH for such actions as a "$2,500 grant to researchers in Virginia, who wanted to know why people were unruly and ill-mannered and why so many of them lied and cheated when they played tennis."[287] The reason they were rude, as Senator Proxmire pointed out, was that "More people wanted to play tennis than there were courts available!"[288] As for why the Arlington, Virginia, tennis players cheated. . . . well, one man's "In!" is another man's "Out!"

And so the endowment, linked to its more famous sibling, grew. As with the NEA, the NEH experienced its growth spurt during the administration of the president so despised by so large a portion of the intellectual class, Richard Nixon. Its budget swelled from $5.6 million in FY 1969, the year before the Nixon budget, to $79.1 million in FY 1975 before reaching its high-water mark, in real dollars, of $145.2 million in FY 1979, $150.1 million in FY 1980, and $151.3 million in FY 1981.

Once Again: The Reagan Threat

But then came Ronald Reagan, whose tentative efforts at slicing the budgets of the endowments largely came a cropper but who assumed a sinister countenance in the mythology of federal support of intellectuals. The first Reagan budget requested $77 million for the NEH in FY 1982, which barely equaled half of its budget of the previous year.

To repel the Reagan assault, a coalition of "academic humanists, libraries, archives, museums, schools, filmmakers and other public programmers, humanities centers, and the state humanities councils" gathered in 1981 under the umbrella of the National Humanities Alliance to advocate for greater funding and visibility for the humanities. Today it consists of over one hundred "national, state and local member organizations and institutions, including: scholarly and professional associations; higher education associations; organizations of museums, libraries, historical societies and state humanities councils; university-based and independent humanities research centers; and colleges and universities."[289] It is, in effect, a lobby. (State humanities councils tend to be less visible and less generously funded than do state arts councils, and are therefore weaker lobbying forces.) The Reagan assault, as it were, was repelled. The NEH wound up with $130.56 million in FY 1982, or only a 14 percent dip from FY 1981.

If the NEH's perceived frumpiness insulated it from the controversies that scorched the NEA, it also lowered its profile. The NEH, as Stephen R. Graubard has written, "lacked brio, and indeed at times seemed positively dowdy; as the 'ugly sister,' it did not attract a great deal of press attention; its congressional hearings were not crowded; they were not the great public events stage-managed by the NEA."[290] Its soberness, its staidness, had the effect of blunting full-scale attacks on the endowments, which since birth had been linked in a kind of fraternal twinning. If the NEH never lit up the night sky with fireworks, nor did it become an irresistible floating target. It was too close to the ground ever really to crash.

This is not to imply that the NEH and its chairmanship have not served as political footballs. In the wake of Ronald Reagan's 1980 election, the post of chairman looked likely to be awarded to Professor M. E. Bradford of the University of Dallas, a respected scholar of American history and literature. Bradford, a Texan, hailed from the traditionalist conservative wing of the Reagan coalition. He had been a supporter of Alabama Governor George C. Wallace for president in 1968 and 1972, but as Wallaceites had been courted by Reagan this seemed not to be a disqualification. He had also been critical, in scholarly discourse, of Abraham Lincoln, and it was on this point that the neoconservative faction of the Reagan coalition chose to attack Bradford. There was a long history of Southern literary men being less than admiring of Lincoln, but they had typically been yellow-dog Democrats, not Republican appointees.

The neoconservative candidate for NEH director, William Bennett, had a much skimpier academic record than did Bradford, but he lacked an anti-Lincoln paper trail (or much of any paper trail), and he emerged the victor in the internecine conflict. In 2003, Bradford's University of Dallas colleague Thomas H. Landess related an amusing story of Bradford's vetting for NEH chairman by Holmes Tuttle, the wealthy automobile dealer, fund-raiser, and member of Reagan's "Kitchen Cabinet" who was screening potential administration officials.[291]

Early in the screening process, writes Landess, Tuttle:

> . . . . summoned Bradford to the Old Executive Office Building and waved the professor's fifteen-page bibliography under his nose.
>
> "The trouble is, you've published too much. Too many targets. Take this thing you wrote about homosexuals."

> Bradford said he had written nothing about homosexuals.
>
> "What's this, then?"
>
> The Car Salesman ran his forefinger down the lengthy list of items, one page after another, until he found the item he was looking for. Then he passed the bibliography across the desk and jabbed at a line.
>
> "There."
>
> The listing was an article on Bishop Richard Corbet[t]'s "The Fairies Farewell,"—a light 17th-century lyric about the loss of belief in the supernatural.
>
> Bradford burst out laughing—a tactical error.
>
> The Car Salesman was indignant.
>
> Bradford attempted to placate him by explaining that the poem was not about homosexuals, but about literal fairies, the kind that fly around on gossamer wings and do good deeds, e.g., the tooth fairy. It was like trying to explain trigonometry to a cat.[292]

Bradford was a goner.

The tussle over the NEH chairmanship recalled what is often said of faculty politics: the battles are so bitter because the stakes are so small. The endowment's accomplishments were, even in the judgment of its supporters, modest. Senator Orrin Hatch (R-UT), chairman of the Senate committee that oversaw the reauthorization of the two endowments in 1985, had words of praise for the NEA while saying of the unprepossessing NEH, "It is interesting to note that the decline [in humanities scholarship] came after the humanities were given their own agency, the NEH, for the specific purpose of encouraging the study of the humanities."[293]

Government-Approved History and Culture

As the culture wars of the 1990s heated up, the NEH was singed, though not seriously burnt. One of the most entertaining battles was set off when in July 1991 the Senate Labor and Human Resources Committee rejected, by one vote, the nomination of literary critic Carol Iannone to the Advisory Council of the National Endowment for the Humanities.

Her critics asserted that Iannone lacked the scholarly credentials for the position. She possessed a doctorate and was an adjunct professor at New York University, but her publications had largely been confined to *Commentary*, the monthly magazine of the American Jewish Committee, which since the 1970s had gained a reputation as the bastion of neoconservatism. In particular her foes had cited a *Commentary* essay by Iannone, "Literature by Quota," in which she argued that certain African American writers, among them Alice Walker and Gloria Naylor, had received a bevy of prestigious awards due to their color rather than the content of their books.[294]

After the committee vote, Senator Daniel Patrick Moynihan, the New York Democrat and a sometime contributor to *Commentary*, took to the Senate floor on July 19 to make what he called, with his usual puckishness, some "good-natured" remarks, which he began with a "melancholy acknowledgment of the further intellectual decline of the Democratic party." He added, "I almost said demise, but will leave bad enough alone."[295]

After tracing the intellectual lineage of *Commentary*, many of whose most notable writers had been "frequently Trotskyites" before the turn toward neoconservatism, he spoke of the ethnic and social-class divisions within the Democratic Party, which Moynihan had written up for *Commentary* in a much-discussed cover story of 1961, "Bosses and Reformers: A Profile of the New York Democrats." Drawing from the lessons of that essay, Moynihan dropped his bombshell: "I very much fear Professor Iannone's troubles arose not from the quality of her work but from her genes, social and otherwise. She is an Italian, Catholic ethnic with a working-class background."[296]

As if carried away by disgust with his party, Moynihan concluded that Iannone's "future should be bright. She has been banned in Boston. No greater fortune ever attended the struggling novelist of the 1930s. Sales would soar outside of Boston. Professor Iannone has now been banned in the Democratic party. What greater fortune could befall an American intellectual in this decadent *fin de siècle*. I wish her well."[297]

The *Wall Street Journal* ran a sixty-eight-word excerpt of Moynihan's remarks, which he had delivered to an empty Senate chamber. In response, Stanley N. Katz, president of the American Council of Learned Societies, fired off an angry letter to Moynihan which the senator then read into the *Congressional Record*. Dr. Katz said that he was "outraged" by Moynihan's statement, or at least the paragraph or so he had read. The ACLS had been leading the anti-Iannone forces, with their ally Senator Ted Kennedy (D-MA), and Katz was incensed to learn that Moynihan was "accusing Iannone's opponents of religious, class, and ethnic prejudice." Then Katz took his outrage a bridge too far: "Something like 300,000 postdoctoral scholars belong to the fifty-one organizations we represent, and you have attacked the integrity of each and every one of them. You have certainly insulted me personally, as a public opponent of the nomination."[298]

This was like tossing a fat softball to Moynihan, who knew how to swing a disputatious bat. Speaking from the Senate floor on August 1, he first reproved Katz for basing his outburst on a brief excerpt rather than the full statement. (Though the full statement was hardly less critical of the anti-Iannone crowd.) "There would have been no great problem obtaining the full text" of his remarks, said Moynihan. "The *Congressional Record* reaches New York. In the event the mails have proved deficient, I would happily have had a copy sent over from my New York Office. I would even have faxed a copy!"

Touché. But Moynihan next took aim at Katz's grandiloquence. What, he asked, "is this business of my having attacked 'Something like 300,000 postdoctoral scholars belong[ing] to fifty-one organizations.' '[E]ach and every one of them?' This gets close to newspeak. Evidently, I have offended The People, 'each and every one' of whom will now rise—altogether, now—in righteous wrath. There is a whiff of the totalitarian mode in all this. . . .I certainly do not like hearing from Dr. Katz that he speaks for me," said Moynihan, who noted his memberships in the American Philosophical Society, the American Academy of Arts and Sciences, and the American Antiquarian Society, each of them constituent societies of the ACLS.

Moynihan huffed, "I do not care one bit for the idea that an executive of the ACLS would claim to speak individually for 300,000 American—and foreign—scholars whose irrepressible practice is to speak for themselves."[299]

The National Endowment for the Humanities was politicized, as the Iannone fracas demonstrated, but then as a politically created entity it had to be, at least outside the fantasies of those who imagine that the administration of such bodies can be left to a pristine clique of experts who are untainted by passions, opinions, prejudices, irrational preferences, friendships, enmities—in other words, by experts who are not human beings. As for the American Council of Learned Societies, it was among those organizations that, according to Frances Stonor Saunders, was a conduit for CIA subsidies to intellectuals. Its administrative hands were not clean.

***

The biggest ideological battle in the history of the NEH was set off by a Republican nominee, Lynne Cheney, who was appointed by President Reagan to succeed William Bennett. On Cheney's watch, the NEH commissioned a set of National History Standards to be drawn up by a team at the National Center for History in the Schools, led by UCLA professor Gary Nash. A grant in the amount of $1.6 million was executed. These standards were to guide the teaching of history in grades 5–12. If this sounds like a strange project for a Republican administration, recall that it was under President Reagan that his US Department of Education, working through the National Commission on Excellence in Education, produced *A Nation at Risk* (1983), a clarion call for greater federal involvement in the theretofore local and state province of education. Thus Chairwoman Cheney was acting in this Reaganite tradition of education centralization. But as the Bush administration gave way to the Clinton administration, Cheney, now the former chairwoman of NEH, viewed the nascent national standards warily.

More than two years in the making, and the recipient of grants not only from the National Endowment for the Humanities but also the Department of Education, the standards set off an immediate storm of protest. The response from the right was ire and outrage. John Leo, a columnist for *US News & World Report*, charged that the standards denigrated the European founders of the American Republic as "dedicated largely to oppression, injustice, gender bias and rape of the natural world," while Native Americans and African Americans are "romanticize[d]" as flawless. Albert Shanker, president of the AFL-CIO affiliated American Federation of Teachers, remarked, "No other nation in the world teaches a national history that leaves its children feeling negative about their own country—this would be the first."[300]

One of the most searching investigations of the National History Standards was written for *Commentary* by Walter A. MacDougall, Professor of International Relations and History at the University of Pennsylvania. He found them biased, ahistorical, devoted inordinately to boosting the esteem of women and African Americans, neglectful of Christianity, and transcendently boring. The one "consistent ideological thread" is feminism. The litany of tendentiousness is long, but MacDougall offers this brief glimpse: "Standards invite students to appreciate Aztec 'architecture, skills, labor system, and agriculture,' but ignore the Aztec religion of human sacrifice; depict Genghis Khan through the eyes of a papal legate whose cultural biases pupils are told to discern; ask students to indict John D. Rockefeller; assess Ronald

Reagan as 'an agent of selfishness'; and contrast the ecological virtue of Native American culture with our rapacious industrialism."[301]

You get the idea.

MacDougall is quite amusing when he discusses "assignments that are impossibly difficult for most high-schoolers ('Research the core and periphery thesis of Immanuel Wallerstein'), impossibly time-consuming ('Using books like *The Scarlet Pimpernel* and *A Tale of Two Cities*, assess the accuracy of such literary accounts in describing the French Revolution'), or simply impossible ('Write a dialogue between a Muslim and a Hindu on what they see as the reasons for the spread of Christian missions, what the impact will be on their faiths, and how best to resist the appeals of Christian missionaries'). Crackle, snore, or make things up?"[302]

Gary Nash, father of the much-reviled standards, defended the minification of Thomas Edison, among others, with the immortal line, "As far as the absence of particular people such as Thomas Edison, also missing are great black inventors and great female inventors."[303] This was multiculturalism run amok, almost to the point of self-parody.

In January 1995, the Senate, by a vote of 99–1, condemned the standards in a sense of the Senate resolution. The sole nay voter, Senator Bennett Johnston (D-LA), dissented because he wanted more teeth in the condemnation. A spokeswoman for the resolution's sponsor, Senator Slade Gorton (R-WA), explained, "There were few references to George Washington. In 31 course standards, they failed to mention the Constitution. There was no mention of Paul Revere, Benjamin Franklin, Thomas Edison and some of America's other historical figures who really made America a better place."[304]

This was yet another in the long line of quarrels between those who wished to use the resources and the imprimatur of the federal government to endorse a dogma, a philosophy, a way of looking at the world. It will not be the last. Though the history standards are long forgotten, they have been succeeded by No Child Left Behind, Common Core, and sundry other proposals for the nationalization of the curriculum. As long as the power to impose a particular worldview on a captive audience of schoolchildren exists, rival partisans will contend for that power.

If, during the culture wars of the early-mid 1990s, the defenders of the National Endowment for the Arts marched (perhaps misleadingly) under a "free speech" banner, the National Endowment for the Humanities was bathed in a different light, thanks to President

Clinton's nomination of University of Pennsylvania president Sheldon Hackney to chair the NEA. Hackney was a Southern liberal, a native of Birmingham, Alabama, who earned a doctorate in history at Yale under the notable historian C. Vann Woodward. (His in-laws, Virginia and Clifford Durr, were prominent Alabama leftists who were frequently red-baited for their activism.) Hackney chose academic administration over teaching and research. He served as president of Tulane University before moving to Penn in 1981. Hackney, who was from a prosperous Birmingham family, moved easily within prominent social circles, and this social standing would prove valuable in his confirmation fight, as his powerful summer neighbors on Martha's Vineyard came to his assistance.

In his memoir about his NEH confirmation ordeal, *The Politics of Presidential Appointment: A Memoir of the Culture War*, Hackney explains that by good fortune, his Martha's Vineyard golfing pal, Vernon Jordan, was heading the Clinton transition team. The connection paid off: Sheldon Hackney was tapped for the position of NEH chairman. But a funny thing happened on the way to the NEH. Sheldon Hackney became the academic poster boy for censorship in the service of political correctness. Indeed, Ralph Reed, the lobbyist who headed the Christian Coalition, ordained him as "The Pope of Political Correctness."[305]

Two University of Pennsylvania free-speech issues came to a head in early 1993. The timing was disastrous for Hackney, as this was the period in which the Clinton administration was putting its team into place. The first incident to come to public attention was the theft of 14,000 copies of the university's student newspaper, *The Daily Pennsylvanian*, by students identifying themselves as "The Black Community." They had objected to the writings of a *DP* columnist and instead of engaging him in debate, they stole and trashed the newspapers.

You might think that the president of a university would respond to such an assault on basic values with a strong endorsement of a free press and a vigorous exchange of ideas. Hackney, to his later regret, issued a mealy-mouthed statement about how "two important University values now stand in conflict. There can be no compromise regarding the First Amendment right of an independent publication to express whatever views it chooses. At the same time, there can be no ignoring the pain that expression may cause. I deeply regret that these recent events may mask the continuing efforts the University is making towards a comfortable and permanent minority presence in a diverse and civil University community. Whatever the consequences in the weeks ahead, the University will continue to work diligently and persistently toward both goals."[306]

Not exactly a ringing endorsement of the liberty of the press. Hackney had equivocated, failing to make clear that he was condemning, in no uncertain terms, the theft of the papers. Although he claimed that those responsible would be punished, not a single student was ever given so much as a slap on the wrist for this crime.

This might have been written off as typical behind-covering by a politically correct college administrator if not for a contemporaneous case that came to be known as the Water Buffalo Incident. On the evening of January 13, 1993, a number of African American Delta Sigma Theta sorority sisters were "singing and dancing loudly outside a high-rise residence hall." Students in the high rise shouted at them to keep it down. There is dispute about just what was said, but the nub of the controversy was the demand by one student, freshman Eden Jacobowitz, who was writing an English paper, to the revelers: "Shut up, you water buffalo. If you want a party, there's a zoo a mile from here." (Jacobowitz had earlier tried the polite, "Please keep quiet," to no avail.)[307]

The women filed a formal complaint. The charge, bizarrely, was that "water buffalo" was a racial epithet. Alan Charles Kors, a civil libertarian who taught history at Penn, took on the role of Jacobowitz's advisor. Kors canvassed experts in African American linguistics and history, none of whom had ever heard "water buffalo" used as a racially offensive term. As Kors later explained in *The Shadow University: The Betrayal of Liberty on America's Campuses* (1998), a book he coauthored with civil-liberties attorney Harvey A. Silvergate:

> The whole case took on a new light, however, when the world-renowned Israeli scholar, Dan Ben-Amos, whose field is African folklore, replied. "What would water buffalo have to do with Africans or African-Americans?" he asked. Informed about the facts of the case, Ben-Amos asked if the student were Israeli or spoke modern Hebrew. Learning that Eden's parents were both Israeli and that he had attended a Hebrew-language high school, Ben-Amos explained that "*Behema* is Hebrew slang for a thoughtless or rowdy person, and, literally, can best be translated as 'water buffalo.' It has absolutely no racial connotation." When Kors asked Jacobowitz, "What's the first thing that comes into your mind if I say 'b'ehema,'" Eden said, "Wow.... that's amazing. In my yeshiva, we called each other *behema* all the time, and the teachers and rabbi would call us that if we misbehaved." He supplied a list of students and teachers from his school who would be glad to testify about it.[308]

Nevertheless, Jacobowitz was put through the ringer by Penn's judicial inquiry officer, who formally charged the student with racial harassment. Eden was subjected to what his advisor Kors called a "kangaroo court." Sheldon Hackney did not lift a finger to stay this travesty, though in his defense, he pointed out that "*the Penn system was set up specifically to exclude the president and the provost*" from the process, an exclusion he later deplored.[309] [Italics in original]

Hackney was roasted in the press for this instance of p.c. gone wild. The *Forward*, a Jewish daily, headlined its story of April 23, "Pennsylvania Preparing to Buffalo a Yeshiva Boy." On April 26, the *Wall Street Journal* editorially denounced Penn for making Jacobowitz "the latest victim of the ideological fever known as political correctness." The *Journal* editorialist went on to remark that it was "not irrelevant to note that the head of this institution, Sheldon Hackney, is President Clinton's nominee to head the National Endowment for the Humanities and a man, university spokesmen insist, committed to free speech."[310]

A month of scrambling ensued, as the university, under widespread mockery, alternately threatened and pled with Jacobowitz and Kors to settle matters. Finally, the women dropped the charges, Jacobowitz apologized for calling them water buffalo, and a major obstacle to Sheldon Hackney's confirmation had been removed. Hackney presented his best civil libertarian face to the Senate Committee on Labor and Human Resources, under whose umbrella the NEH fell. He assured Senator Nancy Kassebaum (R-KS) that the charge of racial harassment was not justified, and he confessed that "I have come to feel that even though civility is very important in an educational setting, it is a mistake to try to enforce it among members of the campus community through rules and penalties administered through a judicial system."[311]

The Committee, thus mollified, approved the nomination by a vote of 17–0. The unanimity did not carry over to the Senate floor, where twenty-two Republicans and Democrat Joe Lieberman (CT) voted against Hackney, who would serve four years as chairman before giving way to William R. Ferris, a Southern folklorist whose popularity was such that when George W. Bush took office, Mississippi's two Republican US senators lobbied him to reappoint Ferris. (Bush instead appointed Bruce Cole, an art historian.)

The Republicans who were swept into the House by the 1994 midterm election succeeded in slicing the NEH budget from $172 million in FY 1995 to $110 million in FY 1996. The perception that Hackney was in thrall to political correctness did not help: the agency's appropriation was stuck around $110 million until rising slightly to $115 million in FY 2000 and $120 million in FY 2001, the last budget of the Clinton era.

As NEH chairman, Sheldon Hackney's signal achievement was a series of forums called "A National Conversation on American Pluralism and Identity," which he hoped would stimulate discussion about what Americans held in common. The conversation was a dud: as the *New York Times* noted in its obituary for Mr. Hackney, "the 'conversations' begun by Mr. Hackney were not highly publicized and not particularly popular on the right or the left for different reasons."[312] But when one has failed to defend the free exchange of ideas in one very visible position, it is difficult to convince people to converse under his auspices in another position.

In January 1995, at the height of the cultural wars of the mid-1990s, a former NEH chairman, William Bennett, testified before the House Appropriations Subcommittee on the Interior in favor of abolishing the NEH. The agency had met with his approval fourteen years earlier, when he bested M.E. Bradford in the conservative struggle for the chairmanship, but the arrival of the Gingrich Contract with America Republican Congress had apparently changed his mind. Bennett now held that "the federal government should not be in the business of subsidizing the humanities and the arts." He sounded a positively libertarian note, saying that "it seems to me that the central question the 104th Congress needs to address is one which Representatives and Senators almost never ask anymore; namely, is this enterprise one in which the federal government ought to be involved?"

Bennett, citing theater critic and NEA advocate Robert Brustein's praise of the endowments for giving the "stamp of approval" to worthy projects, asks, "Do we want a government agency to have that function? Do we want to invest it with the power of putting its official 'stamp of approval.' . . . upon any particular work of art or scholarship?"

This was precisely what Bennett's Republican successor Lynne Cheney was doing when she authorized the National History Standards, apparently confident in the belief that Republicans would occupy the catbird seat for a long enough time to see the standards through to completion and dissemination.

Bennett sought to tie the NEH to the NEA scandals. Conceding that the projects funded by the former were "less pornographic," he insisted that they were nevertheless politically tendentious, instancing NEH funding of the Modern Language Association, which had recently sponsored convention panels on such pressing matters as "Lesbian Tongues

Untied," "Henry James and Queer Performativity," and "Strategies for Feminist Team Teaching of Hispanic Woman Writers."

Bennett ended his rather remarkable performance—his trumpet blast for the abolition of the agency he had recently headed—with another burst of libertarian rhetoric, saying that if scholars and artists and intellectuals truly prize freedom, "they should paint, perform and think freely without any help from, and thus obligation to, the government."[313]

It is doubtful that Bennett convinced anyone not previously committed to the endowment's abolition. Like the NEA, the NEH was never in serious danger of expiry despite the occasional rhetorical blasts from conservative or libertarian-tinged Republicans.

***

When faced with genuine dissent, the first instinct of a government cultural commissar is to run the other way. Consider the Jefferson Lecture, an annual address which has been sponsored by the National Endowment for the Humanities since 1972. The NEH calls the Jefferson Lecture "the highest honor the federal government confers for distinguished intellectual achievement in the humanities."[314] Lecturers in recent years have included filmmaker Martin Scorsese, playwright Arthur Miller, popular historian David McCullough, social critic Tom Wolfe, and Harvard President Drew Gilpin Faust. In its earlier years, the Jefferson Lecture was delivered by, among others, poet-novelist Robert Penn Warren, novelist Saul Bellow, and sociologist Robert Nisbet.

President Obama's first appointee as NEH chair was Jim Leach, a fifteen-term former Iowa Republican congressman. Leach had left Congress involuntarily after the 2006 election. His nomination was not necessarily evidence of Obama graciously reaching across the aisle; former Rep. Leach endorsed Obama in the 2008 election.

In 2012, the Jefferson Lecturer was Wendell Berry, the farmer, poet, novelist, and social critic from Kentucky. Berry's political views are too complicated to fit within the left-right spectrum; the endowment deserves credit for inviting him. He proceeded to deliver a characteristically thoughtful and passionate address, titled "It All Turns on Affection," about the connections between people, especially country people, and the places in which they live, and the social, cultural, and economic implications of farming land to which one has a powerful familial attachment. In the course of this lecture Berry had harsh words for James Duke, whose surname hangs on a prominent Southern university, and Duke's monopolistic American Tobacco Company. Berry also spoke, with eloquent harshness, of what he viewed as the enemies of the small family farm. As *The American Spectator* noted after the speech, this was a case of a "true Jeffersonian deliver[ing] the Annual Jefferson Lecture."[315]

Immediately after Berry's address, which was greeted with a standing ovation, NEH Chairman Jim Leach hastened to explain, "the views of the speaker do not necessarily reflect the views of the United States government."[316] The disclaimer was delivered partly in jest, and partly not. But it was a reminder that a government that funds ideas and those who express them is not neutral with respect to those ideas.

The endowment remains a secondary presence in support of research in the American academy, and as Stephen R. Graubard argues, this is all to the good, since a "federal bureaucracy, requiring congressional and public approval for its policies. . . . will inevitably live by a political calculus that will compel [it] to avoid the controversial, or opt for the popular, sometimes selecting the meretricious where the alternative is dangerous."[317] This means, in practice, that court historians are to be elevated above dissenters or revisionists, and scholars grazing in the trendiest meadows of centrist multiculturalism will receive the federal grants that the independent-minded do not even bother to apply for.

The most recent round of NEH grants were topped by an award of $1 million to celebrity documentary filmmaker Ken Burns for a ten-part series on the Vietnam War. Given Mr. Burns's track record, it is almost inconceivable that (1) he could not have raised this sum from private or private foundation sources; and (2) the series, however skillfully made, will depart in any way from the broadly conventional wisdom about the war.

The NEH's FY 2015 budget of $146.02 million allocates barely 10 percent, or $14.78 million, to "research programs," which the endowment's scholarly godfathers had once assumed would be its core and reason for being. This is half as much as is spent on administration, and only slightly less than is expended on another core function, "preservation and access" ($15.46 million).[318] No one is raising a fuss about any of this, or about NEH initiatives to strengthen humanities education at the community college level, stage plays featuring Iraq War veterans, or digitize early 20th-century recordings of Native American speech. Even the $1 million to the amply endowed Ken Burns failed to rouse critics. The NEH remains under the radar and outside the realm of controversy—as it has for most of its half-century of existence.

Notes

1. George Biddle, "The Government and the Arts: A Proposal by George Biddle, With Comment and Criticisms by Others," *Harper's Magazine* 200 (October 1943): 427.
2. Ibid., 428.
3. Ibid., 433.
4. Larson, *The Reluctant Patron*, 23.
5. Grieve, *The Federal Art Project and the Creation of Middlebrow Culture*, 168.
6. John Sloan, *John Sloan on Drawing and Painting: Gist of Art* (Mineola, NY: Dover, 2000/1939), 28–29.
7. Larson, *The Reluctant Patron*, 67.
8. Joseph P. Fried, "Frank Thompson, 70; Career In Congress Ended With Abscam," *New York Times*, July 24, 1989.
9. Paul Mickle, "1980: Stung!" *The Trentonian*, accessed October 12, 2015, http://www.capitalcentury.com/1980.html.
10. Thompson, "Are the Communists Right in Calling Us Cultural Barbarians?," 5.
11. Ibid., 5, 10.
12. Arthur Schlesinger Jr., "Notes on a National Cultural Policy," *Daedalus* 89, no. 2 (Spring 1960): 399.
13. Donna M. Binkiewicz, *Federalizing the Muse: United States Arts Policy and the National Endowment for the Arts, 1965–1980* (Chapel Hill: University of North Carolina Press, 2004), 63.
14. Michael Kammen, "Culture and the State in America," *Journal of American History* 83, no. 3 (December 1996): 801.
15. Larson, *The Reluctant Patron*, 123.
16. William J. Baumol and William G. Bowen, *Performing Arts—The Economic Dilemma* (New York: Twentieth Century Fund, 1966), 369.
17. Larson, *The Reluctant Patron*, 83.
18. Ibid., 51.
19. "Government Subsidy: A Dangerous Expedient," *Musical America* (Vol. 69, No. 11 September 1949): 14.
20. Arthur Schlesinger Jr., *A Thousand Days: John F. Kennedy in the White House* (Boston, MA: Houghton Mifflin, 1965), 729.
21. Baumol and Bowen, *Performing Arts*, 348.
22. Zimmer and Toepler, "The Subsidized Muse," 42.
23. "Jackie near Victory in Drive for Culture in Nation's Capitol," Associated Press, The Hendersonville (NC) *Times-News*, June 12, 1962.
24. Hyde, "Being Good Ancestors," 9.
25. See note 23 above.
26. Colm Toibin, "How to Be a Wife," *London Review of Books*, June 6, 2002.
27. Gore Vidal, "Writers and the World," in *Homage to Daniel Shays: Collected Essays, 1952–1972* (New York: Random House, 1972), 215.
28. Schlesinger, *A Thousand Days*, 730–1.
29. John Whitcomb and Claire Whitcomb, *Real Life at the White House: 200 Years of Daily Life at America's Most Famous Residence* (New York: Taylor & Francis, 2002), 355.
30. Arthur J. Goldberg, "To Come to the Aid of the Arts," *New York Times Magazine*, March 11, 1962.
31. Larson, *The Reluctant Patron*, 158, 162.

32. Baumol and Bowen, *Performing Arts*, 370.
33. Eric Pace, "August Heckscher, 83, Dies; Advocate for Parks and Arts," *New York Times*, April 7, 1997.
34. Schlesinger, *A Thousand Days*, 734.
35. John Brademas, "Government, the Arts, and the Public Happiness," *Music Educators Journal* 52, no. 5 (April–May 1966): 42.
36. "The Arts and the National Government," Report to the President Submitted by August Heckscher, Special Consultant on the Arts, May 28, 1963 (Washington, DC: U.S. Government Printing Office, 1963), 1.
37. Ibid., 2.
38. Ibid., 4, 9.
39. Ibid., 28.
40. John F. Kennedy to August Heckscher, June 10, 1963, in ibid., vii.
41. "Statement by the President Establishing the President's Advisory Council on the Arts," in ibid., 33.
42. Alvin Toffler, *The Culture Consumers: Art and Affluence in America* (New York: St. Martin's, 1964), 208.
43. Neeli Cherkorski, *Ferlinghetti* (New York: Doubleday, 1979), 208.
44. "President John F. Kennedy: Remarks at Amherst College," October 26, 1963, accessed October 12, 2015, http://arts.gov/about/kennedy.
45. Larson, *The Reluctant Patron*, 181.
46. After the President's assassination, the new National Cultural Center, a public-private partnership whose enabling legislation had been signed by President Eisenhower, was renamed the John F. Kennedy Center for the Performing Arts.
47. Michael Macdonald Mooney, *The Ministry of Culture: Connections Among Art, Money and Politics* (New York: Wyndham Books, 1980), 249.
48. Scott MacKay, "The Life and Times of an Uncommon Man: Sen. Claiborne Pell," October 20, 2011, accessed October 12, 2015, http://wrnipoliticsblog.wordpress.com/2011/10/20/the-life-and-times-of-an-uncommon-man-sen-claborne-pell.
49. Livingston Biddle, *Our Government and the Arts: A Perspective from the Inside* (New York: ACA Books, 1988), 28.
50. Larson, *The Reluctant Patron*, 95–96.
51. Ibid., 131–2.
52. Biddle, *Our Government and the Arts*, 38.
53. Ibid., 39.
54. Ibid., 40.
55. Ibid., 50–51.
56. Larson, *The Reluctant Patron*, 206.
57. Stanley Kauffmann, "Can Culture Explode? Notes on Subsidizing the Arts," *Commentary* 40, no. 2 (August 1965): 21.
58. Richard Kostelanetz, "The New Benefactors," *Liberty*, January 1990, 60.
59. John D. Rockefeller 3rd, "Foreword by the Chairman," *The Performing Arts: Problems and Prospects* (New York: McGraw-Hill, 1965), vi.
60. Ibid., 6, 13.
61. Ibid., ix.
62. Ibid., 21, 15.
63. Ibid., 43.

64. Ibid., 111–2.
65. Ibid., 113.
66. Ibid., 145.
67. Ibid., 206.
68. "Foundation on the Arts and Humanities," *CQ Almanac 1965*, accessed October 12, 2015, http://library.cqpress.com/cqalmanac/document.php?id=cqal65-1259837.
69. Biddle, *Our Government and the Arts*, 176.
70. "Foundation on the Arts and Humanities," *CQ Almanac 1965*.
71. http://www.neh.gov/about/history/national-foundation-arts-and-humanities-act-1965-pl-89-209.
72. Lyndon B. Johnson, "Remarks at the Signing of the Arts and Humanities Bill," September 29, 1965, accessed October 12, 2015, http://www.presidency.ucsb.edu/ws/?pid=27279.
73. Baumol and Bowen, *Performing Arts*, 3.
74. Ibid., 68.
75. Ibid., 404–5.
76. Ibid., viii–ix.
77. Ibid., 8, 96.
78. Ibid., 97.
79. Eric F. Goldman, *The Tragedy of Lyndon B. Johnson* (New York: Knopf, 1969), 418.
80. John Rodden and John Rossi, "Kultur Clash at the White House," *Kenyon Review* 29, no. 4 (Fall 2007): 161.
81. Goldman, *The Tragedy of Lyndon B. Johnson*, 419, 453.
82. "Bess Abell Turned Secretarial Skills into Summit Position," *Sarasota Herald-Tribune*, UPI, July 7, 1978.
83. Goldman, *The Tragedy of Lyndon B. Johnson*, 420.
84. Ibid., 428.
85. Ibid., 423–4.
86. Ibid., 427.
87. Ibid., 445–6.
88. Ibid., 450–2, 448.
89. Ibid., 456–7.
90. Ibid., 461, 463.
91. Ibid., 466.
92. Rodden and Rossi, "Kultur Clash at the White House," 174.
93. Ibid., 167.
94. Goldman, *The Tragedy of Lyndon B. Johnson*, 471.
95. Rodden and Rossi, "Kultur Clash at the White House," 176.
96. Goldman, *The Tragedy of Lyndon B. Johnson*, 474.
97. Rodden and Rossi, "Kultur Clash at the White House," 177.
98. Eric Pace, "Roger L. Stevens, Real Estate Magnate, Producer and Fund-Raiser, is Dead at 87," *New York Times*, February 4, 1998.
99. Stefan Toepler and Annette Zimmer, "The State and the Non-Profit Sector in the Provision of Arts and Culture: The Cases of Germany and the United States," *European Journal of Cultural Policy* 3, no. 2 (1997): 294.
100. "Arts, Recreation, and Travel," Table 1234, accessed October 12, 2015, http://www.census.gov/prod/2011pubs/12statab/arts.pdf.

101. Bauerlein, *National Endowment for the Arts*, 19.
102. Ibid., 27.
103. Baumol and Bowen, *Performing Arts*, 374.
104. Roberta Smith, "Michael Werboff, 99, Portraitist Whose Subjects Included Kings," *New York Times*, April 14, 1996.
105. Margaret Jane Wyszomirski, "The Politics of Art: Nancy Hanks and the National Endowment for the Arts," in *Leadership and Innovation*, eds. Jameson W. Doig and Erwin C. Hargrove (Baltimore, MD: Johns Hopkins University Press, 1987), 171–2, accessed October 12, 2015, http://ksuweb.kennesaw.edu/~uzimmerm/Notes/Entrep.Hanks.pdf.
106. Ronald Berman, *Culture & Politics* (Lanham, MD: University Press of America, 1984), 9–10.
107. Wyszomirski, "The Politics of Art," 178.
108. Joel Whitney, "The *Paris Review*, the Cold War, and the CIA," salon.com, May 27, 2012.
109. Aram Saroyan, "The Most Expensive Word in History," *Mother Jones* (August 1981): 36.
110. Michael Whitney Straight, *Nancy Hanks: An Intimate Portrait: The Creation of a National Commitment to the Arts* (Durham, NC: Duke University Press, 1988), 158.
111. Ibid., 158–9.
112. Biddle, *Our Government and the Arts*, 218.
113. George Plimpton, "Introductory Note," *Mother Jones* (August 1981): 36.
114. Stigler, "The Intellectual and the Marketplace," 82.
115. Kauffmann, "Can Culture Explode?," 20.
116. Erica Jong, *Fear of Flying* (New York: Signet, 1973), acknowledgements.
117. Paul Theroux, "Hapless Organ," *New Statesman*, April 19, 1974, accessed October 12, 2015, http://www.enotes.com/topics/erica–jong/critical–essays/jong–erica–1943.
118. Roy Fuller, "Taxpayers, the Arts and Big Balloonz," *Encounter* 49, no. 4 (October 1977): 44.
119. Ibid., 45.
120. Jonathan Yardley, "When Art Goes on the Dole," *Civilization* 2, no. 5 (September/October 1995): 34.
121. Fuller, "Taxpayers, the Arts and Big Balloonz," 47.
122. Roy Shaw, "The Arts Council & Poetic Injustice," *Encounter*, November 1977, 90.
123. Ibid., 93.
124. Amis, "An Arts Policy?," 84, 86.
125. Ibid., 89.
126. Biddle, *Our Government and the Arts*, 289.
127. Wyszomirski, "The Politics of Art," 185.
128. Bauerlein, 37–38.
129. Wyszomirski, "The Politics of Art," 181.
130. Kammen, "Culture and the State in America," 796.
131. Berman, *Culture & Politics*, 148.
132. Hilton Kramer, "The Presidency and the Arts," *New York Times*, October 31, 1976.

133. "Visual Art in Utah," accessed October 12, 2015, http://heritage.utah.gov/arts-and-museums/visual-public-art.
134. Baumol and Bowen, *Performing Arts*, 350.
135. Ryan C. MacPherson, "Broadening the Tastes of the Public Good: How the National Endowment for the Arts Subsidizes 'Sexual Identities' for the New Civil Polytheism," *The Family in America* 28, no. 4 (Fall 2014): 431.
136. Kammen, "Culture and the State in America," 796.
137. Dick Netzer, *The Subsidized Muse: Public Support for the Arts in the United States* (New York: Cambridge University Press, 1978), 90.
138. Kostelanetz, "The New Benefactors," 58.
139. Fox, "Revisiting the Politics of Art Museums," 43.
140. Netzer, *The Subsidized Muse*, 84.
141. "Michael Straight," *The Telegraph*, January 17, 2004, accessed October 12, 2015, http://www.telegraph.co.uk/news/obituaries/1451875/Michael-Straight.html.
142. Bauerlein, 81.
143. Hilary Masters, "Go Down Dignified: The NEA Writing Fellowships," *Georgia Review* 35, no. 2 (Summer 1981): 233.
144. Ibid., 234.
145. Ibid., 239, 243.
146. Amy Stolls and Jon Parrish Peede, "Literature," in *National Endowment for the Arts: A History 1965–2008*, ed. Mark Bauerlein (Washington, DC: National Endowment for the Arts, 2008), 189.
147. Don Ball, ed., *NEA Literature Fellowships: 40 Years of Supporting American Writers* (Washington, DC: National Endowment for the Arts, March 2006), 7.
148. Ibid., 20.
149. Ibid., 23.
150. Kevin V. Mulcahy, "Government and the Arts in the United States," 323.
151. For more on the assault on the NEA as a piece of the "defunding the left" campaign, see Jerome L. Himmelstein and Mayer Zald, "American Conservatism and Government Funding of the Social Sciences and the Arts," *Sociological Inquiry* 54, no. 2 (April 1984): 171–87.
152. Biddle, *Our Government and the Arts*, 493.
153. Toni Morrison, "Cutting the Endowment: An Argument," *Washington Post*, March 22, 1981.
154. Alan L. Feld, Michael O'Hare, and J. Mark Davidson Schuster, *Patrons Despite Themselves: Taxpayers and Arts Policy* (New York: New York University Press, 1983), 75.
155. Ibid., 83.
156. Most museum administrators and advocates acknowledge that their visitors are unrepresentative of the general population. For strategies to diversify the museum clientele, see, for instance, Jan Larson, "The Museum Is Open," *American Demographics* 16 (November 1994): 32–38.
157. Cowen, *Good and Plenty*, 29.
158. Baumol and Bowen, *Performing Arts*, 376–7.
159. van den Haag, "Should the Government Subsidize the Arts?," 66.
160. "Arts, Recreation, and Travel," Table 1238, accessed October 12, 2015, http://www.census.gov/prod/2011pubs/12statab/arts.pdf.
161. Ibid.

162. Arthur C. Brooks, "Who opposes government arts funding?," *Public Choice* 108, no. 3/3 (2001): 355.
163. Ibid., 363.
164. Ibid., 366.
165. Robert Reinhold, "Scientists at U.S. Agency Troubled About Future," *New York Times*, July 8, 1981.
166. Kenneth Prewitt and David L. Sills, "Federal Funding for the Social Sciences: Threats and Responses," *ASA Footnotes* 9 (December 1981): 4–5.
167. Robert Reinhold, "Social Scientists Fight For Government Funds," *New York Times*, July 29, 1981.
168. Constance Holden, "Dark Days for Social Research," *Science* 211, no. 4489 (March 27, 1981): 1398.
169. Margaret Wyszormirski, "From Public Support for the Arts to Cultural Policy," *Review of Policy Research* 21, no. 4 (2004): 477.
170. Biddle, *Our Government and the Arts*, 505.
171. Wyszormirski, "From Public Support for the Arts to Cultural Policy," 473.
172. Cummings and Katz, "Government and the Arts in the Modern World," 358.
173. Robert D. McFadden, "A Modernized 'Rigoletto' is Attacked," *New York Times*, March 6, 1984.
174. David Bird, "Met in Accord with Protesters over 'Rigoletto,'" *New York Times*, March 13, 1984; Alvaro Ignacio Anillo, "The National Endowment for the Humanities: Control of Funding Versus Academic Freedom," *Vanderbilt Law Review* 45, no. 2 (1992): 461.
175. "National Medal of Arts," accessed October 12, 2015, http://arts.gov/honors/medals.
176. John Frohnmayer, *Leaving Town Alive: Confessions of an Art Warrior* (Boston, MA: Houghton Mifflin, 1993), 29.
177. "A Brief History of 'Piss Christ,'" *ArtInfo*, December 25, 2013, October 12, 2015, http://blogs.artinfo.com/artintheair/2013/12/25/a-brief-history-of-piss-christ/.
178. Bauerlein, *National Endowment for the Arts*, 92. Serrano's creation has not lost its capacity to outrage. In August 2014, protesters at a rally in Ajaccio, Corsica, objected to the display of *Piss Christ* in Corsica's Fesch Museum. MacPherson, "Broadening the Tastes of the Public Good," 413.
179. Gary Indiana, "Gary Indiana on Censorship in the Arts," *Artforum* 28, no. 1 (September 1989): 11–12.
180. Marie Tessier, "Tying Down Federal Funds for the Arts," *Congressional Quarterly Editorial Research Reports* 1, no. 20 (May 25, 1990): 304.
181. MacPherson, "Broadening the Tastes of the Public Good," 422.
182. Frohnmayer, *Leaving Town Alive: Confessions of an Art Warrior*, 36.
183. Tessier, "Tying Down Federal Funds for the Arts," 303, 305.
184. Michael Oreskes, "Senate Votes to Bar U.S. Support of 'Obscene or Indecent' Artwork," *New York Times*, July 27, 1989.
185. Jesse Helms, "Art, the First Amendment, and the NEA Controversy," *Nova Law Review* 14 (1989–90): 317–8.
186. Ibid., 318–9.
187. Ibid., 320.
188. Frohnmayer, *Leaving Town Alive: Confessions of an Art Warrior*, 135.

189. Tessier, "Tying Down Federal Funds for the Arts," 311.
190. Frohnmayer, *Leaving Town Alive: Confessions of an Art Warrior*, 1, 84.
191. Ibid., 2–3.
192. Bauerlein, *National Endowment for the Arts*, 98.
193. Frohnmayer, *Leaving Town Alive: Confessions of an Art Warrior*, 77.
194. Raleigh Douglas Herbert, "National Endowment for the Arts—the Federal Government's Funding of the Arts and the Decency Clause," *Seton Hall Legislative Journal* 18, no. 1 (1993): 422.
195. Frohnmayer, *Leaving Town Alive: Confessions of an Art Warrior*, 152.
196. Kees Vuyk, "The Arts as an Instrument? Notes on the Controversy Surrounding the Value of Art," *International Journal of Cultural Policy* 16 (2010):176.
197. Dustin Kidd, *Legislating Creativity: The Intersections of Art and Politics* (New York: Routledge, 2010), 15.
198. Ibid., 14.
199. Frohnmayer, *Leaving Town Alive: Confessions of an Art Warrior*, 2.
200. Bauerlein, *National Endowment for the Arts*, 115.
201. Alice Goldfarb Marquis, *Art Lessons: Learning from the Rise and fall of Public Arts Funding* (New York: Basic Books, 1995), 247.
202. Cynthia Koch, "The Contest for American Culture: A Leadership Case Study on the NEA and NEH Funding Crisis," *Public Talk*, accessed October 12, 2015, http://www.upenn.edu/pnc/ptkoch.html.
203. Brooks, "Who Opposes Government Arts Funding?," 355.
204. Robert Hughes, "Pulling the Fuse on Culture," *Time*, August 7, 1995.
205. Newt Gingrich, "Cutting Cultural Funding: A Reply," *Time*, August 21, 1995.
206. Kammen, "Culture and the State in America," 793.
207. John Updike, *Odd Jobs: Essays and Criticism* (New York: Random House, 2012/1991), 947.
208. Peter Marks, "NEA Chairman Rocco Landesman's Peoria arts adventure," *Washington Post*, November 9, 2009.
209. Lee Rosenbaum, "He Produces Controversy," *Wall Street Journal*, November 3, 2009.
210. Mike Boehm, "Obama Picks Low-profile Arts Center Executive to Chair the NEA," *Los Angeles Times*, February 12, 2014.
211. "NEA Funding," accessed October 12, 2015, http://www.americanorchestras.org/advocacy-government/nea-funding.html.
212. "FY14 NEA Grants to Orchestras," October 12, 2015, http://www.americanorchestras.org/advocacy-government/nea-funding/nea-funding-opportunities/nea-grantsto-orchestras/fy14.html.
213. Harris, *Federal Art and National Culture*, 2.
214. Bauerlein, *National Endowment for the Arts*, 2.
215. Cowen, *Good and Plenty*, 3.
216. Feld, O'Hare, and Schuster, *Patrons Despite Themselves*, 2. In 1973, the last year for which the authors had complete data, they estimated the size of direct government aid to the arts in the United States at $200 million, while indirect aid was approximately $460 million. Ibid., 212.
217. Feinberg, "Not with My Tax Money," 102.
218. Cowen, *Good and Plenty*, 40. The net transfer as a result of arts-related tax policy, in the view of Feld, O'Hare, and Schuster, is "from the very wealthy to the moderately wealthy and well-educated. Notwithstanding the stated goals of

government support, such as, for example, through the National Endowment for the Arts, poor and moderate-income people apparently do not benefit much." Feld, O'Hare, and Schuster, *Patrons Despite Themselves*, 71.

219. Arthur C. Brooks, "In Search of True Public Arts Support," *Public Budgeting & Financing* 24, no. 2 (June 2004): 99.
220. Ibid., 100.
221. Maria Recio, "Nation's New Arts Promoter-in-Chief Knows the Landscape," September 12, 2014, McClatchy Washington Bureau, accessed October 12, 2015, http://www.mcclatchydc.com/2014/09/12/239686/nations-new-arts-promoter-in-chief.html#storylink=cpy.
222. https://www.kickstarter.com/hello?ref=footer.
223. Steve Hendrix, "To Fund Artistic Dreams, Just Go along with the Crowd: Internet Sites Allow Stalled Creatives to Raise Major Money," *Washington Post*, August 7, 2015.
224. Even if the NEA did vanish, state and local agencies would more than pick up the slack. Tyler Cowen notes, "Even if we take the most modest estimate possible for non-NEA sources. . . . NEA direct expenditures account for less than 10 percent of total direct governmental support for the arts in America." Seen in that light, the forecast of dire consequences for American arts and artists should the NEA disappear seems absurdly overstated. Cowen, *Good and Plenty*, 91.
225. The prospect of centralized culture continues to excite many arts administrators. In recent years, the Center for Arts and Culture, a Washington-based think tank hoping to "broaden and deepen the national conversation on culture," proposed that the Congress and President convene a National Forum on Creativity and Cultural Heritage, a vision that would have the likes of John Sloan and Lawrence Ferlinghetti reaching for their revolvers. The Center, which was funded by the Rockefeller and Ford Foundations, among other elite philanthropic organizations, was dispatched to that great nonprofit in the sky in 2005, its dream unfulfilled, but as an orator once said, the hope lives on and the dream shall never die. "America's Cultural Capital: Recommendations for Structuring the Federal Role," *Journal of Arts Management, Law, and Society* 31, no. 3 (Fall 2001): 180–3.
226. Bennett, *The Doomsday Lobby*, 45–89.
227. "Testimony of Dr. Frank B. Jewett," Hearings on Science Legislation S. 1297 and Related Bills, U.S. Senate Committee on Military Affairs, Subcommittee on War Mobilization, Washington, DC, 442–7, *passim*.
228. Quoted in James L. Penick Jr., Carroll W. Pursell Jr., Morgan B. Sherwood, and Donald C. Swain, eds. *The Politics of American Science: 1939 to the Present* (Chicago: Rand McNally & Co, 1965), 209.
229. Barbara Barksdale Clowse, *Brainpower for the Cold War: The Sputnik Crisis and National Defense Education Act of 1958* (Westport, CT: Greenwood Press, 1981), 59–60.
230. Stephen R. Graubard, "NEH at Twenty: Another View," *Change* 18, no. 1 (January/February 1986): 24.
231. Berman, *Culture & Politics*, 1.
232. *Report of the Commission on the Humanities* (New York: American Council of Learned Societies, 1964), p. v.
233. *Congressional Record*, March 29, 1962, S5487.
234. *Report of the Commission on the Humanities*, v.

235. O. B. Hardison Jr., "NEH at Twenty: Has it Made a Difference?" *Change* 18 (January/February 1986): 13.
236. *Report of the Commission on the Humanities*, vii.
237. Ibid., 1.
238. Ibid., 4.
239. Ibid., 5–6.
240. Ibid., 7.
241. Dwight D. Eisenhower, "Farewell Radio and Television Address to the American People," January 17, 1961, The American Presidency Project, accessed October 12, 2015, www.presidency.ucsb.edu/ws.
242. *Report of the Commission on the Humanities*, 7–8.
243. Joseph P. Martino, *Science Funding: Politics and Porkbarrel* (New Brunswick, NJ: Transaction, 1992), 88.
244. *Report of the Commission on the Humanities*, 8.
245. Ibid., 14, 10.
246. Ibid., 13, 12.
247. Ibid., 8.
248. Ibid., v.
249. Ibid.
250. Ibid., 51–52.
251. Ibid., 54.
252. Ibid., 57.
253. Ibid., 111–2.
254. Ibid., 115.
255. Ibid., 164.
256. Ibid., 206, 199.
257. Ibid., 203, 205.
258. Ibid., 211.
259. Ibid., 77.
260. Ibid., 218.
261. John Higham, "The Schism in American Scholarship," *American Historical Review* 72, no. 1 (October 1966): 2.
262. Kammen, "Culture and the State in America," 805.
263. Anillo, "The National Endowment for the Humanities," 462.
264. Hardison, "NEH at Twenty: Has it Made a Difference?," 12.
265. Jensen, "The Culture Wars, 1965–1995," 17.
266. President Lyndon B. Johnson, "Remarks in Providence at the 200th Anniversary Convocation of Brown University," September 28, 1964, accessed October 12, 2015, http://www.presidency.ucsb.edu/ws/?pid=26534.
267. "How NEH Got Its Start," accessed October 12, 2015, http://www.neh.gov/about/history.
268. Larson, *The Reluctant Patron*, 197.
269. Kauffmann, "Can Culture Explode?," 20.
270. Public Law, 89–209, accessed October 12, 2015, www.gpo.gov.
271. Danielle Cerny, "Electric Keeney Acid Test," *Brown Daily Herald*, September 22, 2004.
272. Berman, *Culture & Politics*, 5.
273. Thomas J. Condon, "Approaches to Funding Support for Humanistic Scholarship," *Computers and the Humanities* 4, no. 1 (September 1969): 92, 95.

274. "Target of Scholars' Criticism Answers," Associated Press, *Palm Beach Post*, June 27, 1971.
275. Mulcahy, "Government and the Arts in the United States," 325.
276. Berman, *Culture & Politics*, 12.
277. Joan Kufrin, "The Tale of the Golden Letter," *New York Magazine*, April 9, 1979, 57.
278. Berman, *Culture & Politics*, 15, 105.
279. Anillo, "The National Endowment for the Humanities," 472.
280. Berman, *Culture & Politics*, 27.
281. "History of NEH Appropriations," accessed October 12, 2015, http://www.statehumanities.org/library/history_neh_approp_2012.pdf.
282. Hardison, "NEH at Twenty: Has it Made a Difference?," 15.
283. Berman, *Culture & Politics*, 6–8.
284. Ibid., 18, 39.
285. Ibid., 66–67.
286. Ibid., p. 105.
287. Richard Severo, "William Proxmire, Senator Who Abhorred Waste, Dies," *New York Times*, December 15, 2005.
288. Robert W. Pelton, *Infernal Revenue: A Jolly Peek at Some of the Scams that Waste Away Your Taxes* (Lincoln, NE: toExcel, 2000/1984), 63.
289. "About NHA," accessed October 12, 2015, http://www.nhalliance.org/about/index.shtml.
290. Graubard, "NEH at Twenty: Another View," 26.
291. Constance L. Hays, "Holmes Tuttle, 83; In 'Kitchen Cabinet' That Aided Reagan," *New York Times*, June 17, 1989.
292. Thomas H. Landess, "Mel Bradford, Old Indian Fighters, and the NEH," accessed October 12, 2015, www.lewrockwell.com, April 25, 2003.
293. Hardison, "NEH at Twenty: Has it Made a Difference?," 12.
294. Carol Iannone, "Literature by Quota," *Commentary* (March 1991): 50–53.
295. Daniel Patrick Moynihan, "The Nomination of Carol Iannone," *Academic Questions* 5, no. 1 (March 1992): 57, 61.
296. Ibid., 63–64.
297. Ibid., 65.
298. Ibid., 58.
299. Ibid., 59.
300. John Leo, "History Standards Assault Western Culture," Spokane *Statesman-Review*, January 31, 1995. For a defense of the standards, see Arnita A. Jones, "Our Stake in the History Standards," *OAH Magazine of History* 9, no. 5 (Spring 1995): 5; Jones was executive secretary of the Organization of American Historians.
301. Walter A. McDougall, "Whose History? Whose Standards?" *Commentary* 99, no. 5 (May 1995): 39, 36.
302. Ibid., 39.
303. Jensen, "The Culture Wars, 1965–1995," 23.
304. "Senate Rejects Standards for Teaching History: Western Civilization Presented Poorly, Gorton Resolution Says," Associated Press, January 19, 1995.
305. Sheldon Hackney, *The Politics of Presidential Appointment: A Memoir of the Culture War* (Montgomery, AL: NewSouth Books, 2002), 15.
306. Ibid., 85.

307. Alan Charles Kors and Harvey A. Silvergate, *The Shadow University: The Betrayal of Liberty on America's Campuses* (New York: Free Press, 1998), accessed October 12, 2015, http://partners.nytimes.com/books/first/k/kors-university.html; unpaginated.
308. Ibid.
309. Hackney, *The Politics of Presidential Appointment*, 91, 95.
310. Ibid., 99–100.
311. Ibid., 230.
312. Paul Vitello, "Sheldon Hackney, Leader in Humanities, Dies at 79," *New York Times*, September 16, 2013.
313. William J. Bennett, "The Case for Abolishing the National Endowment for the Arts and the National Endowment for the Humanities," delivered before the House Appropriations Subcommittee on Interior, January 24, 1995.
314. "Jefferson Lecture," accessed October 12, 2015, http://www.neh.gov/about/awards/jefferson-lecture.
315. Christopher Orlet, "The Affections of Wendell Berry," *The American Spectator*, May 3, 2012, accessed October 12, 2015, http://spectator.org/articles/35591/affections-wendell-berry.
316. Scott Carlson, "'We All Are Implicated': Wendell Berry Laments a Disconnection from Community and the Land," *The Chronicle of Higher Education*, April 23, 2012, accessed October 12, 2015, http://chronicle.com/article/In-Jefferson-Lecture-Wendell/131648/.
317. Graubard, "NEH at Twenty," 27.
318. "Summary of Fiscal Year 2015 Appropriation," accessed October 12, 2015, http://www.neh.gov/files/2015_neh_budget_approp.pdf.

Conclusion

According to *Giving USA* and the Indiana University Lilly Family School of Philanthropy, annual charitable contributions by individuals, foundations, and corporations to the arts, culture, and humanities is approximately $17 billion.[1] This total dwarfs that of the combined budgets of the National Endowments for the Arts and the Humanities (not even 2 percent of that $17 billion), which suggests that perhaps the importance of the endowments has always been more symbolic than practical.

We are coming up on eighty-five years of federal sponsorship of writers, artists, and intellectuals. The programs described herein have been modest in scope but sometimes immodest in aims. Federal One went beyond basic relief for the unemployed and sought, especially in its Theatre and Writers' projects, to change the way Americans viewed their regions and their country. The secret subsidy of modern art during the Cold War sought nothing less than undermining the Soviet Union. The National Endowments for the Arts and Humanities were intended to transform a nation of alleged philistines and gross materialists into cultured men and women.

Were they successful? Americans did view their country differently by the early 1940s, as Federal One had run its course, but an epochal world war contributed far more to that altered vision than did competently written state guides and propagandistic plays. The Soviet Union did fall, though its demise had nothing to do with the triumph of Abstract Expressionism, and the dissolution of what Ronald Reagan termed the "Evil Empire" happened a dozen years after the Congress for Cultural Freedom decamped to that great gravy train in the sky and a quarter century after it had ceased to be of any real significance. As for Americans today cutting a cultured profile. . . . look around and judge for yourself.

And what effect have these programs had on the *artists themselves*? From the start, writers representing various political traditions have doubted that state support would produce better art. We have quoted them throughout this work: skeptics whose concern was not so much political economy as it was authorial independence. Henry Seidel Canby, editor of the *Saturday Review of Literature*, had expressed his doubts during the New Deal-era debate over a bureau of the arts: "In the seventeenth century writers had to cringe and sweat for what money they got," explained Canby. "They had to write fulsome prefaces, or wait for shillings in booksellers' halls. The economic conditions of literary production were terrible—and the output includes one of the chief treasure heaps of English literature."

"Today," Canby continued, "the market of literary wares is organized and over-organized. No good (and celebrated) story-teller or playwright. . . . can fail of a decent reward. And the output is—well, not yet Elizabethan, Jacobean, or even Augustan in its quality."[2] Canby was quick to assure affronted writers that he was not calling for them to panhandle on streetcorners, but he saw no obvious connection between a writer's source of income and the quality of his or her work.

When the NEA and NEH were aborning, Thornton Wilder, playwright, novelist, and thrice the winner of a Pulitzer Prize, criticized the proposed endowment in May 1965, saying, "There are no Miltons dying mute here today." Talent will out, according to Wilder, who joked that in many towns, "anyone who can play the scales is rushed off to Vienna to study music" with monies "raised by the local music appreciation club."[3] This is wild exaggeration, to be sure, though in our age the number of talented artists whose light is hidden under bushel baskets is severely limited.

During the culture war disputes of the 1990s, Shelby Foote, the novelist and author of a three-volume history of the Civil War that seems likely to endure as a great American work of art, said in response to a question about writers receiving monies from the NEA that "I'm very much against it. I'm for subsidizing the arts—opera, the theater, symphony orchestras, and so forth—but I think creative people should be left alone. It takes away from what you're doing. Even a grant does that. I think making just enough to pay the light bill is an affirmation of your commitment."[4]

Most cutting of all, perhaps, was poet Richard Moore, who in the 1970s fulminated that:

> it isn't just that the money we give to artists is being *wasted.* It is doing *positive harm.* An arts bureaucracy has grown up in the last few years to formulate the applications, select the judges, and give

> the right sort of ballyhoo to the recipients. There is no other way for such a system to work. And there is no way to make such a system honest. But supposing that it *is* honest, it cripples nevertheless. Only mediocrity can destroy art. And in every bureaucracy, mediocrity luxuriates. Where do the judges come from? The writers' union, of course. The solid citizens of art who have enough of a reputation to be chosen and nothing better to do than such hackwork. And they will reward those who are like themselves. They will constitute a self-perpetuating and endlessly stultifying organization that will ensure the banishment of true talent to madness and outer darkness. Precisely that, I suspect in the depths of my heart, is the true purpose of such a system: to stamp all creativity out of a society which has grown too brittle to endure it; and for that reason I am afraid that my objection to such Government involvement in the arts may be a cry in the wilderness.[5]

If so, it is a terribly eloquent cry. Hyperbole has been present in these disputes since the beginning. During the debate over the National Foundation on the Arts and Humanities Act, freshman Rep. Marion Gene Snyder (R-KY) depicted a future that looked like a hybrid of the nightmares of Kurt Vonnegut and Ayn Rand: "The curtain comes down on this final act with all local drama clubs, municipal symphonies, private entertainers, radio and TV stations—either under the direction of the newly created Fine Art Department or enjoined from functioning for want of a license. All art forms have become standardized. Progress is possible only through recognition by the bureaucracy. No script, song, play, poem, book, or opera is attributed to any one individual. All artistic efforts are the work of the establishment."[6]

Nothing even approaching this has happened. But the government-sanctioned culture industry *has* promoted favored art forms and movements—e.g., the CIA's modernism, the progressive liberalism of Federal One, or an NEA from which political conservatives are notable by their absence—and how could it have been otherwise? Whenever tax dollars are to be distributed, the mechanism for the distribution thereof will be contested over by those who desire access to those dollars. They may coat their efforts in high-minded language or professed ideals, and in many cases their rhetoric is sincere, but at bottom, it is a mere, even sordid, scramble for loot.

In 1976, the neoconservative critic Hilton Kramer could write that "Everyone now agrees that the Government has an obligation to subsidize the arts in this country." By "everyone" he meant those within his circumscribed orbit, of course, rather like the film critic Pauline Kael, who was baffled by Richard Nixon's landslide victory in 1972 since everyone she knew had voted for McGovern.[7]

Forty years later, Kramer's statement is less true. There remains, in the hinterlands, a voiceless constituency—Kramer, Robert Hughes, and their contemporary versions would no doubt call them philistines—who are unreconciled to government subsidy of arts. But the elite consensus is uncracked. The NEA and NEH are in no immediate danger of dissolution, or even severe budget cuts, but nor are their budgets rising. The emergence of private and voluntaristic fundraising mechanisms such as Kickstarter may nudge the endowments further to the margins. Meanwhile, the libertarian critique of politics has gained a toehold in American discourse and has given a modicum of intellectual respectability to an antisubsidy cause whose noisy and colorful tradition has included Beat poets, agrarian novelists, anarchist artists, upper-crust patrons of symphony orchestras, and just plain old ordinary painters and fiddlers and story-tellers who practice their art without any benevolent intrusion whatsoever by government—and they like it that way.

Notes

1. "Giving USA: Americans Gave $335.17 Billion to Charity in 2013; Total Approaches Pre-Recession Peak," June 17, 2014, accessed October 12, 2015, http://www.philanthropy.iupui.edu/news/article/giving-usa-2014.
2. Henry Seidel Canby, "Should Authors Go on Salary?," *Saturday Review of Literature*, November 26, 1932.
3. Biddle, *Our Government and the Arts*, 167.
4. "Live with *TAE*," *The American Enterprise*, January/February 2000, 16.
5. Quoted in Masters, "Go Down Dignified: The NEA Writing Fellowships," 244.
6. Larson, *The Reluctant Patron*, 193.
7. Kramer, "The Presidency and the Arts."

Index

T